SAILING
INTO THE
PAST

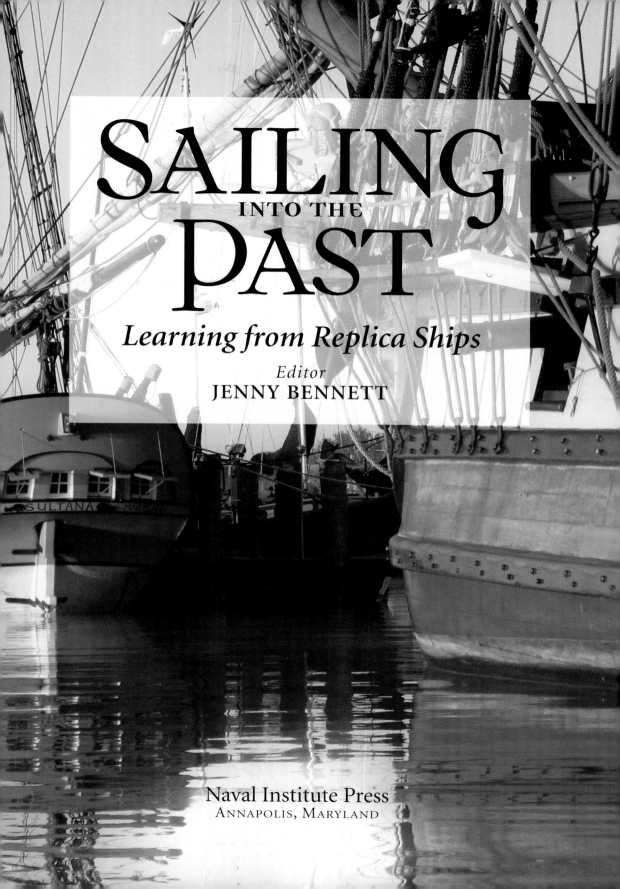

SAILING
INTO THE
PAST

Learning from Replica Ships

Editor
JENNY BENNETT

Naval Institute Press
ANNAPOLIS, MARYLAND

Editor
Jenny Bennett

Contributors
Burkhard Bange
Douglas Brooks
Nick Burningham
Andrew Davis
Wolf-Dieter Hoheisel
Rikke Johansen
Antonia Macarthur
Seán McGrail
Drew McMullen
Colin Palmer
Boris Rankov
Richard Woodman
Peter Wrike

Copyright © Seaforth Publishing 2009
Text copyright © individual contributors 2009

First published in Great Britain in 2009 by
Seaforth Publishing,
Pen & Sword Books Ltd,
47 Church Street,
Barnsley S70 2AS

Published and distributed in the
United States of America and Canada by the
Naval Institute Press,
291 Wood Road, Annapolis,
Maryland 21402-5034

www.nip.org

Library of Congress Control Number: 2009935180

ISBN 978 1 59114 811 1

Printed in China through Printworks International Ltd.

Frontispiece: *Sultana* at rest Chestertown, alongside the visiting replicas
Kalmar Nyckel (right) and *Pride of Baltimore* II.

(Christopher Cerino)

CONTENTS

THE RISE OF THE REPLICA

FOR THOSE OF US who dream of being able to experience life in another time, another place, the rise of the replica ship in modern culture offers new and exciting possibilities. Now, even in the dawn of the twenty-first century, it is possible to bend one's back to the oar of a trireme, hunker down on the floorboards of a Viking longship on a gruelling ocean voyage, stand on a yard high above a wooden deck and bend hemp lines to cotton canvas. To do any of these is to be transported into another age, when life was surely more fundamental than anything most of us are likely to experience in our everyday modern lives.

But is there more to the replica than the fulfillment of dreams? And how do we balance the desire of historians and archaeologists to 'get it right' at any cost with the need to offset the high price of building a ship? We live in a bureaucratic and litigious world in which a fully-operational passenger-carrying vessel must be equipped with safety features never before considered necessary, and once such features are incorporated the status of 'replica' is instantly compromised. Can a ship built to eighteenth-century plans with eighteenth-century techniques and materials be deemed 'authentic' if it carries a diesel engine and electric ovens? And if we agree that such a hybrid cannot truly be a replica is there any justification for its construction? And what of those replicas built not from plans but from research, hypothesis and historical theory? Can we ever definitively say, 'this is it, just as it would have been'? And, if not, is there a defence for building such a vessel?

Well, yes, for there is surely no other man-made artefact of such extraordinary complexity, such longevity in our collective history, such wide-reaching variety of which we have such limited hands-on experience than the sailing vessel. And in the absence of an original, only the replica – compromised or not – can give us much of the knowledge we seek. Without the replica trireme, longship, caravel, bark it would surely be impossible to truly understand them.

This book is a 'behind the scenes' look at some of the most authentic and noteworthy re-creations of sailing vessels through the ages. Their individual stories reveal a common thread and purpose: to recreate something that no longer survives in its original form and seek practical truths about ancient craft; to further our understanding of the achievements of our ancestors and, in so doing, learn more about ourselves and our place in history; to take the hypotheses of academics and turn them into realities that will either prove or disprove the theories.

During the twentieth century a sea change occurred in the building of historic vessels. Where once it was enough to take a wooden hull, carve some decorative

woodwork onto a sterncastle, and hoist a few square sails to claim it as the 'true' *Golden Hinde*, today even the most casual observer demands that we 'prove it'. Thus, the replicas described in this volume are representative of a new breed: a breed founded in solid research that has been assembled over many decades and is still growing. In choosing which, of the many, examples should be included we selected vessels that each represent a different era of seafaring and for which there are no extant prototypes; that, of their type, are as authentic as could be, given our current knowledge and the compromises brought to bear by modern society; that are exceptional in their quality of build and level of research. Certainly there are others that could have been included but this book is not a directory, rather it is a cross section that illustrates the rise of the replica and reveals the on-going developments in the search for authenticity and use of such vessels.

No doubt, within a few years, new evidence will have been unearthed to contradict some of the findings even of these most respected examples. Nevertheless, they prove that the building of such reconstructions is invaluable in our pursuit of historical understanding. The sailing vessel, large and small, has been central to human history: it took men to war, carried goods between far-flung nations, explored uncharted, even unknown, lands. While we could theorise and argue about the settling of Polynesia by the South Americans, if Thor Heyerdahl had not built *Kon-Tiki*, would we have ever known that a primitive reed boat could sail across thousands of miles of the Pacific Ocean? And if no one had reconstructed and sailed a Viking longship would we have truly believed that such vessels could sail to windward and could, therefore, have sailed from Scandinavia to North America? Inevitably, as our latterday replicas bring answers to questions, they beg ever more questions, but as the puzzles are solved these extraordinary reconstructions bring us closer to a fuller understanding and enable us to sail ever more purposefully into the past.

JENNY BENNETT

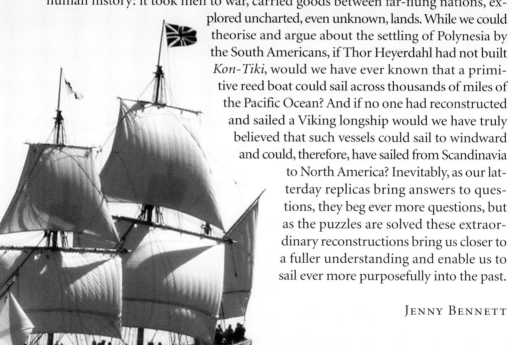

1 Sailing into the Past

The sailing vessel, in all its many guises, was a noble creation. William Morris, that great nineteenth-century aesthete, said that one should possess nothing that was neither useful nor beautiful; while his contemporary, John Ruskin, said: 'Take it all in all, a ship is the most honourable thing a man has ever produced.' While all sailing vessels were useful they were not always beautiful, though the majority were and certainly those of the late nineteenth century – the products of the Clyde, the Wear and Aberdeen – were as near to the sublime in their union of fitness for purpose with satisfaction to the eye as was possible. All, however, have their own enchantment.

For myself it was this seduction of the eye that first caught my attention. On my weary and resentful way to school I used to pass a small antiques shop, in the window of which, one day, were two handsome prints of full-rigged sailing ships. Enquiry revealed the pictures to be a guinea each, a prodigious sum for a twelve-year-old schoolboy who had but two shillings and sixpence a week. Having decided that an accumulation of birthday money might secure one of the prints, I had only to decide which one – *Blackadder* or *Cimba*? I eventually plumped for the former, on the grounds that the image was more interesting, and the ship was perhaps built by John Willis as an improvement on the *Cutty Sark*, which was then much in the news as an appeal to save her had just been launched. As it turned out, *Blackadder* was a dismal failure and suffered a series of dismastings owing to some faulty work aloft, but I have the oak-framed print still. The original painting was by Jack Spurling and, though I did not know it at the time, he had caught the freshness of the open ocean, the sharp, stinging bite of the wind and its harping in taut rigging while the lofty sails, each yard braced a little further around than the one below, drove the ship onwards.

In those post-war days images of great sailing ships were all one had. Even the *Cutty Sark* was to go into dry-dock and, in 1956, she lacked anything that could be called a rig. There was one old barque that I had seen in

Ramsgate harbour about seven years earlier. She was a restaurant – a project doomed to failure in those days of austerity – and some fool had renamed her *Bounty*. Her real name was *Alastor* and she was almost the last sailing vessel to bring a cargo up the Thames. As a small boy I heard of the ritual sinking off the Owers of the old 74-gun line-of-battle ship *Implacable*; only later did I learn that, like *Victory*, she was a survivor of Trafalgar, having been built and commissioned as the French *Duguay Trouin* and captured a fortnight after the battle off Cape Ortegal by Rear Admiral Sir Richard Strachan. About the same time as her sinking, in 1948, the impoverished Labour government decided to scrap the brigantine *Research*. Constructed of non-magnetic materials at considerable expense on the eve of war, she had been intended as a Royal Research Ship but was laid up on the River Dart for the duration of hostilities. Her scrapping seemed an act of national vandalism, as disappointing as the sinking of the *Implacable*.

Thereafter, sailing ships were encountered only in books: Alan Villiers's *Joseph Conrad*; Adrian Seligman's *Cap Pilar*. But in the same year that *Cutty Sark* made the headlines, the first Sail Training Race, precursor of the Tall Ships races, was run. There were pictures in the newspapers: topsail schooners and the Dartmouth cadets manning Niarchos's superb three-masted schooner *Creole* as they left Torbay bound for Lisbon. For a boy nurturing the desire to go to sea in the Merchant Service, the fact that the cadets of the School of Navigation at Warsash beat the Royal Navy was gratifying. That their vessel, *Moyana*, opened up and sank on the way home to the Hamble only added the spice of excitement to the whole, wonderful affair. Then came the disastrous news of the loss of *Pamir*, a big, powerful, four-masted barque – a type of sailing vessel Alan Villiers had convinced me through his seductive writings in his *Way of a Ship* was the epitome of the wind-driven cargo-carrier. She had gone down in heavy weather in the South Atlantic and taken a crew of young German cadets with her. It was dreadful and I bought

FIGURE 1

The clipper *Anglesey* running up Channel, off Dover. The refined clipper of the mid-nineteenth century marked the apogee of the wooden sailing ship; thereafter, the technology of iron and steel permitted the building of far larger ships, the four- and five-masted barques, but these lasted for only a few decades. Their demise marked the death of the sailing ship after countless ages during which man harnessed sail and wind to navigate the seas. The replica enables us to witness again the skills and some of the experiences of our forefathers.
(© The National Maritime Museum, Greenwich, London)

three copies of the *Daily Express* that carried the story of one survivor, the cook.

Thus did I become fascinated with the history of sail – at a distance, second and third hand.

The history of sailing vessels is complex and varied. Their earliest appearance on the lakes and rivers of the world can be attributed to three motives: fish, war, trade; and probably these were all roughly contemporaneous. Wherever in the world men built hulls capable of rigging a mast and hoisting a sail, there can have been little variation in early hull form – one type suiting all purposes and relying upon local building materials and methods, along with the developmental cunning of those who set about the task. Once craft moved out of sheltered waters, however, purpose increasingly dominated design, perhaps bending or even breaking tradition. Local sea conditions, strength of tides and tidal range, existence of prevailing, seasonal or daily winds, would all dominate and dictate the optimum form of a sailing vessel.

Much of the influence of local conditions may still be seen in the variable nature of small craft across the world – craft that differ greatly yet perform similar functions. For example, though both use timber and retain traditional hull-forms, the inshore fishing coble of the northeast of England is quite dissimilar to the *jangada* of northeast Brazil. Once seafarers began to voyage further away from their home waters, they were not slow to adopt foreign techniques and practices that proved superior to their own. Thus, by the time the early European maritime states, Portugal and Spain, were venturing forth on their expeditions of discovery, their squadrons were dominated by two types of vessel: the ship-rigged *não* and the *caravel*. The former, which bore both the square sail of northern Europe and the lateen of the Mediterranean and Arab tradition, was full-hulled and capable of carrying a cargo of some quantity; the latter was ideal for advanced reconnaissance, not least because it possessed the extraordinary capability of reconfiguring its rig with three variations, all of which lent themselves to different circumstances. The lateen-rigged *caravela latina* was best at windward work; the *caravela redonda* split her sail area between lateen and square to obtain a more general functionality; the *caravela de armada*, with

only her foremast square-rigged as a proto-barquentine, proved suitable for long passages, worked to windward tolerably well and, most importantly, provided a relatively stable platform for artillery, hence its name.

These hulls were constructed by planking a frame of ribs erected upon a keel and tied fore-and-aft by stringers, a method which not only would become universal for the ocean-going wooden vessel, but also would

eventually prove practical with new materials such as iron and then steel. The so-called North European tradition of clenched planking stiffened by framework built superb and elegant hulls capable of ocean voyaging, but could not increase in size and strength to accommodate either heavy cargo or artillery and would be reserved for small, fast craft.

However, the Europeans were neither preeminent nor the first to explore the open seas.

FIGURE 2

The carrack was the bulk carrier of its day, by the beginning of the sixteenth century able to load more than 1,000 tons and carry as many as 1,000 passengers, and with the introduction of the topsail the type anticipated 400 years of square-rigged sail. This is one of the few contemporary paintings of ships of this era and a wonderful representation of the first generation of ocean-going merchantmen, full of information. The vessels either side of the main ship are thought to depict the same vessel on different tacks.
(© The National Maritime Museum, Greenwich, London)

When the Portuguese reached the Indian Ocean they discovered the Arabs to be accomplished navigators and builders of superb ocean-going *dhows* while the Chinese were, at that critical moment, just retreating from the notion of seeking new lands. Notwithstanding this consequential decision of the distant emperor, the great fleets of junks commanded by Admiral Zheng were vastly more impressive than the single *não* and two *caravels* of Admiral Christopher Columbus. Indeed, there are those who regard the Chinese junk as, perhaps, the most efficient of all sailing rigs: versatile, easily handled and economical. Whether or not it was truly capable of powering vessels of considerable size is still a matter of some conjecture, but it seems likely.

Nevertheless, in a world where human life came cheap, economics did not much intrude and it was the aggressive European states that developed large, ocean-going sailing vessels that tended not to seek windward efficiency – considered by many mariners to be perverse – but made the best use of favourable winds using the square rig. Of course, a square-rig ship has to be capable of some windward work and so a judicious mixture of lateen and triangular sails hoisting on stays was incorporated to form the classic, three-masted 'full-rigged ship'. This, in essence, is what Columbus's *Santa Maria* was and precisely what the *Cutty Sark* was, 400 years later; the difference between them was simply one of refinement due in part to economics and in part to the necessity for a tea clipper to work to windward against the prevailing monsoon of the eastern seas. The refinements consisted of taller masts, stronger rigging, wider yards and a slimmer hull built with some knowledge of hydrodynamics and stability. Sails were better cut and made of stronger material; there were more of them and their area was divided into manageable sizes; the running rigging was more sophisticated and crews had developed multiple expertises – in the nineteenth-century God was less frequently evoked when the sky darkened and the wind rose.

Although nature was the seaman's enemy, it was also his driving force and, happily for the ocean voyager, there was a global wind system that lent itself to ship developments –

FIGURE 3
Pamir, the last of the sailing bulk carriers to carry cargo – grain - round Cape Horn, photographed in a gale during that voyage in 1949. The four-masted barque has come to symbolise the last romantic days of sail.
(Seaforth)

though it took some time to discover it in its entirety. When the friar-seaman Urdaneta discovered the 'Great Gyre' in the Pacific in 1565 and was able to conduct a não – which had arrived in the Philippines by way of the constantly westward-blowing trade winds – *back* towards New Spain, he put Acapulco on the map, initiating the longest-used single seabound trade route in history – it existed until 1815. Whither the wind blew became the loci for trade: ports developed from which goods were dispersed, either directly inland or along the adjacent littoral in smaller, coastal craft always constrained in their navigation by tortuous channels and therefore more likely to use some form of fore-and-aft rig.

Square rig remained in use on the very last, big, cargo-carrying sailing vessels – the traditional ship rig acquiring a fourth mast in the

late nineteenth century (in one single example, the German-flagged *Preussen*, a fifth) before the expense of a larger crew persuaded shipowners to dispense with the yards on the fourth (jigger) mast and extend its gaff-rigged spanker by means of one or two topsails. (The practice had already proved successful on the mizzen mast of a full-rigged ship, converting her to a barque, usually with little significant reduction in performance but significant savings in both gear and manpower.) The adoption of the four-masted barque, with its massive steel-hull scantlings, steel spars, steel-wire standing rigging, and wire and chain running-gear, was probably the apogee of the development of the ocean-going 'windjammer' – an ugly, but somehow fitting, noun. There were a number of five-masted barques, of which the best known are probably the

highly efficient *Potosi* and the ill-fated *København*, but the four-masted barque became the world's last standard long-haul bulk cargo sailing vessel, still carrying grain from Australia to Europe on the very eve of the Second World War. Impounding the several Finnish and German barques on the outbreak of hostilities saved many of them, but attempts to reinvigorate commercial sail after the war were not successful and ended with the disastrous voyage of the *Pamir* that attracted my attention in 1956; her sister-ship *Passat* has been laid up ever since and is now a static exhibit at Travemunde on the Baltic.

Between the galleons of Urdaneta and the big barques of Gustav Erikson – the canny shipowner from Mariehamn in the Åland Islands, who bought up the redundant tonnage of the great European shipowners in the first half of the twentieth century – lay 500 years of development. On the oceans there had been, by and large, a convergence of design. But in coastal waters local demands, traditions and available building materials maintained vernacular distinction to the very end of the sailing era so that even near-neighbours, such as the Netherlands and England, produced coastal and fishing craft of wide difference even though they were in frequent contact and often borrowed or shared common design features. Occasionally, too, a particular rig would prove enduring in one trade long after it became outmoded in another – the best example being the long life of the medieval sprit-rig in

the Thames and English coastal sailing barge, or the square sail in the Humber keel. However, what appear over-conservative anachronisms were actually forms of refinement that lent themselves to their particular working environment: that so seemingly unwieldy a rig as the spritsail ketch of the Thames sailing-barge could carry up to 200 tons of lading through the tide-riven estuarine shallows at speeds rivalling those of a later motor-coaster, speaks for itself.

Coastal and offshore sea areas saw a great deal of development, some of it remarkably sophisticated. The exceptional handiness of

the brig was demonstrated by masters bringing coal from the Tyne to the Thames, and was a wonder to all who observed it working up a crowded, narrowing and tidal river, tacking, backing and filling, making stern-boards and dredging anchors or turning short around using a club-haul. And what of those elegant and yacht-like working craft, the Grand Banks fishing schooners of Maine and Massachusetts? Or the *baggala* and *sambuk*, the *dhoni* and *pattamar*, along with other coastal craft of the Arabian Sea, Persian Gulf and Indian coasts; the *zebec* of the Mediterranean, even the bat-winged Foochow junk has its own pleasing configuration to those with an eclectic eye.

I have mentioned several ships by name, many of which achieved unique historical status by virtue of one attribute or another. Such maritime icons stand on their own merits, yet there is another side to the story: the generic. Certain ship *types* have been extraordinarily important. While the position of, say, the Norse longship, is readily perceptible through its frequent mention in the Sagas and its associations with the Vikings, there are other specific types that had profound impacts upon human history: the Greek galley, for example, the Roman cargo-ship used for conveying Egyptian grain to Ostia, port of Rome; the Hanseatic cog, which wove a vast network of trading patterns across the waters of northwest Europe; the versatile Dutch *fluyt* which, like the caravel, could be adapted for different purposes but possessed the great advantage of being handled by a minimal crew and was copied or captured in considerable numbers by the British, who called them 'fly-boats'; the emigrant ship of the mid nineteenth century, which facilitated a vast diaspora of displaced, disadvantaged and starving people from Europe to North America and Australia – and this list does not even mention the several generations of men-of-war whose naval exploits had such an impact upon history, particularly British history. But, whatever their influences, all have slipped into history and, were it not for the twentieth-century rise of the replica, no one would now have the opportunity to experience, first hand, their qualities, capabilities or, indeed, deficiencies.

Of course, one significant factor that no amount of studying ship construction and faithful replication can take into account was the inherent skill of the contemporary masters. A moderately competent crew could be licked into shape but the success of a sailing ship depended upon the seamanship of her commander, as well as his financial acumen in finding her cargoes. Even such a renowned thoroughbred as the *Cutty Sark* disappointed her owner, John Willis, throughout her career in the China tea trade. It was not until Captain Richard Woodget joined her as master – by which time she had been relegated to the Australian wool-trade – that she began to show her true qualities. The post-1945 era in sail suffered from a lack of expertise but time and the revived interest in sail, coupled with the opportunities to train and qualify in square rig, have provided a small new pool of expert sailing-ship masters, women as well as men.

To summarise the history of the sailing ship and its fascination to an age in which it plays no direct commercial or martial part must suffer from those generalisations attending all such overviews. Yet the 6,000-year history of sail continues to exert a powerful influence upon our imaginations. Yacht sailing is a widely enjoyed sport, both in its cruising and racing forms, while there is more serious investment in two other aspects of sail, both of which require considerable commercial interest. The first is the hi-tech sailing cruise-liner, which marries a modernised version of the sailing ship with powered control systems that obviate the risk to human life and limb inherent in the old, traditional forms of seafaring under sail. Whether these craft fall within the aesthetic or utilitarian criteria of Morris and Ruskin is debatable, for they lack the lines of their predecessors, but nevertheless they represent a reinvigoration of the large sailing ship and, in general, are powered by a 'clean' and renewable energy source. The second revival is more commercially uncertain, but reflects a closer relationship with the old tradition – the replica ship, which, in turn, falls into two categories. Neither is a true replica in the absolute sense of the word, since modern regulations require the fitting of safety equipment, and the absence of an auxiliary engine is today largely inconceivable. However, in a vessel such as the *Endeavour* replica (Chapter 12), these considerations are dealt with by subtle concealment and artifice so that the external appearance and most of the ship's working practices remain authentic to the last quarter of the eighteenth century. Other such replicas are the French cutter *Restronguet* or the Swedish East Indiaman *Götheburg* and the Dutch *jacht Duyfken* (Chapter 8). These specifically named craft represent the great majority of modern replicas, having been inspired by an original vessel with a national or local connection, each indissolubly linked with the means by which finances are raised and running costs and operational objectives are defined.

There are also reconstructions of a *type* of ship, the most obvious examples being the American topsail schooner *Pride of Baltimore* (Chapter 13) and *Stad Amsterdam,* a non-specific reconstruction of an extreme clipper. Such vessels are intended to pay their way and have, perforce, to make concessions to tradition and embrace modern regulations. Nevertheless they provide valuable insights into how things were conducted by our forebears while at the same time providing the adventurous among us with unique, life-enhancing and life-affirming opportunities.

Despite the differences, both types of replica have developed from the common inspiration arising out of an admiration for the utilitarian beauty of various forms of sailing ship and a thirst for a greater understanding of things past. Today they comprise an astonishing inventory spanning many centuries and many types. Such is the richness of our enthusiasm that there are now several East Indiamen, while the example of an extreme clipper in *Stad Amsterdam* finds its counterpoint in the Irish emigrant ships *Dunbrody* and *Jeanie Johnston.* Indeed, unlike the gloomy days of my post-war childhood, when the best that could be hoped for an old sailing ship was her preservation in a graving-dock, today the future of the replica ship seems assured, with people from all walks of life finding something deeply satisfying in sailing into the past.

RICHARD WOODMAN

2 EXPERIMENTAL ARCHAEOLOGY: REPLICAS AND RECONSTRUCTIONS

I first heard the term 'replica' used in an archaeological sense in 1973, during my second year as an Assistant Keeper at the National Maritime Museum, Greenwich. At the time I was helping master boatbuilder Harold Kimber of Highbridge, Somerset, to build a copy (Figure 1)of the Gokstad *faering* (Figure 2). This ninth-century AD four-oared boat had been excavated in 1880 from a royal burial mound near Sandefjord on the west side of Oslo fjord, some sixty miles south of Oslo, Norway. Some forty to fifty years after excavation, when the elements had been conserved and reassembled, she was put on display in the Viking Ship Hall at Bigdøy near Oslo. While I was preparing a museum publication on the building and trials of the faering 'replica', I read Professor John Coles's 1966 article, 'Experimental Archaeology', and then his 1973 book, *Archaeology by Experiment*. I began to consider the idea that, with some rejigging of our aims and methods, we might claim that our faering project was, actually, an aspect of Experimental Boat Archaeology – a process sometimes used in the evaluation of excavated boats and ships.

However, to build our boat, Harold Kimber had used lines drawings and construction plans of the reassembled faering recently prepared by curator Arne-Emil Christensen of the Viking Ship Museum in Oslo. With hindsight I realise that our work was not truly experimental archaeology but, rather, was more akin to the building of a post-medieval vessel for which naval architect's drawings or similarly comprehensive records exist. In short, we had not been involved in experimentation but had built a replica – as accurate a copy as we could make of the shape and structure of the original faering in Oslo.

Replicas and reconstructions

The experience of building the Greenwich faering led me to the conclusion that within the activity generally known as 'replica building', there is a spectrum of projects: at one end are the projects based on comprehensive, usually recent, evidence: a surviving vessel; plans and photographs; detailed technical descriptions; living traditions. Such vessels may best be called 'replicas' – defined in the Oxford English Dictionary as a 'reproduction', 'facsimile', 'copy', or 'model' of an original object. An example of such a replica is HM Bark *Endeavour* (Chapter 12). At the other end of the spectrum are those projects based on incomplete, usually ancient, evidence such as an excavated wreck or early depiction or model. The outcome of research – a scale drawing or model – may be called a 'hypothetical reconstruction' and the subsequent full-scale boat or ship, a 'floating hypothesis'. Examples of such reconstructions are the fourteenth-century AD Bremen cog, based on the excavated remains of one particular vessel (Chapter 6) and the fifth-century BC Athenian trireme, based on ancient descriptions and illustrations of the type (Chapter 4).

For such replicas as, say, HM Bark *Endeavour*, there is little doubt about the shape, structure and rigging, and thus there is little, if any, experimental work to be done until the seagoing phase. On the other hand, the direct evidence for ancient vessels is invariably incomplete (especially for the upper hull, ends, rigging and steering) and much work has to be put into the hypothetical reconstruction of the missing parts – it may even be that reconstruction proves impossible or that several equally possible reconstructions may be devised.

The main motivation for building 'replicas' is probably to emulate predecessors and to understand better their lives in the boatyard and at sea: in effect, replica builders accept a challenge to build and sail a vessel *similar* to those used in the recent past. Such considerations may also be in the minds of those intending to devise a hypothetical reconstruction and then build a floating hypothesis, but their main aim must surely be to formulate

building procedures and sailing trials that will enable them to answer questions about Man's maritime past. In effect, their intention is to undertake an archaeological experiment.

Between these two groups are vessels that are neither fully replicas nor fully floating hypotheses: for example, consider the attempts made between 1892 and 1992 to devise 'reconstructions' of Columbus's three-ship flotilla of his first transatlantic voyage. The evidence for such vessels is neither as full nor as firm as is needed for projects aimed at designing, building and testing replicas and floating hypotheses. The value of such 'in-between' projects and their contribution to our knowledge of the past is uncertain. The evidence used as a basis for determining the ancient design is usually far from compre-hensive and can appear diffuse. It is doubtful whether anything new can be learnt about the original prototype, and it may be that the originators of such projects do not have this in mind. Nevertheless, such undertakings are not without value: when adequately planned and supervised, projects that result in a 'look-alike' vessel (a 'visual' rather than a 'structural' replica), with no other claim to authenticity, may yet offer knowledge about ancient skills if the participants use authentic woodworking

tools and procedures. Furthermore, working the resultant vessel at sea should increase our understanding of the problems faced by our predecessors.

Project aims

The arguments presented above lead to the conclusion that establishing the aims of a replica reconstruction project is a very important task; nevertheless, the aims of some projects have not been made clear in their published reports and it may be that they were never defined. Some projects appear to have been inspired by historical nostalgia or national prestige; others may have been motivated by thoughts of 'learning about oneself', or even by a wish for self-aggrandisement. For an archaeologically motivated project, however, it is essential that there be an overriding archaeological and/or historical aim. For example, the main aim could be 'To design, build and use an authentic reconstruction of a particular vessel, or type of vessel, in order to increase knowledge and understanding of technological, economic and social achievements in earlier times'. Once the aims are defined, then the degree of authenticity to be achieved, and the building

FIGURE 1
The Greenwich replica *faering* in Mutton Cove, Plymouth.

techniques to be used and those to be avoided should become clear, as should the hypotheses to be tested and the questions to be answered by seagoing trials. Furthermore, the resources needed to achieve these targets should become more readily established.

Archaeological projects

The methods used in building Harold Kimber's Gokstad faering replica in 1973 and her subsequent sea trials off Plymouth in 1974 were far less sophisticated than those used today by archaeologists to determine the original form and structure of a boat or ship represented by incomplete, disarranged and inarticulate excavated remains (Figure 3). Such a process begins after the remains have been recovered and moved to a laboratory where each element is recorded in detail, followed either by reassembly (usually after conservation) to form the original hull shape – as had been attempted in Oslo with the Gokstad faering – or by building small-scale models of each of the structural elements (Figure 4). Whichever method is used, the incomplete vessel or model that emerges is then recorded; the resultant construction drawing or small-scale model represents the excavated vessel 'as found' but with displaced timbers reinstated, fragmented timbers made whole, distorted, compressed and shrunken timbers rectified and the vessel rotated to its probable attitude when afloat. This 'as-found'

drawing or model becomes the basis for the attempted reconstruction (Figure 5) of the original ship or boat by 'filling in the missing pieces', using rigorously argued procedures. In its turn, this reconstruction becomes the blueprint for building a full-scale floating hypothesis. In effect, there are four stages in this process:

1   Establish the aims of the project and systematically assemble, work through and re-evaluate all evidence for the excavated vessel.

2   Model every plank and framing timber excavated, and build a small-scale, 'as-found', model of the hull.

3   If sufficient evidence exists, use the Stage 2 model or drawing and other valid evidence to reconstruct the full form, structure, propulsion outfit and steering arrangements of the original craft – there may be variant details in this hypothetical reconstruction.

4   The Stage 3, small-scale reconstruction model or drawing may then be used as a basis for building a full-scale model (floating hypothesis) to be tested afloat.

The post-excavation research undertaken in several recent boat archaeological projects have included aspects of Stages 1, 2 and 3 but Stage 4 has not been attempted. Examples of

FIGURE 2
The Gokstad *faering* of AD 850 on display in the Viking Ship Hall at Bigdøy, near Oslo.

FIGURE 3
The fragmented and disturbed remains of five eleventh-century Viking vessels within a cofferdam at Skuldelev in Roskilde fjord in 1962.

FIGURE 4
An 'as-found' model of the AD 300 Romano-Celtic boat from Barland's Farm, Gwent.

this include: the prehistoric boats Ferriby 1, Brigg 2, and Hasholme; the Barland's Farm boat of Roman date, and the medieval boat from Graveney.[1] In each of these projects the original vessel's performance was estimated from the Stage 3 small-scale reconstruction drawing or model, using naval architectural calculations, rather than being deduced from sea trials of a full-scale reconstruction.

The question may be asked: are performance figures obtained by such methods sufficient or, if financial resources were to become available, should a full-scale model be built and tested? Before such questions can be answered, the methods used and the results obtained by Stages 1, 2 and 3 should be evaluated by an impartial and informed body of specialists who would examine the excavated timbers, the site archive, the research archive and any publications, to determine whether the reconstruction proposed at the end of Stage 3 is a valid one, based on authentic evidence and rigorous arguments. This group should then ensure that the proposed Stage 4 research (building and testing a full-scale reconstruction model) conforms to

FIGURE 5
A reconstruction model
of the Barland's Farm
boat.

FIGURE 8
Floating reconstructions of the five Skuldelev
vessels.
(Werner Karrasch, The Viking Ship Museum, Denmark)

experimental principles such as those discussed by Coles (1977), Coates et al (1995), Crumlin-Pedersen and McGrail (2006).[2] Furthermore, the expected outcome, in terms of significant additions to knowledge about those ancient vessels, must be shown to be commensurate with anticipated costs.

Alternative reconstructions

Excavated evidence for propulsion outfits and steering arrangements is rare, so it is unlikely that, in the Stage 3 research, there will be one unique solution to the reconstruction problem: at the least, alternative propulsion and steering arrangements compatible with the surviving remains will have to be suggested. This was the case during post-excavation research on the Romano-Celtic boat from Barland's Farm and, in the resulting publication, both a square sail and a lugsail were suggested as alternatives for propulsion by sail; rowing, it was thought, could have been in the sit-pull or stand-push mode; steering could have been by steering oar or

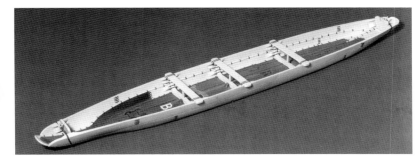

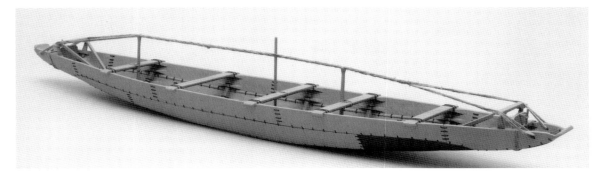

side rudder. Since, in all these examples, the modifications needed to the hull would be minimal, it should be relatively simple to arrange for all the alternatives to be tested during sea trials if any floating hypothesis were to be built.

For two of the six aforementioned ancient projects, however, there are more fundamental uncertainties. Alternative reconstructions have been published for each of the Bronze Age sewn-plank boats, Ferriby 1 (Figure 6 & 7) and Brigg 2, which have significantly different hull shapes. No single full-scale model could include both alternatives. The competing reconstructions, in each case, appear to be based on different ideas as to what was excavated and thus the solution may well be for an impartial and informed group of specialists to undertake an audit of the evidence from which the two pairs of alternatives have been derived. Such a reassessment of the Dover boat evidence is now being undertaken as the published reconstruction has been disputed.[3]

After a series of sea trials of the trireme *Olympias* – the Anglo-Greek floating hypothesis of an Athenian warship of the fifth century BC (Chapter 4) – further research cast doubt on the length of the ancient cubit that

had been used as a module when designing the reconstruction. If the revised modular cubit now identified were to be used to redesign the trireme, oarsmen would be able to apply more power to their stroke, but there would be a different shape of hull. Moreover, it has been estimated that it would cost £1,000,000 to build and fit-out another full-scale trireme; a second full-scale model therefore seems unlikely.

Types of experimental boat reconstruction
Early vessels are dealt with in Part I of this volume, and recent boats and ships in Part II. The original vessels that are the prototypes for the reconstructions discussed in Part I were not formally designed, whereas those in Part II are from periods when ships were 'designed', and specifications, naval architectural drawings and accurate contemporary iconography of many of them have survived.

There are other differences between the two. In the early group, indirect evidence from other contemporary or earlier wrecks, representations and documents has to be used to 'fill in the gaps' in the excavated remains or, in some cases, to design much of the reconstruction. Furthermore, the ancient techniques used to build the original craft are no longer generally in use and it is necessary for the experimenters to learn different techniques and force themselves to think in a way that may well be alien to twenty-first century minds. On the other hand, replica builders in the second group, generally have to use shipbuilding techniques that were used within living memory and, indeed, are still used today in places such as the Indian subcontinent. In this case, directly relevant data may be used to build a substantially accurate replica.

A further distinction can be made by dividing the projects into two groups typified, on the one hand, by the reconstructed Athenian trireme *Olympias* and, on the other, by the reconstructed Viking Age vessels *Skuldelev 1, 2, 3, 5* and *6* (Figure 8). The trireme is an example of a 'Representative' approach to the subject: the designed reconstruction is a synthesis of the character-istic features of a historically identified class of vessel recognised in, and mainly based on, iconographic and documentary evidence. The vessel built is intended to be a typical example of that class. On the other hand, much of the evidence used in the reconstruction of each of the five Skuldelev vessels has been derived directly from the appropriate excavated remains: these are 'Specific' reconstructions. Towards the end of his Introduction to this volume, Richard Woodman similarly contrasts replicas of specifically named craft (for example the Dutch *jacht Duyfken*) with those of ship types (for example 'topsail schooner' or 'extreme clipper').

Of the vessels in the 'early' section of this volume the trireme (Chapter 4) and caravel (Chapter 7) are 'Representative' recon-structions; the Skuldelevs (Chapter 5) and cog (Chapter 6) are 'Specific'. In the 'later' section, the Jamestown fleet (Chapter 9) *Duyfken* (Chapter 8), *Sultana* (Chapter 11) and *Endeavour* (Chapter 12) all appear to be 'Specific' replicas; while the Japanese *edo* (Chapter 10) and *Pride of Baltimore* (Chapter 13) would seem to be 'Representative'.

Whether the representative or the specific approach is used in a particular case depends on whether the primary basis for the proposed reconstruction is for a class of vessel (a trireme, or late-fifteenth-century seagoing ship, for example), in which case the recon-struction would be 'Representative'; or whether that basis is a single vessel (an excavated boat or ship, or naval architectural drawings), in which case the reconstruction would be 'Specific'. The specific and repre-sentative approaches to experimental arch-aeology are both potentially valid ways of finding out more about the past. Both require high-quality evidence, the rigorous present-ation of arguments, the logically developed formulation of a reconstruction, the authentic building of a full-scale model and scientifically based trials. Both types also use all forms of evidence available – excavated, textual, iconographic, ethnographic and environ-mental – and the natural physical laws.

The value of replicas and reconstructions

Replicas
A 'specific' project based on a prototype for which comprehensive structural evidence survives, and from a period when building and sailing techniques are well-documented, should result in an authentic replica. Although little new information may be gained about the past, the participants in, and observers of, such experiments, as well as the general public, may well come to appreciate more vividly the skills and knowledge of shipbuilders and seamen of earlier days, possibly leading to a deeper understanding of the importance of sailing ships and an appreciation of the skills needed in their design, building and use.

Hypothetical reconstructions
On the other hand, an experiment – specific or representative – aiming to design and build a reconstruction of an early vessel from a shipbuilding and seafaring environment about which incomplete technical information has come down to us, could have the potential to increase knowledge about those aspects of earlier times, especially if the project aims to answer specific questions. Much has been learnt from the trireme and Skuldelev experiments, and something has been learnt from almost every experiment in which only partial evidence for the prototype has

survived. Projects that have made little contribution to our knowledge of ancient technology and seafaring probably foundered in their early stages for not having clearly defined aims and because the originators' ideas were not circulated for criticism at an early stage. Furthermore, few experimenters appear to have built a small-scale 'as-found' model as a preliminary step in their research, and several have not yet been published in a manner that would enable their archaeological/historical value to be evaluated.

Although the outcome of a boat archaeological experiment very much depends on the rigour and accuracy in the practical work of building and testing a 'floating hypothesis', the earlier transformation of the boat as excavated – incomplete and disarranged – into a reconstruction, small-scale drawing or model has an even greater influence on the potential of that experiment to increase knowledge of the past. This transformation is an essential prerequisite to building and trials. A start has been made on the compilation of a guide to best practice for boat archaeological experiments – see the article 'Experimental boat and ship archaeology: principles and methods' in the *International Journal of Nautical Archaeology*, Vol 24 – and a consensus on what should be best practice in archaeological experiments could well emerge if the multi-disciplinary readers of this volume were now to read that article and the papers by John Coles in 1977, Ole Crumlin-Pedersen in 1995 and Ole Crumlin-Pedersen with Seán McGrail in 2006 and then publish an informed criticism.

Seán McGrail

REFERENCES

Blue, L. Hocker, F. & Englert, A. (eds). 2006. *Connected by the Sea* ISBSA 10. Oxford

Brown, D.K. 1998. 'Experimental boat archaeology seen as reverse engineering'. Unpublished paper, privately circulated.

Clark, P. (ed.) 2004. *Dover Bronze Age Boat*. Swindon

—— 2004 *Dover Bronze Age Boat in Context*. Oxford

Coates, J. et al 1995. 'Experimental boat and ship archaeology', *International Journal of Nautical Archaeology*, 24: 293–301

Coles, J.M. 1966. 'Experimental archaeology'. *Proc. Soc. Antiquaries of Scotland*, 99: 1–20

—— 1973. *Archaeology by Experiment*. London

—— 1977. 'Experimental archaeology: theory & principles'. *Sources & Techniques in Boat Archaeology*, McGrail, S. (ed). Oxford

Crumlin-Pedersen, O. 1995. 'Experimental archaeology and ships'. *International Journal of Nautical Archaeology*, 24: 303–16

Crumlin-Pedersen, O. & McGrail, S. 2006. 'Some principles for the reconstruction of ancient boat structures'. *International Journal of Nautical Archaeology*, 35: 53–57

Crumlin-Pedersen, O. & Olsen, O. 2002. *Skuldelev Ships* 1. 'Ships and Boats of the North', 4.1, Roskilde

Fenwick, V. (ed.) 1978. *Graveney Boat*, Oxford

Gifford, E. & Gifford, J. 1996. 'Sailing performance of Anglo-Saxon ships as derived from the building and trials of half-scale models of Sutton Hoo and Graveney ships'. *Mariner's Mirror*, 82: 131–53

—— 2004. 'Use of half-scale models in archaeological research' in Clark, P. (ed): 67–81

Gifford, E., Gifford, J. & Coates, J. 2006. 'Construction & trials of a half-scale model of the Early Bronze Age ship, Ferriby 1, to assess the capability of the full-size ship' in Blue, L. Hocker, F. & Englert, A. (eds): 57–62

McGrail, S. 1976. *Building & Trials of the Replica of an Ancient Boat: the Gokstad Faering*. Maritime Monograph 11. Greenwich

—— 1993. 'Experimental Archaeology & the Trireme' in Shaw, T. (ed) 4–10

—— 2004. *Boats of the World* 2nd edition. Oxford

—— 2006. 'Experimental boat archaeology: has it a future?' in Blue, L. et al (eds): 8–15

Millett, M. & McGrail, S. 1987. 'Archaeology of the Hasholme logboat'. *Archaeological Journal* 144: 69–155

Morrison, J.S., Coates, J.F. & Rankov, B.N. 2000. *Athenian Trireme*. Cambridge

Nayling, N. & McGrail, S. 2004. *Barland's Farm Romano-Celtic Boat*. CBA Research Report 138. York

Rankov, B.N. forthcoming. Proceedings of a Trireme Conference at Oxford in 1998

Roberts, O. 1992. 'Brigg 'raft' re-assessed as a round bilge Bronze Age boat'. *International Journal of Nautical Archaeology*, 21: 245–58

Shaw, T. (ed). 1993. *Trireme Project*. Oxford

Wright, E.V. 1990. *Ferriby Boats: Seacraft of the Bronze Age*. London

NOTES

[1] Ferriby 1, Brigg 2, and the Hasholme find are all prehistoric boats excavated from foreshore and land sites in the Humber estuary region on England's East Coast. Ferriby 1 and Brigg 2 are Bronze Age sewn-plank boats dated to around 1780 BC and 800 BC respectively. The Hasholme find is a logboat some 13m in length (one of the largest of the European logboats) and dated around 300 BC. In 1984 the remains were excavated from a field – now below sea level – which in the Iron Age had been a tidal creek of the River Humber. See Wright, 1990; McGrail 2004; Millett & McGrail (1987).

The Barland's Farm boat is a Celtic plank boat built frame first towards the end of the Roman period, around AD 300. The remains were excavated in 1993 from a river bed – now a land site – east of Newport, Gwent, on the northern shores of the Severn Estuary. See Nayling & McGrail (2004)

The Graveney clinker-built boat of around AD 900 was excavated from the southern shores of the Thames estuary in 1970. She had been a small sail-powered coastal trading vessel. See Fenwick (1978).

[2] In a paper presented at the first conference on Boat and Ship Archaeology held in 1976 at the National Maritime Museum, Greenwich, Professor John Coles drew attention to the lack of rules and procedures that would guide the hypothetical reconstruction of excavated vessels and the subsequent building and trials of full-scale models. Two decades later, in 1995, Dr John Coates (formerly Chief Naval Architect at the UK Ministry of Defence) and nine colleagues published a paper aimed at filling that gap. In 2006 Ole Crumlin-Pedersen (formerly of the Viking Ship Museum, Roskilde) and Seán McGrail published an article describing the principles that have to be followed if attempts to reconstruct the original vessel from excavated remains are to lead to reliable results.

[3] The remains of the sewn-plank boat from Dover were excavated in 1992; she is dated to around 1550 BC. See Clark (2004).

3 MEASURING PERFORMANCE UNDER SAIL

The natural interface, where sky meets sea, is a difficult place to inhabit. It is the boundary between two fluids that differ in density by a factor of one thousand, where the energy from one whips up the surface of the other. In the air the flow patterns are gusty and unsteady, while in the water they can be a steady tidal current, the orbital motion of a lazy swell, or the turbulence of a breaking crest. A sailing vessel has to operate across this complex boundary, with its hull in the dense water, its sails in the turbulent air. As a result, measuring the performance of the vessel is no easy matter. The forces on the hull and sails are very variable in both magnitude and direction. To make matters worse, the presence of the vessel modifies the flow patterns, which means that measurements taken with onboard instruments are subject to unavoidable error.

However, as with any measurements, it is important to consider what is to be measured and why. Is the aim to get a full,

comprehensive picture of a vessel's performance in all conditions, or a 'quick and dirty' assessment of windward ability and a rough idea of passage speeds? The full picture is usually presented as a 'polar diagram', a graphical presentation that shows the variation of boat speed in different wind speeds over a range of angles to the wind. Figure 1 shows a typical polar diagram for a sailing yacht, obtained from a computer simulation program. With the information in this diagram it is, in theory, possible to determine the sailing speed under almost any condition and thus estimate how passage times vary with wind speed and direction and how the speed made good to windward varies with wind speed.

Unfortunately theory and practice are not the same thing and when attempts are made to measure the variation of boat speed with wind speed and direction, a great deal of scatter appears. A measured polar diagram is shown in Figure 1 and again in Figure 2 – the result of experiments on a replica Japanese sailing trader conducted by a skilled and well-equipped team of engineers and naval architects (Chapter 10).[1] It is immediately apparent that there is a considerable variability in the results. For example, there is almost 30 per cent difference in recorded boat speed when close hauled on port and starboard tacks (even though the speed axis is the ratio of boat speed to wind speed, a data reduction that might be expected to minimise the scatter).

These results – like many others – show that, even with a substantial budget and access to highly qualified teams of sailors and scientists, the complete measurement of sailing performance is very difficult indeed. The question is why, and what options are there for alternative approaches?

The challenges of measurement

Initially, let us consider the question in the simplest case of boats sailing in calm waters with no tidal streams. Here the water in which the boat is sailing is more or less stationary, so the only variable is the wind – and what a variable that is.

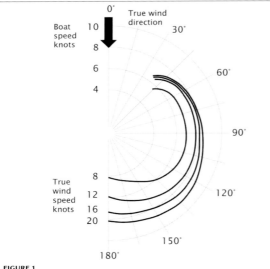

FIGURE 1

A typical polar diagram for a sailing yacht, obtained from a computer simulation program. The wind is blowing from the top of the diagram and the dark lines show how the boat speed varies with true wind direction over a range of wind speed. Note that as the wind rises, the speed lines become closer together because the resistance of the boat increases rapidly due to the build up of the wave-making component of that resistance. (This diagram does not take account of the effect of waves.)

Figure 3 shows the output from wind speed and direction instruments over a period of 25 seconds.[2] Even when the direction measurements are smoothed by damping the wind vane, there are variations of up to 25° in one second. While a skilled helmsman might be able to detect a change of wind direction during one second, it is altogether another matter to make the boat respond, unless it is a small dinghy. Larger vessels are condemned to sail through these rapid changes, although they might be able to respond to the more general longer-term shifts that are apparent from the damped trace.

The wind speed shows less rapid variation but nevertheless varies by as much as 3 knots in one second, which from a starting level of 6 knots represents a 50 per cent increase. This doubles the resulting forces produced by the rig, which has the potential to increase the speed by 30 per cent or more (depending upon the steepness of the resistance curve at the sailing point). However, since the driving force from the sails is typically $\frac{1}{100}$ the weight of the boat, a doubling of the driving force will only produce an acceleration of 0.1 m/sec², which means it will take many seconds for the speed to increase by 30 per cent. By this time the wind has changed again, long before the boat has 'caught up' with the previous change. Because it takes time to accelerate a vessel, the driving force from the rig is not immediately translated into increased speed, so there is a time lag between the measured wind speed and the boat speed.

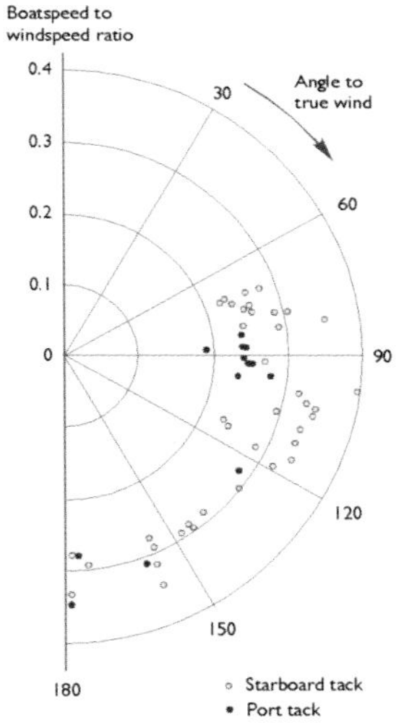

Difficulties of onboard measurement

Unfortunately this variability in wind speed and direction is only part of the reason why it is so difficult to measure sailing performance. The sails themselves influence the flow patterns around the boat to such an extent that measurements taken with instruments located in the standard position at the masthead can have substantial errors. In fact, the masthead is one of the worst places to locate wind instruments.[3] Here the error in wind direction (when close hauled) can be as much as 7° (to windward). In 2002 a report revealed similar errors at the masthead but also showed that as the heading moves away from close hauled, the errors reduce to 2° to 3° only, so results on reaching and running courses are more reliable.[4]

FIGURE 2
Measured polar performance diagram for *Naniwa-maru* – replica of a Japanese sailing trader (see Chapter 10). The graph shows the variation of boat speed to wind speed ratio over a range of headings relative to the true wind direction. It shows that in calm water the vessel could not sail closer than 75 degrees to the wind. There was also a large difference in performance between the port and starboard tacks, for reasons that the experimenters could not understand.

Boatspeed to windspeed ratio
0.4
0.3
0.2
0.1
0
Angle to true wind
30
60
90
120
150
180
○ Starboard tack
● Port tack

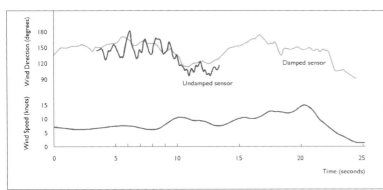

FIGURE 3
Measurements of wind speed and direction over a period of 25 seconds. Traces of damped and undamped wind vane are compared and show substantial variations in wind direction that occur at a frequency that cannot be followed by any but the most manoeuvrable dinghy. The wind speed variations represent a change in driving force of as much as 100%, taking place in a matter of seconds.

Wind Direction (degrees)
180
150
120
90
Wind Speed (knots)
15
10
5
0

Damped sensor
Undamped sensor

Time (seconds)
0   5   10   15   20   25

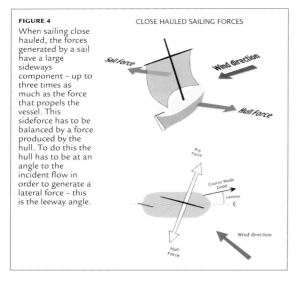

FIGURE 4
When sailing close hauled, the forces generated by a sail have a large sideways component – up to three times as much as the force that propels the vessel. This sideforce has to be balanced by a force produced by the hull. To do this the hull has to be at an angle to the incident flow in order to generate a lateral force – this is the leeway angle.

respectable 45° to the wind rather than the actual 75° – a big difference.

This shows that it is important to know the leeway angle if reliable estimates of windward performance are to be made – yet it is actually one of the most difficult variables to measure. Like the sails, the hull influences the flow field around itself, so attempts to tow drag devices over the stern and measure the angle with the hull centreline are fraught with difficulty.[5] If the line is short the drag device will be strongly affected by the hull downwash and wake; if it is long it will deflect under the influence of the wind. A vane mounted on a frame ahead of the vessel has been used but it is complex and vulnerable.

Effects of waves and tidal streams
Thus far the discussion has been limited to

Leeway
When a vessel sails close to the wind, the sails generate large lateral forces as well as forces that drive the vessel forwards, in the ratio of as much as three to one (Figure 4). This means that the hull must produce an equal and opposite force and, to do this, has to run at an angle to the water flowing past it – the leeway angle. This has the effect of turning the bow of the boat towards the wind relative to the course actually sailed, which in turn reduces the apparent wind angle as judged from the boat. While leeway angles for sailing yachts may be small (a matter of a few degrees), those for more traditionally shaped vessels can be large – as much as 15° or more.

Figure 5 shows the geometry of a sailing vessel working to windward and achieving a course made good that is at 75° to the true wind direction. Assuming that its speed is 40 per cent of the true wind speed, the vessel will experience an apparent wind that is 15° closer to the bow than the true wind. If it is sailing with 15° of leeway, this means that *from the point of view of people on board*, the wind they feel on their faces will be 30° closer to the bow than the real wind is to the course made good. Thus, if the observers are not able to estimate the leeway angle or the difference between real and apparent wind directions, they may conclude that their vessel is sailing at a

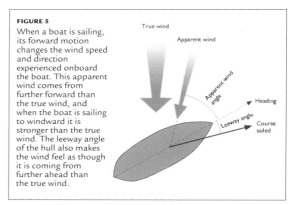

FIGURE 5
When a boat is sailing, its forward motion changes the wind speed and direction experienced onboard the boat. This apparent wind comes from further forward than the true wind, and when the boat is sailing to windward it is stronger than the true wind. The leeway angle of the hull also makes the wind feel as though it is coming from further ahead than the true wind.

measurements recorded in flat water and non-tidal conditions; add the effects of waves and tidal currents and the results become even more problematic. It is very difficult to measure tidal streams accurately. Estimates can be made from tidal diamonds on charts and from tidal atlases, but the results are location-specific and vary considerably with the position in the neap/spring cycle. It is generally easier to estimate the direction of the current than its speed. If speed under reaching conditions is required, it is often possible to arrange to sail across the current or on reciprocal runs with and against the current. This is not generally possible for close-hauled tests when the sailing course is dictated by the wind direction. If the recordings are based on GPS position readings (and thus the speed and position over the ground), a vessel sailing at 5 knots through the water against a current of 1 knot will record an angle to the true wind that is about 10° less than it should be. This error is, of course, avoided if the boat is the frame of reference but, as noted above, that introduces other errors.

If the tests are carried out in waves, another level of complexity applies. Not only do the waves increase the fluctuations in the measured signals but also they have a significant effect upon the resistance of the hull, an effect that is dependent upon the height and length of the waves and their angle to the course of the vessel. Even under relatively moderate sea conditions, a head sea

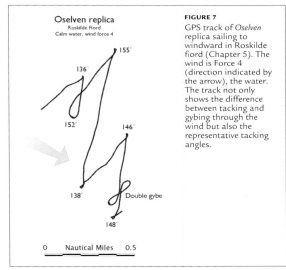

FIGURE 7

GPS track of *Oselven* replica sailing to windward in Roskilde fiord (Chapter 5). The wind is Force 4 (direction indicated by the arrow), the water. The track not only shows the difference between tacking and gybing through the wind but also the representative tacking angles.

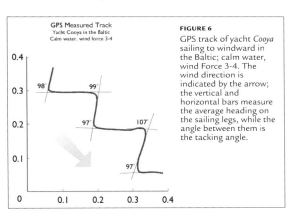

FIGURE 6

GPS track of yacht *Cooya* sailing to windward in the Baltic; calm water, wind Force 3-4. The wind direction is indicated by the arrow; the vertical and horizontal bars measure the average heading on the sailing legs, while the angle between them is the tacking angle.

FIGURE 8

GPS track of *Roar Ege* replica sailing in Roskilde fjord (Chapter 5). The wind is strong, Force 6-7, but the water calm due to the very limited fetch in the narrow part of the fjord. Tacking and gybing manoeuvres are recorded, demonstrating the large distance lost to windward by adopting the safer gybing manoeuvre.

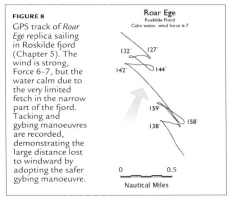

can double the resistance of a boat while the motions it causes also reduce the effectiveness of the sails due to the pitching and rolling.

All this may be rather depressing reading for those who want fully to quantify the performance of replicas and it certainly means that many of the reported results should be viewed very critically. In particular, statements based upon on-board visual observations of instrument read-outs are likely to be extremely unreliable.

Priorities for measuring replica performance

It is clear from the foregoing that the measurement of the whole range of performance requires high levels of technical skills and

equipment as well as a test area free of tidal currents and where waves are small. It will need many days of testing to find all the right conditions and, depending upon the approach adopted, a chase boat may be needed in addition to the replica itself. All these requirements are likely to overstretch the budget and capabilities of all but the very best funded of organisations. Given such difficulties, what options do sailors of replicas have for measuring the performance of their vessels? Are there any 'quick and dirty' methods good enough to establish an order of merit and give a generalised measure of windward capability? Can anything useful be done on a shoestring, using readily available instrumentation?

FIGURE 9
The replica of a typical
Japanese coastal trading
ship, *Naniwa-maru*, during
sailing trials in Osaka Bay,
seen here running before
the wind (Chapter 7). The
great bellying sail, while a
powerful driver
downwind, was pretty
well impossible to set
successfully upwind. The
soft materials and the
shape made it difficult to
flatten.

FIGURE 10
Prior to conducting sailing
trials experts at the Viking
Ship Museum in Roskilde
explain the sails and
controls on the replica of
a small Viking boat.

FIGURE 11

The barge yacht *Rosie Probert* aground in the Humber Estuary. Her fine bow and leeboards are clear in this picture. She is a half model of a Thames barge and though in tests she pointed well when tacking, she made a lot of leeway and showed that onboard instruments only tell half the story.

FIGURE 12

GPS record of the track sailed by *Rosie Probert* when beating against a Force 4–5 wind in an almost flat sea with no tidal stream. She achieved an angle to the true wind of 85° whereas the onboard impression was of sailing much closer to the wind.

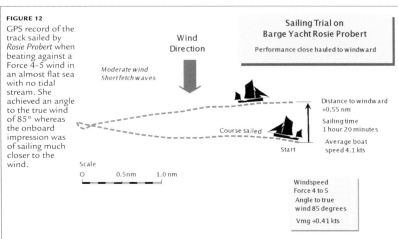

Wind Direction

Sailing Trial on
Barge Yacht Rosie Probert

Performance close hauled to windward

Moderate wind
Short fetch waves

Distance to windward
+0.55 nm

Course sailed

Sailing time
1 hour 20 minutes

Start

Average boat
speed 4.1 kts

Scale

0   0.5nm   1.0 nm

Windspeed
Force 4 to 5
Angle to true
wind 85 degrees

Vmg +0.41 kts

If the carried instruments are standard, then on-board measurements of boat speed and heading plus wind speed and direction will give very limited results. At the very least, measurements must be time-averaged – not easy with modern digital read-outs – so some form of data recording is necessary. Numbers snatched instantaneously from the log and wind speed indicator are almost worthless. When the wind is from aft or around to the beam, the distortions of air flow over the sails will have less influence on the instruments than when close hauled, so time-averaged measurements from on-board instruments can be informative and it should be possible to obtain at least an envelope of the range of performance in different wind speeds. When compared to yachts, trading and voyaging vessels are slow for their size, so their resistance is dominated by the frictional component, and the wind-speed-to-boat-speed ratio is likely to be reasonably constant. This means that tests in one wind speed can be extrapolated to another to provide a calculated envelope of boat speed in different winds.

However, when the wind moves forward of the beam, on-board instrumentation becomes unreliable. To measure both the angle of the apparent wind to the boat and the leeway angle simultaneously and accurately is almost impossible. However, all these are indirect variables used to calculate what matters: the angle sailed against the wind. If this can be determined directly then apparent wind and leeway become irrelevant; fortunately for the replica sailor, new technology in the form of low-cost GPS systems has made this possible.

Use of GPS tracking to record tacking angle
A GPS allows the speed and track of a boat to be recorded with great accuracy. Therefore, if a test site with low (or known) tidal currents is available, the potential exists for accurate results. Of course, the GPS does not give measurements of wind speed and direction but if these are not required as inputs to a calculation of windward performance, they do not have to be known with high accuracy. A combination of readings from conventional instruments and the judgement of the sailor can provide adequate answers.

With the record of the boat's track from a GPS it is possible to measure directly the tacking angle – the change of course when a vessel goes from one tack to another. In practice the actual speed made good will also depend upon the ability of the sailor to work the wind shifts and the ground lost during tacking, but the tacking angle is a measure of the vessel's underlying performance potential. It therefore provides a very useful figure of merit that can be used to assess the windward performance and compare it to the results of other vessels.

The tacking angle can be measured from GPS track data and, if records are made over a number of tacks, an averaged value can be obtained. It is also possible to obtain average

boat speed through the water from GPS tracks and, when combined with estimates of the average wind speed during the tests, the actual speed made good can be calculated.

A number of PC-based marine navigation packages that interface with GPS systems are available and the results can be analysed directly on the screen or downloaded for additional analysis. It is also possible to interface handheld GPS units with laptops or small handheld computers (PDAs); indeed, some PDAs are now available with integral GPS capability. There are many dedicated GPS data-logging systems becoming available. Using an iPAQ PDA in a waterproof bag connected to a Garmin handheld GPS, I put together a robust system that I have used on a variety of sailing vessels – from my own 8.5m (27ft 10in) yacht to Viking ship replicas at Roskilde (Chapter 5).

Sample results – yachts and Viking ships
Figure 6 shows the results obtained sailing a 1914 vintage cruising yacht, *Cooya*, in the Baltic. In calm water and a gentle breeze she tacked through an average of 99°, giving a sailing angle to the wind of 50°. The same instrumentation system was used to track two different Viking ship replicas sailed by the Roskilde Ship Museum. First was the small *Oselven* (Figure 7) sailing in a Force 4 breeze, close to the windward shore, in very small waves. The tacking angles varied from 136° to 155°, giving an average of 146° and thus an angle to the true wind of 73°. It is also clear from the traces just how much ground is lost by gybing through the wind (safer in a square-rigged boat) rather than tacking. Later in the day the wind increased to Force 5 or more and the average tacking angle dropped to 151°.

Measurements were also taken on the larger *Roar Ege* when working down Roskilde Fjord into winds at times touching Force 7 (Figure 8). For safety reasons the ship was gybed on many occasions and, as the trace shows, when this manoeuvre is carried out in restricted water very little ground is made to windward. The average tacking angle for this Viking ship was 144°, or an angle to the true wind of 72° – no doubt if there had been

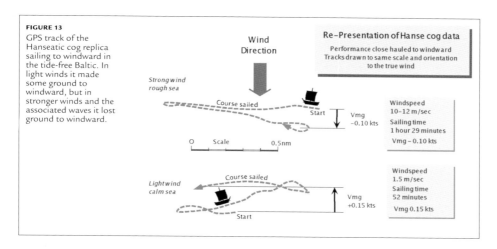

FIGURE 13
GPS track of the Hanseatic cog replica sailing to windward in the tide-free Baltic. In light winds it made some ground to windward, but in stronger winds and the associated waves it lost ground to windward.

waves to match the wind speed, this angle would have been substantially greater.

Hanse cog

Another example of this measuring technique was used during the sailing trials of the Hanseatic cog replica (Chapter 6).[6] Trials were conducted in the Baltic, where tidal-current effects were small. The vessel's position was recorded with a GPS, thus providing a record of track and speed. Two sets of results were presented – one in a light wind of around 1.5 metres per second (Force 2), the other in 10 to 12 metres per second (Force 5–6). They are re-plotted in Figure 13 and show that, while the cog could make ground to windward in the light winds, it lost ground against the strong wind and associated waves. While not stated by the authors, it is very likely that the impression from on board the vessel was of progress being made to windward as the apparent wind angle would have been well forward of the beam. The authors remarked:

Can cogs beat against the wind? The polar plots show the maximally attainable angle of closeness to the true wind to be between 67 and 75 degrees, depending on sail size and wind speed. These are course angles that can be sailed for at least short periods of time, resulting in a Vmg [Velocity made good] value of approximately one knot. Over longer distances, however, Vmg is

only attained in very light winds in sheltered water, i.e. without seaway. Such were the results of measurements of speed and distance over ground with the aid of GPS devices. Taking two tacking manoeuvres into account, at wind speeds of Beaufort 2 and using the total sail area, the Vmg amounted to 0.63 knots in ballast condition. In load condition with two reefs in the sail and sailing at SSW 6 on a moderate sea in an area off Warnemünde, the cog was forced to turn 0.1 nautical miles away from the wind. In completely unloaded condition, sailing with one reef at ESE 5 to 6 in the Strander Bay, the loss of closeness to the wind was higher – 0.2 nautical miles over distances of 1.8 and 2.4 nautical miles. In such situations the leeway is quite considerable. It reaches 10 to 15 degrees and can climb even higher when the sheet is hauled too close…. Thus Hanse cogs can hardly have beaten against the wind; they are suitable only for reaches.

The use of GPS track data is simple and effective and, were it widely adopted by replica sailors, it is possible to imagine a database being established where results are deposited. It would then be possible for other researchers to access the data, knowing that it was all similarly obtained and therefore directly comparable. This might then allow us to build a fuller picture of the sailing capabilities of ancient vessels.

Model testing and computer models

Thus far we have addressed the measurement of the performance of full-scale replicas – budget constraints generally preclude any other forms of testing. However, if resources are available, analytical, wind-tunnel and towing-tank tests can produce useful additional data.[7,8,9] With the rise of computer power, it is also becoming possible to create computer models using Computational Fluid Dynamics (CFD) tools as a way to avoid the high costs of wind-tunnel and towing-tank tests. However, these methods must be applied to traditional vessels with caution – the flexibility of materials used for the masts, rigging and sails can lead to considerable stretch and, therefore, changes in the shape of the sails. Also the surface finish on the hull, even when new, is a great deal rougher than assumed for high-performance sailing vessels, so suitable corrections must be applied to tank test results. It is worth noting that since the majority of the resistance to motion of sailing trading vessels is frictional it is particularly sensitive to hull roughness. For example, the fouling of a hull after one season in tropical waters can more than double the frictional resistance of the hull, a factor that can clearly have a very marked effect on passage times and windward ability.

Conclusions

The interface 'twixt wind and water is a demanding environment. Even with sophisticated instrumentation and data processing, it is very difficult to obtain an accurate and comprehensive characterisation of the performance of a sailing vessel. In the future, a combination of model testing and computer simulation may provide a solution but we will need to model real materials and real conditions in ways not currently possible. In the meantime, the availability of low cost GPS provides a way forward. While such systems do not enable every aspect of performance to be measured, they can produce data that is sufficient to estimate passage speeds and establish at least an order of merit for windward performance and how it varies with the conditions. Simple measurements of the tacking angle are all that are needed to estimate windward ability and, since it is quick and easy to obtain such measurements, they can be repeated in a range of different combinations of wind and waves. While these cannot be used to put the data onto a comprehensive polar performance plot, they can provide the practical sailor with a way not only to compare the performance of different craft but also to gain an impression of how our ancestors fared at sea.

COLIN PALMER

NOTES
[1] Nomoto, K, Masuyama, Y. & Sakurai, A. 2001. Sailing Performance of 'Namiwa-maru', a Full Scale Reconstruction of Sailing Trader of Japanese Heritage. In, *Proceedings of the 15th Chesapeake Sailing Yacht Symposium*. USA, Chesapeake Sailing Yacht Symposium.
[2] Gatehouse, R. N. B., 1968, The Design of Sailing Instruments. In *Instrument Sailing, the Measurement of Full-Scale Performance and its Relation to Predicted Performance*. SUYR Report 22, Southampton University.
[3] Marchaj, C. A. 1979 *Aero-Hydrodynamics of Sailing*. Granada Publishing, London.
[4] Hansen, H., Jackson, P & Hochkirch, K. 2002. Comparison of Wind Tunnel and Full-Scale Aerodynamic Sail Force Measurements. High Performance Yacht Design Conference, Auckland, New Zealand.
[5] Grant, P. H. & Stephens, O. J., 1997. On Test Measurements in Full Scale Test Programs. In

Proceedings of the 13th Chesapeake Sailing Yacht Symposium, Annapolis, USA.
[6] Brandt, H. & Hochkirch, K. 1995. The sailing properties of the Hanse cog in comparison with other cargo sailships. *Ship Technology Research* Vol. 42, No. 1.
[7] Masuyama, Y Sakurai, A, Fukasawa, T., and Aoki, K. 2005. Comparison of tacking and wearing performance between a Japanese traditional square rig and a Chinese lug rig. SNAME, *Proceedings of the 17th Chesapeake Sailing Yacht Symposium*.
[8] Nestorson, M. 2004. Reconstruction of the Technical Properties of the Göta wreck. Report No. X-04/155. Department of Shipping and Marine Technology, Chalmers University of Technology, Gothenburg, Sweden.
[9] Olsson, M. 2005. Performance Predictions for the East Indiaman Gotheborg. Report No: X-05/164. Department of Shipping and Marine Technology, Chalmers University of Technology, Gothenburg, Sweden.

PART I

ANCIENT
AND
MEDIEVAL SHIPS

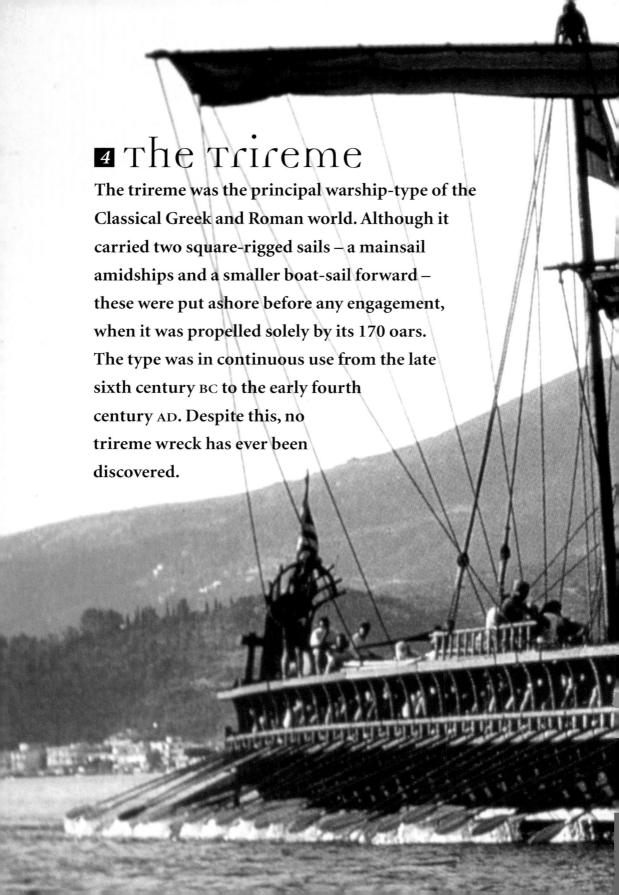

4 the trireme

The trireme was the principal warship-type of the Classical Greek and Roman world. Although it carried two square-rigged sails – a mainsail amidships and a smaller boat-sail forward – these were put ashore before any engagement, when it was propelled solely by its 170 oars. The type was in continuous use from the late sixth century BC to the early fourth century AD. Despite this, no trireme wreck has ever been discovered.

Our knowledge of the trireme is thus derived entirely from a variety of indirect sources, including reliefs and vase-paintings, ancient literature, inscriptions and various indications from mainly land-based archaeology. It is not, therefore, possible to build anything that can reasonably be called a 'replica', although over the last 500 years there have been several attempts at what may be termed 'hypothetical reconstructions', mainly on paper but also physical. The most recent of these projects culminated in the building of the Hellenic Navy vessel *Olympias* (Figure 1), the subject of five series of sea trials between 1987 and 1994.

History of the trireme

The trireme was ultimately derived from the oared vessels of the Aegean and Eastern Mediterranean in the later second millennium BC. From around 900 BC, oared ships with a pronounced forefoot appear regularly and in some detail on Greek vases and are often shown carrying warriors who fight from the decks. Their oars appear to have been arranged on a single level with one man working each oar. Such single-level vessels were used for centuries, and in the later period had twenty, thirty or even fifty rowers. They were often used to carry important individuals, as troop transports, or as scouting vessels.

By the latter part of the eight century BC, a new type of ship appears in Greek vase paintings and on Assyrian reliefs, with oars arranged on two levels, allowing the construction of shorter and more manoeuvrable vessels with the same oarpower as before. *Pentekontores* ('fifty-oars') were usually privately owned as oared merchantmen capable of taking cargoes smaller than could be carried by sailing vessels, but with the invaluable ability to make way against unfavourable winds. They could be used by the same owners for both trade and piracy, and were often commandeered by rulers or states to form ad hoc war-fleets. Both Homer and vase-paintings of the sixth century BC imply that longer two-level vessels (*nees dikrotoi*) also existed, with possibly up to 120 oars,[1] but it is the pentekontors that appear most frequently in literary sources.[2]

The subsequent development of the trireme was a natural progression from the pentekontor, achieved by adding a third level of rowers at the top. This was done either by making the hull broader and deeper, so that the top level of rowers – the thranites (*thranitai*) – rowed over the topwale while both the mid-level zygians (*zygioi*) and lowest-level thalamians (*thalamioi*) rowed through oarports, or by attaching seats for the thranites and an outrigger bracket at the top of a hull. The trireme probably did not emerge, however, until the late sixth century BC. Although the historian Thucydides, writing at the end of the fifth century BC, attributes its invention to the Corinthians around 700 BC, there is reason to believe that credit should instead be given to the Phoenicians who lived on the coast of modern Syria and Lebanon a century and a half later.[3] However, the earliest clear reference we have to a trireme (*trieres*) is in a fragment by the Greek poet Hipponax, from Ephesus on the coast of Asia Minor, writing in the 530s BC.[4]

It is probably no coincidence that the first recorded naval battle to involve ramming tactics dates to this same period. It was fought around 535 BC off Alalia in Corsica between refugees from Phocaea in Asia Minor and a combined Etruscan and Carthaginian fleet. According to historian Herodotus, the Phocaeans won the battle but lost their entire fleet, with forty ships destroyed and twenty rendered useless because 'their rams were twisted off'.[5]

We know from inscriptions that in the fourth century BC triremes had 170 oars, of which 62 were for *thranitai*, 54 for *zygioi* and 54 for *thalamioi*, giving 31, 27 and 27 rooms at the three levels respectively. Each oar was rowed by one man.[6] Such a vessel, displacing around 48 tonnes fully manned, would have been about the same length and manoeuvrability as the largest two-level ships but would have had up to 70 per cent more oarpower. This would have given it an advantage of up to 1 knot in sprint speed and around 2.5 knots more than an ordinary pentekontor at both cruising and ramming speeds, more than cancelling out the pentekontor's advantage in manoeuvrability.

This extra margin of performance would

have justified the considerable increase in cost represented by such vessels, in terms of both the hulls and the much larger crews needed to operate them. The expense would, in turn, explain why it was the Phoenicians and other states subject to Persian rule that were the first to develop and adopt the type – only a wealthy empire could have afforded to equip a fleet of such vessels.[7] For a while the Greek states struggled to keep up.

Within a few years, however, Athens had been transformed by the discovery of silver at Laurion on the southeast tip of the Attic peninsula, and in 483 BC a skilful and far-sighted politician by the name of Themistocles persuaded the Athenian assembly to spend their windfall on the acquisition of a new 100-strong trireme fleet. A further 100 were added soon afterwards when it became apparent that the Persians were again about to invade.[8] These 200 ships formed the backbone of the combined Greek fleet which, in 480 BC, faced Persia's triremes in the waters between the southern coast of Attica and the island of Salamis.[9] It was the greatest trireme battle of antiquity and resulted in a total Greek victory that paved the way for the final repulse of the invasion in the following year. The trireme was now the dominant warship type of the Eastern Mediterranean.[10]

After the Persian withdrawal from Greece, Athens began to use her fleet to carve out an empire and by the 320s BC had some 380 triremes.

Eventually new ship-types came to prominence.[11] At the beginning of the fourth century AD, the *penteres* (*quinquereme* or 'five') had been invented at Syracuse and introduced alongside the city's triremes.[12] This was a three-level ship with twice the displacement of a trireme and an oarcrew of around 300 men. It was significantly slower – by nearly 2 knots – than a trireme in a sprint and slightly slower when cruising, but could carry seventy-five troops on deck compared to a maximum of forty for a trireme. Possibly by 367 BC, the Syracusans had developed an even larger type, the *hexeres* ('six'), with two men to an oar on all three levels.[13] Meanwhile, the Carthaginians in North Africa

had invented the lighter and more economical *tetreres* (*quadrireme* or 'four'),[14] a two-level vessel with two men to each oar. All these types could be used for both ramming and fighting from the decks and marked a move towards a mixed style of naval warfare.

Through the next century ever larger 'polyremes' were developed in Macedonia, Syria and Egypt, some of them with double hulls and perhaps up to seven men to an oar. The trireme, however, continued in use alongside fours and fives both at Carthage, until her destruction in 146 BC, and at Rome. The main technological development of this period was the enclosure of the upper level or levels or even the entire oarsystems of triremes and above within a wooden oar-box, which both performed the function of an outrigger and offered the rowers protection from missiles and artillery.

The last recorded use of polyremes was in the Egyptian-supplied fleet of Antony and Cleopatra at the battle of Actium in 31 BC, which was defeated by the generally smaller vessels of Octavian, the first Roman emperor.[15] Henceforth, the Mediterranean became a Roman lake completely surrounded by Roman territory or that of subject allies, and only Roman fleets or those sanctioned by Rome operated within it. The most common ship type was once again the trireme.

The last known record of a trireme fleet in action was in AD 324 when the Eastern emperor, Licinius, was defeated near the mouth of the Dardanelles by the much smaller vessels of the Western emperor, Constantine, who soon after became sole ruler from his new capital of Constantinople.[16] Thereafter, we do not hear of triremes again and the fifth-century historian Zosimus tells us that the secret of their construction had been lost by his day.[17]

Earlier reconstructions

The history of attempts to reconstruct the ancient trireme and other types of oared warship is unusually long, going back to the Renaissance.[18] Galleys were then still in use in the Mediterranean and there was an eagerness to unlock the secrets of the ancient polyremes in order to improve contemporary design.

There were two different types of

oarsystem known during the Renaissance. One employed several oars, each pulled by one man, of similar gearing but slightly different lengths rowed from the same bench; this was known as rowing *alla zenzile*. The other employed one long oar to each bench, pulled by up to eight oarsmen; this was known as rowing *a scaloccio*.[19] It was naturally assumed by most sixteenth-century scholars that the same systems were used in antiquity, and the Renaissance types were even given classical names – *triremi* for *alla zenzile* vessels rowed with three oars to a bench, and so on. Soon, however, some scholars began to question this. In 1591, Sir Henry Savile, who taught Greek to Elizabeth I, argued from ancient texts and depictions that most Greek and Roman warships were multi-level vessels.[20] Soon afterwards, in 1606, the great French scholar Josephus Justus Scaliger suggested that the numbers in the names of ships indicated the number of levels of oars.[21]

Nevertheless, the single-level *a scaloccio* arrangement in particular continued to have

FIGURE 1
The *Olympias* trireme reconstruction

FIGURE 2
Cast of the Lenormant relief found on the Acropolis of Athens in 1852, showing three-level ship under oar.

its advocates, with some postulating *a scaloccio* oars arranged in steps, often with successively more men per oar with each step upwards. And so the debate continued through the seventeenth and eighteenth centuries. One important contribution came from a man whose practical experience gave his opinions some weight. In 1727 Jean Antoine Barras de la Penne, captain of one of the (*a scaloccio*) galleys of Louis XIV, put forward what was seen as a cogent argument against multi-level vessels: that they would require oars of significantly different lengths at the different levels and it would therefore be impossible for the rowers to keep in time.[22] Despite this, with the development of archaeology and the emergence of more and more visual material, by the early nineteenth century most scholars had come to accept some sort of multi-level system.

A new impetus for reconstruction of the trireme arose in the early nineteenth century out of the interest shown by western travellers in the shipsheds of the Piraeus, which had housed the triremes of Classical Athens – it was realised that these sheds could give an indication of the actual dimensions of the vessels. In 1840 a series of inscriptions was published, which had been found in the vicinity of the sheds and contained fourth-century BC inventories of individual Athenian triremes and their equipment. These inscriptions gave vital details of items such as the oars, which were recorded in three groups – thranites (sixty-two per ship), zygians (fifty-four) and thalamians (fifty-four) – with an additional thirty spares, which were either 9 or 9½ cubits long.[23]

Then, in 1852, a French archaeologist by the name of François Lenormant found a 52cm-long marble relief on the Acropolis that was immediately recognised as depicting the central portion of a three-level ship, the top level being rowed through outriggers. Because it almost certainly depicted an Athenian ship of around 400 BC, this could only be a trireme (Figure 2). Unfortunately, a reconstruction based on the relief, which was built in 1861 on the orders of the emperor Napoleon III, failed to impress and the credibility of the three-level theory was badly dented.[24]

Meanwhile, the remains in the Piraeus continued to attract attention and in 1885, a Greek schoolteacher, Iakob Dragatzes, conducted excavations on some well-preserved shipsheds in Zea harbour, assisted by the eminent German archaeologist Wilhelm Dörpfeld, who drew the plans and sections.[25] Dörpfeld's meticulous draughtsmanship still provides the best evidence for the dimensions of an Athenian trireme of the fourth century BC.

Following the Napoleonic débâcle, however, a scholarly reaction set in against

multi-level theories. One of the most influential of the reactionaries was Dr (later Sir) William Woodthorpe Tarn. In 1905 he published a paper in which he argued that ships with four or more levels of oars were a physical impossibility and that if the ship on the Lenormant relief were a three-level ship, it would have been impossible to row for the very reason put forward by Barras de la Penne in 1727. He deduced that the Lenormant relief showed a single-level ship and advocated an *alla zenzile* solution, as had been put forward by the Italian admiral, Luigi Fincati.[26]

FIGURE 3
The late John Morrison on board *Olympias*. Morrison was highly influential in twentieth-century trireme research and the eventual building of the full-scale replica.

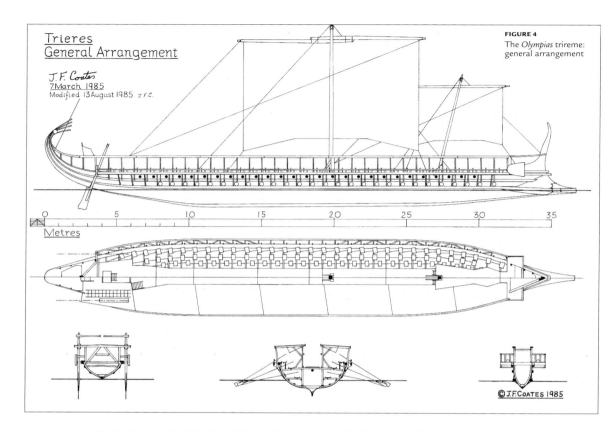

Trieres
General Arrangement

J. F. Coates
7 March 1985
Modified 13 August 1985 J.F.C.

FIGURE 4
The *Olympias* trireme:
general arrangement

Metres

© J.F. Coates 1985

Tarn's view took hold in English-speaking scholarship and held sway for the next three-quarters of a century. When the distinguished American historian Chester G. Starr produced his article on the 'Trireme' for the second edition of the *Oxford Classical Dictionary*, published in 1970 and not superseded until 1996, he was able to write that 'The long-accepted view that the rowers sat in three superimposed banks is now generally rejected; it seems probable that, the rowing-benches being slanted forward, the rowers sat three on a bench, each rower pulling an individual oar.'[27]

The *Olympias* reconstruction
John Morrison (1913–2000) (Figure 3) first became interested in the trireme controversy in the late 1930s. He took to heart Barras de la Penne's observation about oar lengths but drew exactly the opposite conclusion, having noted that only two lengths of spare oars were recorded in the naval inventory inscriptions and that these differed from each other by only half a cubit (about 22cm). Morrison argued that it was, in fact, possible for oars of the same length to be arranged over three levels. Morrison's father, Sinclair, built a model based on the Lenormant relief to demonstrate the arrangement and the findings were published in *The Mariner's Mirror* in 1941 and the *Classical Quarterly* in 1947.[28] There, Morrison also explained the numbers in the names of different ship types as referring not to levels of oars but to the files of rowers on each side of the ship. Thus, a trireme had one rower per oar at three levels, a quadrireme two per oar at two levels, a quinquereme two per oar at two levels and one to an oar at the lowest level, and so on. These propositions failed to find favour with the academic community, and Tarn, a Fellow of Morrison's own college, Trinity, Cambridge, advised him to stick to philosophy.

Morrison was not deterred, however, and returned to the topic in 1968 in *Greek Oared Ships 900–322 BC*, which he wrote with Roddi Williams of Durham University. The literary evidence had been known for centuries but the book brought it all together for the first time, citing the texts in the original languages and explaining them in English. It also added recent archaeological discoveries and a large collection of visual evidence from Greek vases, coins, models and reliefs. Morrison's former pupil, David Blackman, provided a chapter summarising the shipshed evidence for the dimensions of ancient vessels.[29] The value of the book as a major resource for the field of ancient maritime studies was recognised immediately but once again Morrison's three-level reconstruction of the trireme failed to convince.

Finally, when Morrison retired as the first President of Wolfson College, Cambridge in 1980, he decided to follow the lead of previous participants in the trireme controversy and entered into a collaboration with a naval architect. This was John Coates, who had himself just retired as Chief Naval Architect and Deputy Director of Ship Design at the British Ministry of Defence. Coates had a strong interest in historical wooden vessels. His role was, as he put it, 'quite simply to take the historical requirements, laid before us so clearly by Morrison and Williams in their book *Greek Oared Ships*, to treat them as Owner's or Naval Staff Requirements and design a complete and feasible ship to accord with them'.[30]

Coates was able to make use of a number of important archaeological discoveries that had been published since the appearance of *Greek Oared Ships*. These included the wreck of a merchant sailing vessel of the late fourth century BC found off Kyrenia, Cyprus, in 1967,[31] which provided an excellent example of the mortice-and-tenon construction found in other Classical wrecks. Also important was a Punic wreck or wrecks of the third century BC found off Marsala, Sicily, in 1969, the only ancient seagoing oared vessel(s) so far discovered in the Mediterranean;[32] the wineglass cross-section of their mortice-and-tenon hulls was adopted for the trireme reconstruction. Finally, the bronze ram-sheathing from a second-century BC Cypriot warship larger than a trireme was found off Athlit near

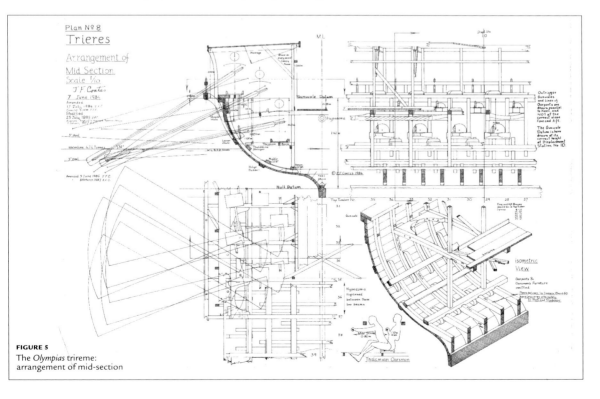

FIGURE 5
The *Olympias* trireme:
arrangement of mid-section

Haifa, Israel, in 1980, with parts of the ship's keel and bow-timbers, confirming the use of mortice-and-tenon construction for warships as well as merchantmen.

On the basis of all the evidence available to him, the key requirements for Coates's design (Figure 4) were to be as follows:

1 The ship would have three levels of oars.

2 There would be sixty-two oars at the upper (thranite) level, fifty-four at the middle (zygian) level and fifty-four at the lowest (thalamian) level. Each oar would be rowed by a single man and, following evidence from the Roman architectural writer, Vitruvius,[33] the longitudinal distance between each thole pin, and therefore the 'room' for each rower, would be 2 cubits (0.888m, based on an Attic cubit of 0.444m). The oars would be 9.5 cubits long (4.22m) in the middle portion of the ship and 9 cubits long (4.05m) at the ends.

3 The ship would have an overall beam of a little less than 5.9m at the widest point (ie the outriggers) and an overall length of around 37m, based on the shipshed remains at Zea.

4 The hull would be of light, shell-first, mortice-and-tenon construction in fir and oak; the ram and its timbers would be scaled from the Athlit ram; the form of the bows and outriggers would be as shown by numerous coins and pottery models of the Classical period; the cross-section of the hull (Figure 5) would be based on that of the Marsala oared vessels; the hull as a whole would be capable of being slipped and launched on a gradient of about 1:10, which is that of the Zea sheds.

5 The ship would be steered by two rudders, each fitted with a tiller and attached through the outrigger on either side of the stern, and capable of being stowed in a horizontal position, as shown on the Lindos relief from Rhodes (Figure 6).

6 The ship would carry a mainmast and a small boat-mast forward; the sails would be

FIGURE 6
Stern of a second-century BC warship on a relief from Lindos on the island of Rhodes. Note the curve of the aft cut-up and the rudder housed horizontally and out of the water.

square-rigged, fitted with brailing ropes and could be removed and taken ashore.

7 The ship would be stable under oar and sail, capable of achieving sustained cruising speeds under oar of 7 to 8 knots and of still higher sprint speeds in battle, highly manoeuvrable and able to resist the forces generated by ramming, as implied by literary texts.

The initial intention was to publish an improved three-level reconstruction on paper, but soon there was a significant change of direction. In May 1982, Frank Welsh, an author and former banker and industrialist, suggested to Morrison that since he and Coates were aiming to produce a complete design for a trireme, they should take the obvious next step and build a real ship. Welsh, Morrison and Coates together formed the

Trireme Trust and organised a conference at the National Maritime Museum, Greenwich, in April 1983, which resulted in a number of modifications to the design. Subsequently, further improvements were made to the oarsystem on the advice of physicist and rowing coach Timothy Shaw, who served as helmsman and trials director in the reconstruction. The sailing rig was designed by Owain Roberts, who served as the ship's first sailing master.[34]

After the Greenwich conference Coates was invited to Greece by Harry Tzalas of the Hellenic Institute for the Preservation of Nautical Tradition to view the building of the first Kyrenia ship replica. While there, a lecture by Coates at the Hellenic Maritime Museum sparked the interest of senior officers of the Hellenic Navy, which in turn led to an undertaking that, if a reconstruction of an ancient trireme were to be built, the Navy would look after her. A few months later, the Hellenic Navy and Greek Ministry of Culture went still further and announced that they would jointly fund the entire cost of construction if the Trust would provide plans and specifications of the design and a trial-section to guide the builders. Moreover, the Trust would be allowed to carry out trials with the Navy's assistance. It was an impressive demonstration of Greece's interest and pride in her maritime past.

The trial-section, designed to float on a raft of oil-drums and with fifteen port-side rowing positions, was built by the Coventry Boatbuilders' Co-operative and tested at Coombe Abbey. It was exhibited at the 1985 Henley Royal Regatta (Figure 7) where some 200 passing rowers of both sexes tried out the oarsystem and immediately signed up to row the ship at Poros. Construction of the full-sized ship began at the boatyard of the Tzakakos brothers at Keratsini in May 1985.

The hull was built up by the mortice-and-tenon method, strake by strake from the keel. At first three, and later six, shipwrights were employed, overseen by the Hellenic Navy with regular visits by John Coates. The shipbuilders were provided with formers against which they could fit the strakes (Figure 8) but which would later be removed to allow the insertion of floors, futtocks and top timbers. The ship was

FIGURE 7
John Coates demonstrating the trireme trial section at Henley Royal Regatta in July 1985.

eventually launched in the Piraeus on 27 June 1987.[35]

Aims and sea trials

For a variety of reasons the Trust had decided that the ship would not be built 'archaeologically pure', using only authentic materials and tools. Since there were no wrecks to replicate and since the literary texts indicated that various woods might be used to construct triremes, there was no definitive choice available. Moreover, the use of machine tools and easily obtained woods with properties and densities similar to those used in antiquity (eg Douglas fir for silver fir, iroko for Turkey oak) would allow for a very significant reduction in overall cost – although this would still amount to £750,000 at 1987 prices. In addition, the application of modern varnishes and preservatives would ensure longevity.

This meant, of course, that the aims of the reconstruction could not be holistic.[36] It was felt, however, that other reconstruction projects which *were* archaeologically pure – such as the Roskilde Viking vessels (Chapter 5) and the Kyrenia replica – were already investigating aspects such as the use of ancient tools, construction man-hours and durability, and that to adopt such an approach would, to some extent, be duplicating that work. Moreover, by not doing so, one could increase the safety margins – an important consideration in a vessel that would be rowed by 170 volunteers. The demands of safety and crew morale also limited what could be achieved in the sea-trials.[37] Such ships are known to have been

FIGURE 8
Olympias under construction. Note the upright temporary formers being used to determine the shape of the hull, and the mortices already cut into the top surface of the strake being fitted, ready to receive the next strake.

vulnerable to bad weather in antiquity, so rough conditions had to be avoided, and while the oarcrew often welcomed short periods of sailing as an opportunity to take a rest, they found prolonged sailing boring and preferred to row.

The limitations were not considered particularly problematic, since *Olympias* was to be built, in Seán McGrail's felicitous description, as a 'floating hypothesis'.[38] The primary focus of the sea-trials, as determined by the Trust, was to be on the viability of the proposed oarsystem and the related question of performance under oar and whether it matched the evidence of the ancient texts. If the ship could be rowed effectively with three levels of oars, then the main objection to a three-level reconstruction would fall away. The validation of the oarsystem would also allow a more confident reconstruction of the later oared vessels, including the quinqueremes and polyremes. Finally, a successful reconstruction would undoubtedly attract widespread media attention and would publicise a major example of ancient technology to a worldwide audience. The Trust's interests and approach were thus historical and educational rather than archaeological – to understand, explain and present the working and performance of an important artefact from the past, rather than simply to replicate its structure.

The initial trials were conducted at Poros, in August 1987, and a few days later the ship was commissioned as HN Trireme *Olympias*. There followed another four series of trials in 1988, 1990, 1992 and 1994, as well as a visit to London in 1993 to celebrate the 2,500th anniversary of the founding of Greek democracy.[39] In the first year, the Trust's oarcrew was largely composed of British university students, but from 1988 onwards many rowers were recruited and brought over from the United States by the newly formed Trireme Trust USA; others came from all over the world.

The first year's trials were largely occupied with learning how to co-ordinate the rowing. The thranite rowers had a clear view along and out of the ship, were well-ventilated, and soon learned to cope with the relatively steep angle of their oars. The zygians could not see their oar-blades but could see along the ship and benefited from a little cooling breeze. The thalamians found their rowing positions cramped and hot and could see neither out of nor along the ship (Figure 9). The rowing master coaching the crew up on deck could not easily see the oars and the rowers at the same time and had difficulty making himself heard throughout the vessel, even with a megaphone. Keeping the whole crew working in time was difficult and mistakes often caused unfortunate thalamians to get their oars caught in the water ('catching a crab'). This sometimes had alarming results as rowers could be pinned to the cross-beams immediately behind their heads.

Although many of the crew went home after three weeks feeling that the design was essentially flawed and unrowable, a great deal had been learned and the main problems had essentially been solved. The rowers had been organised to work in vertical groups of three, which became known as 'triads'. The thranite of the triad would verbally direct the rowing of the zygian and thalamian, so that they started to move together as a small team. Then, with the help of 'team-leaders' coaching from the central gangway, they would gradually blend in with the triads on either side, so that the crew grew together.

By the beginning of the 1988 trials the crabbing had been reduced and was soon effectively eliminated. Moreover, a microphone and six electronic speakers had been installed to enable the rowing masters to give orders and keep the crew in time. This produced much greater cohesion and gave the crew the ability to recover more quickly from mistakes. The introduction of a piper standing by the mast – in accordance with hints from the ancient texts – allowed the rowing master to concentrate on coaching, since the rowers could pick up the rhythm of suitable tunes and the high-pitched sound could be heard throughout the ship. When the electronic speakers broke down – as they often did – it became possible for two rowing masters to watch each other and simultaneously give orders in different parts of the ship so that everybody could hear.

As communication became easier and experience grew, the rowing also improved (Figure 10) and was aided over the first three years of trials by the shaving down and rebalancing of the oars – which were initially over-engineered and too heavy – and by the re-shaping of the oarblades to reduce clashing. By the end of the 1987 trials the ship could barely manage 7 knots under oars for even a few seconds but in 1988 the same speed was attained easily on the first morning of trials and subsequently an average of 6.65 knots was maintained over 2,000 metres at 38 strokes per minute; a peak speed of 8.0 knots was recorded. In 1990 8.3 knots was attained in a short burst, with a momentary peak speed of just under 9 knots. Over longer distances, 7 knots was averaged for 1 nautical mile (Figure 11) and 4.6 knots averaged while rowing in shifts over a distance of 31 miles en route between Poros and Nafplion. Simultaneous rowing and sailing was also tried out, with 6.6 knots being attained in a 20-knot tailwind. The 1992 trials crew was under-strength numerically and was unable to match these speeds, although their calculated

FIGURE 11
Olympias under oar making 7 knots in August 1990

FIGURE 9
Starboard-side rowers in *Olympias*: *thalamians* at the bottom, *zygians* in the middle and *thranites* on the top

FIGURE 10
Olympias under oar passing through the Corinth Canal in August 1992

power per oar was actually greater than in 1990 and they managed to cover 5.77 nautical miles in one hour of sustained rowing. With an even smaller number of rowers in 1994, however, no improvement was made on any of these figures.

The ship proved extremely manoeuvrable and responsive to the rudders and at higher speeds could be steered easily with one rudder lifted completely and the other half out of the water. Rates of turn were about 3° per second and the ship could be rowed by the whole crew at 7 knots into a complete circle of 110m diameter (3.4 ship lengths) with a speed loss of only 28 per cent. If one side of rowers dropped out and held water, the turn could be tightened to a diameter of 62m (1.9 ship lengths), accomplished in the same time of about two minutes, but with a loss of 50 per cent speed. In another test, by holding water the ship was easily slowed from 5.7 knots to 1.1 knots in only 33m (0.9 ship lengths).

To the surprise of many, the ship also handled extremely well under sail (Figure 12), being stable in winds of up to 25 knots, rolling and heeling 10° to 12° in a 22-knot wind on the beam, and sailing within 65° of the apparent wind, her long keel keeping leeway down to between 5° and 7°. With a 15-knot wind on the quarter, she easily maintained 7 knots under full sail and momentarily touched 10.8 knots in a following gust of 20 knots.

Speeds were calculated quite crudely in 1987 by means of a Dutchman's log, then much more accurately in 1988 using a shore-based geodimeter, which repeatedly measured the ship's position at short intervals by shooting a laser beam at a 360° bank of prisms set up on deck; by 1990 and 1992 hand-held GPS systems had become available. The 1988 data, however, remain particularly valuable, since they were recorded on computer and the printouts show the track of the ship through the water whilst carrying out turning and other manoeuvres.

After the 1994 trials the ship unfortunately became infested with shipworm (*teredo navalis*) and much of her underwater planking had to be replaced. She was taken out of the water and put on display at the Hellenic Navy Museum in Neo Faliro but her hull was then attacked by a fungal disease, which by 2003 was threatening to eat her away altogether. She was cosmetically refurbished in that year at the Elefsina shipyard, in anticipation of her carrying the Olympic flame across the main harbour of the Piraeus just before the opening of the Athens Olympics in August 2004. At the time of writing, although she is no longer fit to undertake sustained trials at sea, *Olympias* is again looking her best and has been provided with a roofed shed as a permanent exhibit of the Navy Museum.

Lessons learned

The principal lesson learned from the *Olympias* reconstruction is clearly that three-level oarsystems can be made to work, thus settling an argument going back to the sixteenth century. In itself this does not prove that the ancient trireme was a three-level ship, but does remove the principal objection. This, in turn, has opened the way for the acceptance of quinqueremes and larger polyremes as ships with up to three levels. Meanwhile, the media attention attracted by the ship and its repeated appearance in books and documentaries have ensured that the educational aims of the Trust were fully achieved. In these aspects, the project has quickly fulfilled all the Trust's hopes and expectations.

Beyond this, however, a great deal has been learned and many more questions have been raised.[40] The performance of the ship under sail is impressive. Her manoeuvrability under oar has exceeded expectations and fully matched both what is implied in the ancient sources and the manoeuvrability of modern warships. The speeds achieved under oar have, however, been disappointing for some. Whether this is fair depends on whether one interprets the ancient texts to imply that triremes normally achieved sustained cruising speeds of around 5 knots under oar – in which case *Olympias* met or exceeded expectations – or whether one adopts a more severe interpretation and regards 7 to 8 knots as achievable. Since the trials have suggested that even with the best possible crew *Olympias* would have difficulty in attaining such a speed, this may imply

FIGURE 12
Olympias under sail in August 1988

that there are some shortcomings in the oar geometry, even allowing for gearing problems caused to the thalamian positions by some minor mistakes in construction.

In particular, it was felt that the room available to the oarsmen restricted their stroke length and therefore the power they could produce. Thus, when a new metrological relief from Salamis was published in 1990[41] showing a long cubit of 0.49m, it was welcomed as enabling the oars to be set 0.98m apart and allowing a significantly longer stroke. This would also permit the position of the cross-beams to be adjusted upwards, so that thalamians could no longer be trapped against them, and the rowing positions could be canted outwards so that rowers would no longer be restricted by the back of the man astern, and could take a stroke limited only by their own physiology. Calculations suggest that canting the rowers in this way would increase their effective power by some 25 per cent. Even though the ship's beam would also be increased from 5.45m to 5.62m at the outrigger and her length from 36.8m to 39.6m, such a trireme, manned by a top-class crew, might be able to cruise at the 7.5 knots demanded by the most severe interpretation of the ancient evidence.

Beyond performance, considerable insight was gained into the practicalities and logistics of operating such a vessel. The difficulties of co-ordination and communication between rowing master and crew have already been described and the trials have shown that these could be overcome. The importance of carrying sufficient drinking water for the oarcrew also became apparent. Trialling at the height of summer, the Trust's rowers were each drinking a litre of water per hour – a conservative amount for athletes exercising in such conditions. This implies the consumption of around 1.7 tonnes of water in a 10-hour rowing day. The daily replenishment of this amount of water, especially when ships were travelling in squadrons and fleets, would have had major logistical implications, which have rarely been considered by historians.

Other operational aspects that came to the fore were the need to minimise movement by non-rowers around the ship while she was under oar to avoid disturbing the balance and rhythm of the ship, and the importance of maintaining morale during long periods of rowing in such cramped conditions. Both issues are hinted at in our sources, but the reconstruction has brought them to life as factors of some importance. It must be stressed that the observations from *Olympias* cannot be used as though they were direct evidence of how things were done in antiquity, but they can sensitise us to the ancient evidence and even raise questions that have not previously been considered.

From the Trireme Trust's point of view, the *Olympias* reconstruction has been a considerable success. It has not, however, been without its critics.[42] Many maritime archaeo-logists have been openly hostile, questioning the legitimacy of any reconstruction not based on material remains. This somewhat misses the point of why the reconstruction was made in the first place, and both discounts the value of other types of evidence and ignores the historical background to the debate. A few scholars have questioned the three-level solution, although the alternative offered – a two-level ship alternating single rowers with two men to a bench *alla zenzile* – is largely based on an interpretation of the so-called Siren Vase depicting Odysseus' ship as a single-level vessel.[43] Most classicists and the general public have, on the other hand, embraced *Olympias* as an authentic representation of an ancient trireme, which has brought its own problems. The very cost of the experiment makes it difficult to replicate, while the attractiveness and very tangibility of *Olympias* as an object make it hard for people to remember that she is only a hypothesis, albeit one based on a good deal of solid evidence.

The Trireme Trust remains convinced that the *Olympias* does reflect – at least in some degree – an ancient reality, and the most recent research has tended to confirm both the details and the general dimensions of John Coates's design. Nevertheless, the long history of the trireme controversy should warn us that the debate is unlikely to be at an end.

BORIS RANKOV

BIBLIOGRAPHY

Alertz, U. 1995. 'The naval architecture and oar systems of medieval and later galleys' in Gardiner and Morrison 1995: 142–62

Barras de la Penne, J.A. 1727. *La Science des Galères*. Paris Bibliothèque Nationale Ms. Fr. 9177-8

Basch, L. 1987. *Le Musée Imaginaire de la Marine Antique*. Athens

Bondioli, M., Burlet, R. and Zysberg, A. 1995. 'Oar mechanics and oar power in medieval and later galleys' in Gardiner and Morrison 1995: 163–205

Coates, J.F. and McGrail, S. (eds) 1984. *The Greek Trireme of the Fifth Century BC*. Greenwich

Coates, J.F. and Morrison, J.S. 1987. 'Authenticity in the replica Athenian *trieres*', *Antiquity* 61: 87-90

Coates, J.F., Platis, S.K. and Shaw J.T. 1990. *The Trireme Trials 1988. Report on the Anglo-Hellenic Sea Trials of Olympias*. Oxford

Coates, J.F. et al. 1995. 'Experimental boat and ship archaeology: principles and methods', *International Journal of Nautical Archaeology* 24: 293–301

Dekoulakou-Sideris, E. 1990. 'A metrological relief from Salamis', *American Journal of Archaeology* 94: 445–51

Dragatzes, I. Kh. 1886. 'Ekthesis peri ton en Peiraiei Anaskaphon (Report of the excavations in Peiraeus)', *Praktika tes en Athenais Arkhaiologikes Etairias tou Etous 1885*. Athens

Gardiner, R. and Morrison, J.S. (eds) 1995. *The Age of the Galley. Mediterranean Oared Vessels since Pre-Classical Times*. London

Fincati, L. 1883. *Le Triremi*. Rome

Frost, H. 1981. *Lilybaeum*. Accademia Nazionale dei Lincei, Notizie degli Scavi di Antichità, Vol. 30 Suppl. Rome

Hammond, N.G.L. and Scullard, H.H. 1970. *The Oxford Classical Dictionary*. 2nd ed. Oxford

Jordan, B. 2000. 'The crews of Athenian triremes', *L'Antiquité Classique* 69: 81–101

Lehmann, L. Th. 1995. *The Polyeric Quest. Renaissance and Baroque Theories about Ancient Men-of-War*. 2nd ed. Amsterdam

McGrail, S. 1992. 'Replicas, reconstructions and floating hypotheses', *International Journal of Nautical Archaeology* 21: 353–5

Morrison, J.S. 1941. 'The Greek Trireme', *The Mariner's Mirror* 27: 14–44

Morrison, J.S. 1947. 'Notes on certain Greek nautical terms', *Classical Quarterly* 41: 122–35

Morrison, J.S. and Coates, J.F. (eds) 1989. *An Athenian Trireme Reconstructed. The British Sea Trials of Olympias, 1987*. BAR International Series 486. Oxford

Morrison, J.S. and Coates, J.F. 1996. *Greek and Roman Oared Warships 399-30 B.C.* Oxford

Morrison, J.S., Coates, J.F. and Rankov, N.B. 2000. *The Athenian Trireme. The History and Reconstruction of an Ancient Greek Warship*. 2nd ed. Cambridge

Morrison, J.S. and Williams, R.T. 1968. *Greek Oared Ships 900–322 B.C.* Cambridge

Rankov, N.B. 1994. 'Reconstructing the past: the operation of the trireme *Olympias* in the light of historical sources', *The Mariner's Mirror* 80: 131–46

Rankov, N.B. 2004. 'Breaking down boundaries: the experience of the multidisciplinary *Olympias* project' in Sauer, E.W. (ed.), *Archaeology and Ancient History: Breaking Down the Boundaries*. London, New York: 49–61

Savile, H. 1591. *The Ende of Nero and the Beginning of Galba: Foure Bookes of the Histories of Cornelius Tacitus*. Oxford

Scaliger, J.J. 1606. *Thesaurus Temporum Eusebii Pamphili Caesareae Palestinae Episcopi*. Leiden

Shaw, J.T. (ed.) 1993. *The Trireme Project. Operational Experience 1987–90. Lessons Learnt*. Oxbow Monograph 31. Oxford

Steffy, J.R. 1985. 'The Kyrenia ship: an interim report on its hull construction', *American Journal of Archaeology* 89.1: 71–101

Steffy, J.R. 1994. *Wooden Shipbuilding and the Interpretation of Shipwrecks*. College Station

Swiny, H.W. and Katzev, M.L. 1973. 'The Kyrenia shipwreck' in Blackman, D.J. (ed.), *Marine Archaeology* (Colston Papers No. 23). London

Tarn, W.W. 1905. 'The Greek Warship', *Journal of Hellenic Studies* 25: 137–73, 204–24

Tilley, A. 1992. 'Three men to a room – a completely different trireme', *Antiquity* 66: 599–610

Tilley, A. 2004. *Seafaring in the Ancient Mediterranean: New Thoughts on Triremes and Other Ancient Ships*. Oxford

Wallinga, H.T. 1993. *Ships and Sea Power before the Great Persian War. The Ancestry of the Ancient Trireme*. Leiden

Welsh, F. 1988. *Building the Trireme*. London

NOTES

[1] Homer, *Iliad* 2.509–10, although the passage only specifies that each of the ships in question carried 120 men.

[2] On the overall development of oared vessels in the Mediterranean, see Morrison and Williams 1968; Gardiner and Morrison 1995.

[3] Cf. Clement of Alexandria, *Stromateis* 1.16.76.

[4] Hipponax frg. 45 Diehl.

[5] Herodotus 1.166.

[6] Thucydides 2.93.2.

[7] Wallinga 1993: 118–29.

[8] Herodotus 7.144; Thucydides 1.14.3; Aristotle *Constitution of the Athenians* 22.7.

[9] Herodotus 8.40–96.

[10] On the emergence of the trireme, see Wallinga 1993; Gardiner and Morrison 1995; Morrison et al. 2000.

[11] The development of the new types in the Hellenistic period is described in Morrison and Coates 1996.

[12] Diodorus Siculus 14.41–42.

[13] Xenagoras Pref. 12.

[14] Aristotle frg. 600.

[15] Dio 50.23.1–3; Florus 2.21; Orosius 6.19.8–9.

[16] Zosimus *New History* 2.22–8.

[17] Zosimus *New History* 5.20.3–4.

[18] For a comprehensive and witty study, see Lehmann 1995.

[19] Alertz 1995; Bondioli et al. 1995.

[20] Lehmann 1995: 65–7 and Morrison et al. 2000: 11–13, both citing Savile 1591.

[21] Lehmann 1995 : 63–5, citing Scaliger 1606.

[22] Barras de la Penne 1727, cited by Morrison et al. 2000: 15.

[23] *IG* 2² 1604–32.

[24] Basch 1987, 31, 39–40; Lehmann 1995, 142–54.

[25] Dragatzes 1886.

[26] Fincati 1883; Tarn 1905 see Morrison et al. 2000: 20–2.

[27] Hammond and Scullard 1970: 1095.

[28] Morrison 1941; 1947.

[29] Morrison and Williams 1968 (chapter by Blackman at pp. 186–92).

[30] Coates and McGrail 1984: 51.

[31] Swiny and Katzev 1973; Steffy 1985; 1994: 42–59.

[32] Frost 1981.

[33] Vitruvius *On Architecture* 1.2.4.

[34] Shaw 1993: 29–47.

[35] For an entertaining and detailed account of the conception and construction of *Olympias*, see Welsh 1988.

[36] For a general discussion of the aims of ship reconstructions, see Coates et al. 1995.

[37] Coates and Morrison 1987; Morrison et al. 2000: 233–6.

[38] McGrail 1992.

[39] Morrison and Coates 1989; Coates, Platis and Shaw 1990; Shaw 1993; Rankov 1994; Morrison et al. 2000: 231–75.

[40] Shaw 1993: 108-9; Morrison et al. 2000: 267–75.

[41] Dekoulakou-Sideris 1990.

[42] See Rankov 2004: 55–7.

[43] Tilley 1992; 2004, followed by Jordan 2000.

5 the viking ships of skuldelev

The Viking Ship Museum in Roskilde, Denmark, launched the reconstruction of the longship *Skuldelev 2* in September 2004. Three years later, sixty men and women sailed the almost 30m-long ship from Roskilde to Ireland's capital city, Dublin, and made the return voyage the following year. The round-trip of about 2,450nm is the culmination – so far – of twenty-five years' work building and sailing Viking ship reconstructions.

The basis for the research behind the reconstructions was the unique find of the five Skuldelev ships excavated from the Roskilde fjord in Denmark in 1962. They had formed part of a complex of underwater barriers created at the end of the eleventh century as a defence for the important trading town and royal seat of Roskilde. The five ships had had all their rigging and loose fittings removed, had been filled with stones and then sunk across the navigation channel outside the village of Skuldelev, about 20km north of Roskilde. Before the excavation it was thought that the part of the barrier in which the ships were lying was simply an underwater stone ridge, but after investigations by divers in 1957–9, the National Museum of Denmark

decided that the ridge should be excavated. In the summer of 1962 a cofferdam was erected around the barrier and the area was drained.

In 1962 marine archaeology was still in its infancy and it was clear from the preliminary underwater observations that the excavation would be extremely difficult – many of the parts were completely or partially covered by each other, complicating not only their recovery but also the documentation of their placement relative to each other. Nevertheless, in under four months not only had five ships been excavated but also the work had set new standards for how ship finds are documented – standards that remain to this day.

During the archaeological investigations it quickly became clear that there were five ships

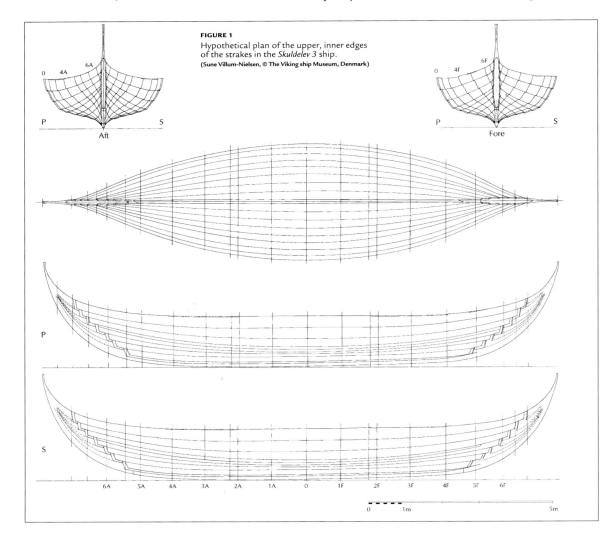

FIGURE 1
Hypothetical plan of the upper, inner edges of the strakes in the *Skuldelev 3* ship.
(Sune Villum-Nielsen, © The Viking ship Museum, Denmark)

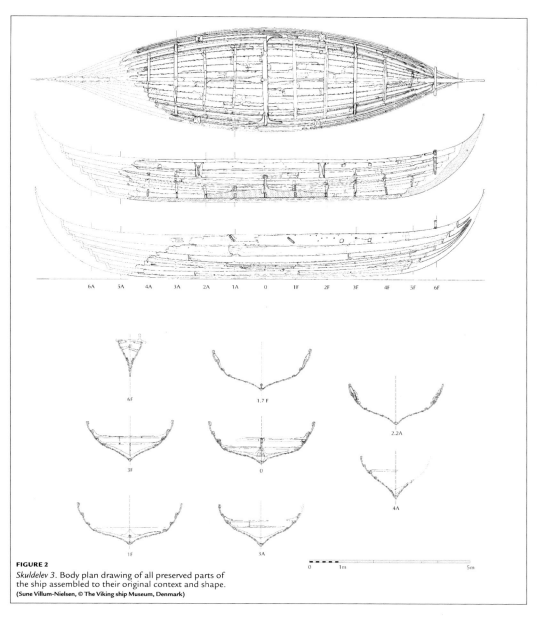

FIGURE 2
Skuldelev 3. Body plan drawing of all preserved parts of
the ship assembled to their original context and shape.
(Sune Villum-Nielsen, © The Viking ship Museum, Denmark)

of various sizes and with very individual
characteristics, but it was not possible to
determine the exact individual hull shapes
since they had been badly distorted by the
weight of the many stones placed on board. It
was decided that the difficult task of
recreating the designs would be tackled at a
later date and so the precise documentation

of the discovery was vital. All the parts and
fragments were comprehensively described,
numbered and photographed. Once the ships
were fully uncovered, they were documented
using photogrammetry and only then were
the thousands of parts and fragments lifted,
washed and sealed in plastic, not only to
prevent drying but also to keep the individual

items together during transport to the conservation laboratory. Here, each of the thousands of parts was measured, drawn and then subjected to a long conservation process before being replaced in its proper context.

Reconstructing the ships

The work of exhibiting the preserved ship parts was a demanding assignment and was not completed until 1993 when the longship, *Skuldelev 2* – last of the five – was finally complete in the exhibition hall of the Viking Ship Museum in Roskilde.

In some cases the long-term conservation of the find has changed the appearance, size or shape of the original ship parts: some have warped and individual planks have shrunk in width. The basis for the subsequent work has therefore been the elaborate and minute recording performed *before* the conservation.

The exact documentation of the original, unpreserved ship parts means that work can continue without subjecting the exhibited ships to repeated examinations and tests. The 1:1 drawings were and are essential for the reconstruction of the ships' original designs – first as drawings and models on the scale of 1:10 and later as sea-going, full-scale reconstructions.

In order to produce models of the ships in their original 3D form, the 1:1 drawings were photographically reduced to a 1:10 scale and

joined together to form complete units – whole plank lengths, for example – that were reproduced in cardboard. The planking and timber frames were then assembled part by part, with original nail holes serving as fixed points for construction. Based on the cardboard models, 'torso-drawings' were prepared showing the relationships of the ships' parts in their original positions, as were drawings of the upper, inner edge of the strakes, which show the design of all the planking and thus make it possible to reconstruct the missing sections.

This graphic representation not only documented the original size of the ships' parts but also safeguarded all preserved traces from the original building and any later repair work, the holes from the dowels and nails, and all wear marks caused during the ships' working lives. The investigations also revealed specific choices of material, which in some cases reflect geographic differences in origin. The meticulous recording of the constructional details, distinctive characteristics and surface finishes has proved to be an important source for determining the standard of craftsmanship and quality of material in each ship and has been indispensable for reconstructing those parts of the ships that were not preserved.

After preparing the reconstruction drawings, the next step was to produce a 1:10 scale reconstruction in wood, which along with the

FIGURE 3
Excavating the Skuldelev Ships within a coffer dam in 1962.
(The Viking Ship Museum, Denmark)

drawings, formed the basis from which the full-sized reconstructions were built.

A treasure trove of ships

The Skuldelev ships were five refined and extremely specialised vessels, which together provide a wonderful insight into the vessel types used in the late Viking Age. All five were clearly built to sail. Their individual constructions and hull designs reflect their intended function in the fields of warfare, trade, goods transportation and fishing. The slender hulls of the longships *Skuldelev 2* and *5* were, to a major extent, determined by the need to be rowed, while the robust beamy construction of *Skuldelev 1* was needed for its more generous cargo capacity.

The ships were all clinker-built and fastened with riveted iron nails. The Nordic technique of building is to construct the ship's hull shell-first and to add the inner frame afterwards. Known as 'shell-first construction', it is the reverse method of the central European technique of 'skeleton-first construction'. The shape of the Nordic hull is formed by stems and keel, on which the planks are clenched together to create an empty shell. The ship's shape is held by floor timbers, horizontal beams (*bitis*) and knees acting as transverse ribs, as well as stringers fastened to the planks with wooden dowels for longitudinal strength (Figure 6). Planks and ribs are cut down to the smallest

FIGURE 4
The archaeologlical remains on display in the Viking Ship Museum in Roskilde, Denmark.
(Werner Karrasch, The Viking Ship Museum, Denmark)

	Skuldelev 1	Skuldelev 2	Skuldelev 3	Skuldelev 5	Skuldelev 6
Date of construction	c1030	1042–3	c1040	c1040	c1040
Origin	Sognefjord region, West Norway	Ireland, Dublin area	West Denmark	Denmark	Sognefjord region, West Norway
Size LxB (m)	16.05 × 4.8	29.3 × 3.8	14 × 3.27	17.3 × 2.47	11.2 × 2.33
Wood species	Pine, lime, oak	Oak	Oak	Oak, pine, ash	Pine, oak
No. of oars	4	60	5	26	14
Cargo capacity (tonnes)	25		4.5–5		2.6
Preserved wood %	70	25	85	65	75
Spacing of floors (cm)	92	72	75	80	94
Function	Cargo	Warfare	Cargo	Warfare	Boat

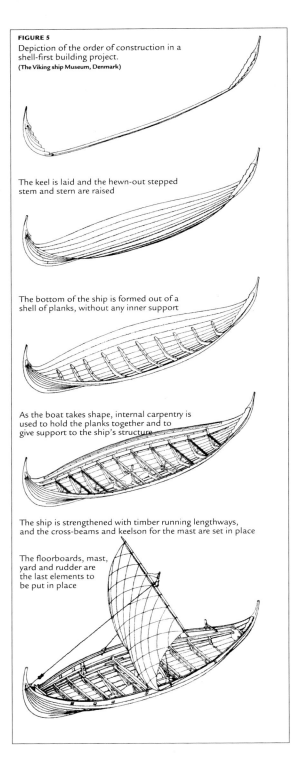

FIGURE 5
Depiction of the order of construction in a shell-first building project.
(The Viking ship Museum, Denmark)

The keel is laid and the hewn-out stepped stem and stern are raised

The bottom of the ship is formed out of a shell of planks, without any inner support

As the boat takes shape, internal carpentry is used to hold the planks together and to give support to the ship's structure

The ship is strengthened with timber running lengthways, and the cross-beams and keelson for the mast are set in place

The floorboards, mast, yard and rudder are the last elements to be put in place

possible dimensions in order to achieve flexible parts that can bend in harmony with others. Indeed, all elements of the build are designed to achieve a light, supple and flexible hull; the technique places major demands on the quality of the building material and the standard of craftsmanship.

Several different varieties of wood were used for the construction of the five Skuldelev ships, and the combination of these varieties in the individual ships depended on where the ships were built and later repaired. *Skuldelev 2* and *3* were mostly made of oak, while *Skuldelev 1* and *6* were mostly made of pine. *Skuldelev 5* was built from planks and ribs of oak together with recycled planks of pine and ash. All the ships had keels of oak – even where the ribs were not predominantly of oak. To a lesser extent linden, elm, birch and beech wood were also used. In all the ships the trunnels were of willow. However, in order to select wood for the reconstructions, it was important to determine not only the species but also the quality and positioning of the grain in each part, so that it would as closely as possible resemble the wood in the original ships.

Flexible hulls
Viking ships were built from newly felled, fresh timber that would have been relatively easy to fashion with the light tools available at the time – the Vikings called fresh oak 'butter-oak', while the dried timber was called 'bone-oak'. Today we refer to such use of fresh wood as wet-wood technology. When building the reconstructions it soon became evident that working with wet wood offers unexpected possibilities and requires special techniques. The method is markedly different from those that use hard, dried timber and, since the technology and skills have been lost, they had to be rediscovered – partly through the study of tool traces left on the original ships and partly through practical experience. The tool traces have revealed that the axe was the most important tool for producing both the planks and the ribs; there is no evidence in the original material that any saw was used (Figure 8).

The planks were split from straight trunks using wooden wedges and axes (Figure 9). The pine planks and the widest of the oak planks were split off, ie the trunk was split into two halves, each of which was hewn into a plank. The majority of the oak planks were radially split – the trunk is split up to four times into two, four, eight and sixteen raw plank workpieces that are then worked with axes into their final shape. For trunks over 1m in diameter, the widest of the raw workpieces can be split again, which means that sixteen to twenty-four planks can be made from one trunk. The splitting technique is important, because the planks are 'reinforced' with the wood's pith ray. The split pieces can then be processed into strong, supple planks that will not fissure or change shape as they dry – an important precondition for the Viking ships' flexibility and strength. Planks thus produced are so flexible that they can be bent easily into shape – Viking-ship planks were neither boiled nor steamed during assembly. The sealing between the planks – the caulking – was made from tarred, three-strand woollen cord. In the reconstruction this has proved very effective, since the woollen cord expands when it becomes wet and thus keeps the laps completely sealed.

An important part of the Skuldelev ships' construction was their framing system, which was comprised of several elements (Figure 6). The ribs were fashioned from grown timbers (Figure 9) – as a basic principle, the shape of a part follows the grain of the wood in order to achieve light, supple and strong components. Below, the ships' internal, transverse reinforcement consisted of floor timbers shaped so that they completely followed the plank shell, to which they were attached with wooden dowels. Above the floor timbers was a horizontal beam, the so-called *biti*, which in *Skuldelev 5* was connected to the side of the ship by axe-fashioned knees. However, the bitis and floor timbers were not nailed to each other – they could move independently without being damaged. For the same reason, the floor timbers were not attached to the keel.

The ships' flexible hulls were created by a carefully thought-out construction, where the vessels' characteristics under sail and at sea were optimised. The strength lay in the strong, supple plank shell and the flexible construction of the frames, which together allowed the hull to flex in the sea and yield to the waves – these open, relatively low-sided craft would have sailed far more smoothly, even more dryly, than higher-sided ships of more rigid construction.

Rigging and square sail

All five ships were designed to sail, but the excavations produced neither sails nor rigging. In fact, no complete rigging or even large sail fragments have been found at any Viking ship or site excavation. There is no doubt, however, that the Vikings used single, large, square sails on their ships, as can be seen in innumerable contemporaneous images.

However, with no original artefacts discovered, the rigging of the Skuldelev ship reconstructions had to be based on the traces

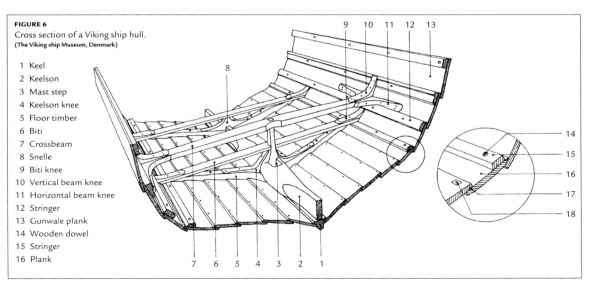

FIGURE 6
Cross section of a Viking ship hull.
(The Viking ship Museum, Denmark)

 1 Keel
 2 Keelson
 3 Mast step
 4 Keelson knee
 5 Floor timber
 6 Biti
 7 Crossbeam
 8 Snelle
 9 Biti knee
10 Vertical beam knee
11 Horizontal beam knee
12 Stringer
13 Gunwale plank
14 Wooden dowel
15 Stringer
16 Plank

of rigging that could be seen on the preserved ship parts: holes where the lines had been made fast; wear marks where they had been led during manoeuvres. Best preserved are the rigging traces on the small cargo ship, *Skuldelev 3*, where practically all are visible. *Skuldelev 1* and *5* also have some rigging traces, but none was found on either *Skuldelev 2* or *Skuldelev 6*.

Those rigging traces that do exist show a pattern that can also be found on the traditional square-sailed boats that were common as fishing vessels on the west coast of Norway right up to modern times. For instance, the work on the Nordland boat, *Rana*, built in 1892, contributed to the interpretation of the three holes found in the upper strake, both to port and starboard, between ribs 2F and 4F on *Skuldelev 3, 1* and *5*. These holes, located just beneath the gunwale, are 37–41mm in diameter and show no signs of wear. Their placement is identical to similar holes in the forebody of the Nordland boat, where they are used to secure

FIGURE 7
Splitting tree trunks for timber the traditional way.
(Werner Karrasch, The Viking Ship Museum, Denmark)

FIGURE 8
No saw was used to construct the Skuldelev ships – ancient or replica – but evidence was found of axes with varied head shapes.
(Werner Karrasch, The Viking Ship Museum, Denmark)

FIGURE 9
Fitting a floor timber in the longship, expertly cut to mirror the lands of the planking.
(Werner Karrasch, The Viking Ship Museum, Denmark)

the sail's tack when going to windward. The tack is tied down to a sturdy pin stuck in to one of the three holes, depending on how close to the wind the boat is sailing. These tack holes are the strongest piece of evidence that the Viking ships were not built just for downwind sailing; they show an allowance for sail trim that would make it possible for the ship to beat to windward. Furthermore, the width of the sail can be determined by the tack holes and the preserved trapezoid holes between ribs 3A and 4A, through which the sheet was run. The distance from the tack holes to the sheet hole indicates the sail's greatest possible width. Sail height, for the reconstructions, has been based entirely on the Nordland boat research.

The traces from the ships' tack and sheet positions, the placing of the mast, the stay-attachment holes, and the well-preserved internal cleats for attaching halyards, all correspond to the rigging on the Nordland boat and together constitute a reliable basis for the reconstruction of the ships' rigging and total sail area.

For example, the sail on *Skuldelev 3* was probably almost square, with a width of 6.5–6.8m and an estimated height of 6.8–7.0m giving a total sail area of 44–46m². The Viking Ship Museum has been criticised for too heavily basing the Skuldelev ship sail reconstructions on newer, ethnographic material, instead of contemporary iconographic material. Indeed, in recent years the 'Roskilde rigging' has been the subject of lively debate. It should be emphasised, however, that the basis for the reconstruction of all the Skuldelev sails is *Skuldelev 3*'s well-documented hull design, which clearly shows that the ship is a sailing ship. The clear rigging traces also rule out that the ship could have had a broad sail, from stem to stern, as illustrated on the Gotland stone. But, of course, this does not mean that other, older types of Viking ships could not have had another type of sail.

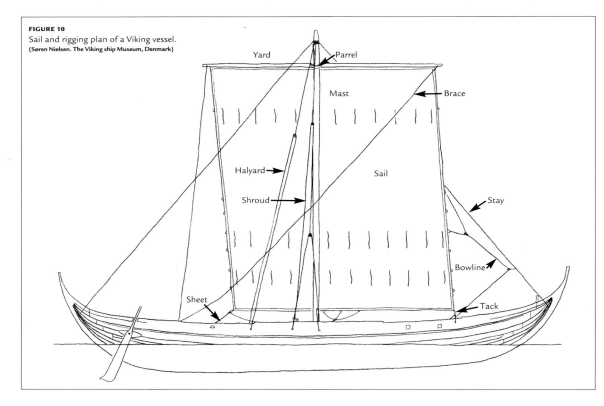

FIGURE 10
Sail and rigging plan of a Viking vessel.
(Søren Nielsen. The Viking ship Museum, Denmark)

Yard · Parrel · Mast · Brace · Halyard · Sail · Shroud · Stay · Bowline · Sheet · Tack

A fleet of Viking ships

After more than forty years of study, we now have a large body of knowledge concerning the construction of the Skuldelev ships and shipbuilding craftsmanship in the Viking Age. Furthermore, interest in the ships as a source of information about social conditions during the Viking Age has increased considerably. Recent research has focused, to a large extent, on dating the ships with dendrochronology. All five of the Skuldelev ships can be placed within quite narrow time bands, though with a great deal of variation among them. *Skuldelev 1* is the best preserved and therefore easiest to place: Sognefjord region, West Norway, c1030. The longship, *Skuldelev 2* – of

which only 25 per cent of the original remains – has been the greatest challenge: Dublin, Ireland, c1042–3. However, despite the small amount of preserved material, those parts of *Skuldelev 2* that were excavated include significant sections of the bottom – all of the keelson and stern, as well as the topsides towards the stern all the way up to the gunwale – and so the ship's most important measuring points are preserved.

With the launch of *Havhingsten fra Glendalough (Sea Stallion of Glendalough)* – the reconstruction of *Skuldelev 2* – the Viking Museum has now finished its world-renowned reconstructions, but research into Viking sailing performance is ongoing. For

Sailing Trials and Voyages

	Skuldelev 1	Skuldelev 2	Skuldelev 3	Skuldelev 5	Skuldelev 6
Name of replica	Ottar	Havhingsten fra Glendalough	Roar Ege	Helge Ask	Kraka Fyr
Year of build	1998–2000	2000–4	1982–4	1990–1	1998
Sail area	90m²	118m²	46m²	50m²	25m²
Top speed under sail	12.5 knots	13.8 knots	8.5 knots	15 knots	8.5 knots
Top speed under oar	1.5 knots	3.4 knots	3.3 knots	5.4 knots	5 knots
Crew	6–12	65–70	5–6	c30	12–14

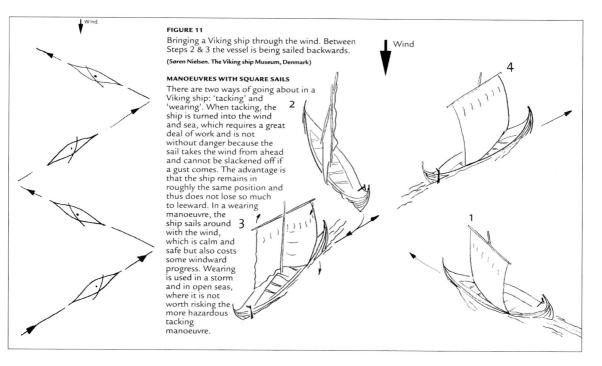

FIGURE 11

Bringing a Viking ship through the wind. Between Steps 2 & 3 the vessel is being sailed backwards.

(Søren Nielsen. The Viking ship Museum, Denmark)

MANOEUVRES WITH SQUARE SAILS

There are two ways of going about in a Viking ship: 'tacking' and 'wearing'. When tacking, the ship is turned into the wind and sea, which requires a great deal of work and is not without danger because the sail takes the wind from ahead and cannot be slackened off if a gust comes. The advantage is that the ship remains in roughly the same position and thus does not lose so much to leeward. In a wearing manoeuvre, the ship sails around with the wind, which is calm and safe but also costs some windward progress. Wearing is used in a storm and in open seas, where it is not worth risking the more hazardous tacking manoeuvre.

the first time in the modern era it is possible to directly compare five Viking ship types and, perhaps, to achieve a greater insight into the characteristics of the construction technology of the individual ships.

A completed, full-scale ship reconstruction waiting to be launched evokes an indescribable curiosity. How will she sail? Will she be seaworthy? Furthermore, the opportunity to test the technology of the past inspires a great deal of speculation about how such ships were originally used. We can never obtain definitive answers to these questions but sailing trials can show us what the ships are capable of and how they perform in a variety of sea and weather conditions.

The first controlled trials were carried out in the autumn of 1984, shortly after the launch of *Skuldelev 3*, the 14m cargo vessel, *Roar Ege*. Max Vinner – who acted as study director from the earliest trials of *Roar Ege* all the way through to the sailing trials of the *Skuldelev 1* reconstruction, *Ottar* in 2003 – formulated the trial objective: '…to discover and document how a Viking ship of the *Skuldelev 3* type was able to handle its cargo

under a variety of natural conditions at sea.' In order to achieve this somewhat abstract objective, four key parameters were drawn up in 1984 as the basis for the sailing trials. They were to record:

• the speed of the ship on different courses relative to wind direction and speed, wave height, and spread of canvas

• the ship's bearing to the wind and drift when working to windward and how the ability to beat against the wind is affected by wave heights and spread of canvas

• the ship's seaworthiness under a variety of wind strengths and wave heights

• the ship's deformations and water flow behaviour around the hull when under sail

The standardised sailing trials show the individual ship's sailing characteristics under specific conditions. Thus, it is important that, as far as possible, all trials, part-trials and manoeuvres are performed multiple times in all weather conditions. The trials must then be repeated under comparable weather conditions in order to describe the ship's speed relative to wind speed and direction, or the ship's performance during manoeuvres such as turning, rowing etc. Through such standardising it is possible to compare the results of any one particular ship with the results of other reconstructions or modern vessels. Since the Skuldelev Ships display such specialised characteristics, it is important to

longship, *Helge Ask*; *Skuldelev 6*, the 11.2m boat, *Kraka Fyr*; and *Skuldelev 1*, the 16m cargo vessel, *Ottar*. At the time of writing, sailing trials with *Skuldelev 2*, the 29.3m longship *The Sea Stallion from Glendalough* have only just begun – the data gathered thus far is being processed and will be published in detail together with the results of the sailing trials of the other reconstructions in Volume II of the Skuldelev monograph due to be published in 2009.

In addition to the results from the official trials, large quantities of data are gathered each year during sailings performed by the boat guilds. These guilds are made up of volunteer Viking-ship enthusiasts who, over several years, have achieved a high level of expertise in sailing the individual ships. Among the reconstructions there is a significant difference of voyage lengths undertaken: some sail only short distances, others sail on 'voyages' of several weeks' duration every summer. The boat guilds keep logbooks of the longer voyages and then deliver them to the Viking Ship Museum for further research.

In recent years, Dr Anton Englert has developed a method for registering data gathered over longer distances – the so-called *trial voyages* – whereby the ships' overall results under sail and oar can be assessed. The Viking Ship Museum now differentiates between 'trial' voyages where the ship's (and the crew's) overall performance is described under the term 'travel speed', and the 'sailing trials' described above where individual factors are isolated for the purpose of describing the ship's sailing characteristics under various conditions. Both methods are used to investigate the ships' significance for traffic, goods transportation and communication routes at sea.

A Viking ship can only sail as close to the wind as its angled square sail will allow. If the ship goes too close to the wind it will loose speed; if the wind comes directly from ahead, the sail will back, causing the ship to move backwards. Thus, it is important for the individual ship to determine its best angle by producing a 'speed rose' that shows the vessel's speed at different angles to the wind.

FIGURE 12
Ottar, built in 1999–2000, a replica of *Skuldelev 1* built in about 1030.
(Werner Karrasch, The Viking Ship Museum, Denmark)

adapt the measurements from the sailing trials to the type of ship. For example, it must be assumed that rowing played a far greater role for the longships, *Skuldelev 2* and *5*, than for the cargo ships, and so the trials for these vessels placed far greater emphasis on manoeuvring under oar. Since the *Roar Ege* trials of 1984, trials have been performed on *Skuldelev 5*, the 17.29m

In order to describe a ship's characteristics, it is important to understand that results depend on several factors: how closely the ship can sail to the wind; the speed on the tacking-legs and the efficiency of the manoeuvres necessary to reach the goal. When beating to windward, the ship works its way forward in a zigzag fashion so, in order to calculate correctly the ship's speed against the wind, the distance to the goal must be divided by the time sailed. This resulting speed against the wind is known as VMG – Velocity Made Good. Of course, the resulting speed against the wind is much slower than the speed actually sailed over the ground on the individual tacks, but it is the VMG that is important, since it shows the speed that the ship achieves against the wind and thus towards the actual goal.

Roar Ege, *a small cargo ship*
Roar Ege was the first reconstructed Skuldelev Ship and the first to undergo a fully developed test programme that provided completely new information about Viking vessels.

The trials showed that the most favourable angle to the wind was 60°, but with the ship's relatively shallow keel, there was a 5–6° drift in calm conditions; this increased quickly to 10° in stronger winds and when the sail was reefed. Nevertheless, the ship can sail as close as 55° to the wind – something very few people expected.

Roar Ege achieved her best VMG in a 9m/s wind under full sail. She achieved 4.8 knots sailing to windward and, if sailed no closer than 66° to the wind, this resulted in a VMG of 2 knots.

In rising winds it became necessary to reef the sail, primarily to reduce the ship's heel and minimise drift and ultimately, in very strong winds, to prevent the ship from capsizing. The sail must be first reefed at 9–10m/s, a fresh breeze. It is lowered part way so that its foot can be rolled up and tied with reef lines. A practised crew can reef in about three minutes.

The best speeds were achieved when sailing beam-on or stern-to the wind. Top speed was measured at 8.5 knots sailing downwind in a 16m/s wind with two reefs in the sail. But it was very rare to sail at top speed; indeed, it is the average speeds that really show a ship's potential. Under favourable wind conditions of 6–7m/s, *Roar Ege* can maintain an average speed of 6.5 knots over a longer distance. This means that the ship can sail 150 nautical miles per day, if she can avoid going to windward.

Roar Ege is equipped with five oars but is definitely not a rowing vessel. She displaces 7.5 tonnes and in trials had a crew of four or five men who, in calm conditions, could achieve a speed under oar of 3.2 knots for very short periods and maintain a speed of 2 knots over distance. In winds of 6m/s and small waves, the crew could maintain a rowing speed of 1.8 knots over a short distance, and with a wind of 10m/s, it was only just possible to maintain the ship's position against the wind. Thus, it must be assumed that the oars were used only during special manoeuvres and when coming in to harbour.

Helge Ask *(Skuldelev 5), a small longship*
Helge Ask is a small vessel with a round bottom and a keel that protrudes only slightly. Her shape is optimised for rowing and many who have viewed the original ship have probably wondered about her performance under sail. *Helge Ask* carries a sail of about 50m² –slightly smaller than the sail on the trading ship *Roar Ege*. She is also much lighter, with a hull weight of only 1.8 tonnes. With equipment, rigging and ballast, the 17.29m vessel weighs just 3.5 tonnes. However, *Helge Ask*'s thirty-man crew constitutes a movable ballast of about 2 tonnes that can be shifted according to the wind direction and, if necessary, right up to the gunwale in strong winds.

Thus, unlike *Roar Ege*, *Helge Ask* has two significant means of propulsion: her sail and twenty-six oars. The greatest measured speed under oar was 5.4 knots, but it is the speed over distance that is important with oars, and *Helge Ask* can maintain a speed of 4–4.5 knots in a light to moderate breeze if all oars are manned. One trial showed that, with twenty of the twenty-six oars manned, *Helge Ask* can be rowed directly into an 8m/s wind at a speed of 3.7 knots if the mast, which produces enormous wind resistance, is taken down – a manoeuvre that can be performed by five or six men in under three minutes while the rest of the crew continue to row. However, if the mast is not lowered, speed drops to about 3 knots, even in wind speeds of only 6–8m/s. In very strong headwinds and counter-currents it was not possible to row the ship forward until the mast was lowered. With the mast down, the ship can be rowed into winds of up to 20–22m/s – the maximum attempted. Rowing *Helge Ask* over a long distance is a challenge, because the crew need to eat and rest. Several different systems that allowed some of the crew to rest while others rowed were tested. The most obvious solution is to let half of the crew – every second oar pair – rest for half an hour. However, this considerably affects the speed, with a reduction of 20–30 per cent. The strain on the other rowers also becomes relatively greater and they quickly tire. A more effective system

FIGURE 13
The longship *The Sea Stallion from Glendalough* during the 2008 sea voyage from Roskilde to Dublin
(Werner Karrasch, The Viking Ship Museum, Denmark)

is rolling breaks, where one or two oar pairs rest at a time. The length of the breaks can be varied, but in our experience, rowers get cold after breaks of more than five minutes and then need a relatively large amount of energy to get 'back into the rhythm'. During *Helge Ask*'s summer voyage, 2001, a complete calm forced the crew to row from a position 4nm east of the Kattegat island of Samsø to Odden harbour on Zealand – a distance of 22nm. Unfortunately, the ship rarely has a full crew during the summer voyages and in this case there were seventeen men on board, sixteen of them

rowing. The 22nm were rowed in six hours, at an average speed of 3.7 knots, even though the crew had rolling breaks of five to fifteen minutes throughout.

Helge Ask's trial voyage demonstrated that she could sail 60° to the wind, just like *Roar Ege*. However, drift was greater so windward progress was less. However, because the ship's rowing function was so integral to her build, it was important to test her performance under sail and under oar in comparable conditions. Thus, sailed and rowed trials were undertaken over the same route, starting from an anchored measuring boat and finishing at a fixed mark directly upwind. As soon as *Helge Ask* had sailed up to the windward mark, she sailed back, downwind, over the same course. The mast was then taken down and the course was rowed, upwind. The trial was repeated several times in increasing wind speeds, and the poorest VMG was measured at 0.8 knots to windward in 17m/s wind, with two reefs in the sail. The best windward VMG under sail was measured at 1.4 knots in 5–7m/s under full sail. The results of the two trials can be seen here:

	Trial 1	Trial 2
Wind	12–17m/s	5–7m/s
VMG to windward	0.8 knots	1.4 knots
With wind astern	7.8 knots	4.2 knots
Rowing to windward	24 oars: 2.9 knots	23 oars: 4.7 knots

With her long, sleek hull, *Helge Ask* has high directional stability, which means that it takes experience and skill to turn her quickly when sailing against the wind and, since the trial voyages were over a relatively short distance, the turns had a major impact on the achieved VMG. Nevertheless, the results show that *Helge Ask* can be rowed 3–3½ times as quickly as she can sail to windward. It is difficult to know whether the ship's poor performance to windward had any influence on her original use, but her poor close-hauled capability should not be written off as useless – it is tiring to row long distances and it is surely sensible to combine the two methods of propulsion: sail long tacking legs against the wind in an open sea with plenty of room and row in narrow

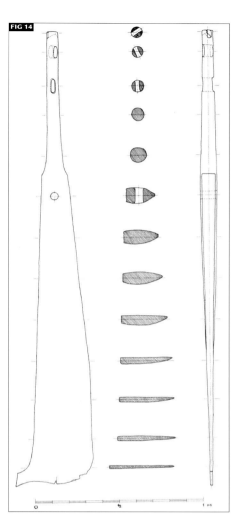

FIG 14

FIG 15

FIGURE 14
The assymetrical side rudder (with cross sectionals) was based on one found in northeast Jutland in 1958.
(The Viking Ship Museum, Denmark)

FIGURES 15
Held in its seat by a leather collar the rudder is easily twisted by the helmsman.
(Werner Karrasch, The Viking Ship Museum, Denmark)

FIGURE 16
Unseated the rudder can be brought up clear of the water.
(Werner Karrasch, The Viking Ship Museum, Denmark)

FIGURE 17
The rudder withy, tightened with wedges.
(Werner Karrasch, The Viking Ship Museum, Denmark)

FIG 16

FIG 17

passages or simply to get upwind before setting the sail to get around a headland or a reef.

Thus far, *Helge Ask*'s top recorded speed is 15 knots, achieved several times over shorter distances with the wind abaft the beam. However, her most interesting speed measurements are those made over longer distances. One of the best examples of a successful voyage was achieved during the summer expedition of 1999, when *Helge Ask* sailed from Hals at Liim fjord's eastern entrance to the Kattegat island of Hjelm – a distance of 70nm. The first section out of the fjord was under oar; when the ship was in open sea, the sail was set in a wind of 8–10m/s from

the north. The 68nm to Hjelm was sailed in slightly increasing winds, which later slackened and finally died so that the final mile had to be rowed. Departure from Hals was at 6am, the sail was set one hour later at 7am and lowered again at 2.30pm. At 3pm, *Helge Ask* was run aground on the beach on Hjelm, giving an average sailing speed of just over 9 knots. If the entire journey's speed is to be calculated, both rowing periods should be included to give a total of 70nm in nine hours, an average of 7.7 knots. This high speed was achieved on a very good day and included no sailing to windward, but if considered together with the results from the sailing trials and other voyaging, it can be imagined that with a well-trained crew of young men who have rowed and sailed since they were six years of age, the ship would be able to bring a message from the royal residence of Roskilde to important towns like Odense or Århus in less than a day.

Ottar, *a sea-going cargo ship*

The reconstruction of *Skuldelev 1*, the large cargo ship, *Ottar*, is very different from both *Roar Ege* and *Helge Ask*. She was clearly built for sea voyages, a fact substantiated by her original construction site in Sognefjord, western Norway. *Ottar* is a cargo ship, but without the original payload, she needs to carry 17 tonnes of ballast stone. The ship's net weight is 7 tonnes and with ballast, sail and rigging she has a total displacement of 25 tonnes. The principal means of propulsion is the 90m² woollen sail, although she also has four oars. Experience shows that it is not possible to row the ship except downwind; even in weak headwinds of 3m/s it is impossible to achieve steerageway. In completely calm weather and on smooth water, *Ottar* has achieved an average speed under oar of 2 knots over 90 minutes. However, when tacking in narrow passages, where efficient turns are vital, the oars make a substantial difference.

Ottar performs well in a fresh breeze and a single reef must be taken in any wind speed greater than 11m/s. The top speed of 12.5 knots has been achieved several times in a fresh breeze abaft the beam. She beats well to windward and, again, the most favourable angle to the wind under full sail is about 60°. With all four reefs taken in – a   reduction in the sail area – *Ottar* can still hold her position against the wind, but gains practically no distance. Sailing trials with a second reconstruction of *Skuldelev 1*, *Saga Siglar*, in the north Atlantic, have shown that she can beat to windward in a fresh wind and large seas with a maintained windward gain of 1.3 knots or 30nm per day. While it may not sound like much over the course of a voyage from, say, Denmark to America, it is absolutely acceptable compared to losing way to leeward while awaiting a favourable wind.

Ottar has made several long voyages, the longest being from Roskilde, Denmark, to Edinburgh, Scotland, and back, but her travels have also included a Baltic voyage and sailing

in the Kattegat and Skagerrak. In 2003 *Ottar* sailed from the Kattegat island of Anholt to Lyngør in southern Norway, a distance of 143nm, in 32 hours and 45 minutes, at an average speed of 4.4 knots. The previous year she sailed 50nm in just eight hours in 8–14m/s winds with an average speed of 6.3 knots. Unfortunately, that voyage was interrupted when the rudder withy broke.

The ships' rudders are all based on the very advanced, asymmetrical side rudder fished up at Vorså in northeast Jutland in 1958 (Figure 14). The design requires an exact balance between the ship's hull, rudder and sail. The rudder is attached to the stern quarter with a withy that passes through the side of the ship and then through the rudder boss – a spacer timber that sits outboard on the side of the ship – to holes in the reinforced rudder frame (Figure 17). The upper part of the rudder is held in the correct position using a seat and strong leather strap. If a shoal requires it, the rudder can be taken out of its seat, ie lifted up (Figure 16). When the rudder is properly designed and fitted and the ship's hull and sail are in balance with each other, there is no problem with the steering, which requires no more energy than is needed to twist the rudder in its two bearings (Figure 15).

However, during the sea voyages of *Ottar* and *The Sea Stallion from Glendalough*, the rudder withy turned out to be the weak point of the ship. When sailing in sheltered Danish waters, the rudder can often be held to the side of the ship by a single length of strong rope. But when sailing in more open waters this has proved to be a poor solution. At sea, the rudder will move up and down, slightly out of step with the ship, and even if wedges are inserted beneath the rope where it passes through the rudder frame, there will always be 'slip' due to the enormous pull on the rudder as the ship slides sideways down a wave. Even a small amount of slip means that the rudder can work in all directions, which wears away at the rope. In recent years trials have been performed with withies made from small beech trees with a maximum diameter of 12–15cm. The wood is twisted, while still on the root, to open the fibres; it becomes so flexible that it can be passed through the rudder frame. Such withies have proven far more durable than rope, especially since the part of the withy that passes through from the rudder to the frame is relatively stiff and provides a hinge effect that does not allow the rudder to work in an unintended manner and thus cause wear.

Ottar's woollen sail, which is treated with yellow ochre and grease in order to increase its ability to hold the wind, was not a total success. Despite several adjustments, the cloth blows out into a deep bunt, which increases the heel of the ship without producing forward motion. An imbalance thus arises between hull and sail, which directly affects the ship's rudder and steerage.

Is there a future for building and sailing viking ship reconstructions?
This question has been asked many times since the successful voyage of the *The Sea Stallion from Glendalough* from Roskilde to Dublin. Many people believe that the goal has now been reached: five ships from Skuldelev have been fully processed from find to reconstructed sailing vessel. But through repeated sailings, both on controlled trials and longer voyages, a pool of sailing experience and data can be collected that will provide new knowledge about sailing characteristics and performance. It is now possible to see the outline of the individual ships' potential and the possibilities they offer.

Building and sailing Viking ships in the modern era has revealed problematic issues with far greater perspectives than could have been imagined when the first keel was laid: There is no doubt that the vessels had an enormous significance for the development and maintenance of Viking society, making it possible for its people to trade, maintain control of their territory, and communicate over great distances. And the enormous consumption of resources must have required a large and stable base of support – to supply the shipbuilders with materials – and a social structure capable of organising the large workforce and producing highly specialised craftsmen, experienced sailors, navigators and skilled strategists. The continued exploration of the Skuldelev ships thus provides an insight into aspects of the past that are most difficult to see clearly and makes the future building and sailing of Viking ship reonstructions imperative.

RIKKE JOHANSEN

BIBLIOGRAPHY
Andersen, Bent & Erik Andersen 1989: *Råsejlet – Dragens Vinge.* Roskilde.
Andersen, Erik 1995: Square sails of wool. In: Olsen, Olaf et al. (eds) *Shipshape. Essays for Ole Crumlin-Pedersen on the occasion of his 60th birthday* February 24th 1995. Roskilde, 249–270.
Andersen, Erik, Bent Andersen, Morten Gøthche & Max Vinner 1980: *Nordlandsbåden – analyseret og prøvesejlet af Vikingeskibshallens Bådelaug.* Copenhagen.
Andersen, Erik, Ole Crumlin-Pedersen, Søren Vadstrup & Max Vinner 1997: *Roar Ege. Skuldelev 3 skibet som arkæologisk eksperiment.* Roskilde.
Bill, Jan, Søren Nielsen, Erik Andersen & Tinna Damgård-Sørensen 2007: *Welcome on board! The Sea Stallion from Glendalough. A Viking longship recreated.* Roskilde.
Crumlin-Pedersen, Ole 1991: *Ship Types and Sizes* AD 800 –1400. Aspects of Maritime Scandinavia AD 200 –1200. Proceedings of the Nordic Seminar on Maritime aspects of Archaeology, Roskilde, 1989. Roskilde 69–82.
Crumlin-Pedersen, Ole & Olaf Olsen (eds) 2002: The Skuldelev Ships I. Topography, Archaeology, History, Conservation and Display. *Ships and Boats of the North* 4.1. Roskilde.
Crumlin-Pedersen, Ole & Max Vinner 1993: *Roar og Helge af Roskilde – om at bygge og sejle med vikingeskibe.* Nationalmuseets Arbejdsmark 1993, 11–29.
Crumlin-Pedersen, Ole & Max Vinner (eds) 1986: *Sailing into the Past.* Proceedings of the International Seminar on Replicas of Ancient and Medieval Vessels, Roskilde, 1984. Roskilde.
Englert, Anton 2006: Trial voyages as a method of experimental archaeology: The aspect of speed. In Blue, Lucy et al. (eds), *Connected by the Sea.* Proceedings of the Tenth International Symposium on Boat and Ship Archaeology Roskilde 2003, 35–42. Oxford.

Englert, Anton 2007: Ohthere's voyages seen from a nautical angle. In Bately, Janet & Anton Englert (eds), Ohthere's Voyages. A late ninth-century account of voyages along the coasts of Norway and Denmark and its cultural context. *Maritime Culture of the North* 1, 117–129. Roskilde.
Finderup, Thomas 2006: History written in tool marks. In Blue, Lucy et al. (eds), *Connected by the Sea.* Proceedings of the Tenth International Symposium on Boat and Ship Archaeology Roskilde 2003, 21–26. Oxford.
Larsen, A.-C., and M. Kryger, W. Karrasch, R. Johansen and L. Dahl Christensen (eds) 2008: *Havhingsten fra Glendalough/ Sea Stallion of Glendalough Roskilde–Dublin 2007.* En forsøgsrejse i billeder/Pictures of a trial voyage. Med fotos af/With photos by Werner Karrasch. Roskilde.
Nielsen, Søren 2006: Experimental archaeology at the Viking Ship Museum in Roskilde. In Blue, Lucy et al. (eds), *Connected by the Sea.* Proceedings of the Tenth International Symposium on Boat and Ship Archaeology Roskilde 2003, 16–20. Oxford.
Olsen, Olaf, Jan Skamby Madsen & Flemming Rieck (eds) 1995: *Shipshape. Essays for Ole Crumlin-Pedersen on the occasion of his 60th birthday* February 24th 1995. Roskilde.
Olsen, Olaf & Ole Crumlin-Pedersen 1978: *Five Viking Ships from Roskilde Fjord.* Copenhagen.
Tørnsø Johansen, Rikke 2002: *Fra Ottars Logbog. Marinarkæologisk Nyhedsbrev fra Roskilde* 18, 28–33. Roskilde.
Vadstrup, Søren 1993: *I vikingernes kølvand.* Roskilde
Vinner, Max 2002: *Viking Ship Museum Boats.* Roskilde.
Vinner, Max 1995: 'A Viking-ship off Cape Farewell 1984'. In: Olsen, Olaf et al. (eds) *Shipshape. Essays for Ole Crumlin-Pedersen on the occasion of his 60th birthday,* February 24th 1995, 289–304. Roskilde.
Vinner, Max 1993: Unnasiling – the seaworthiness of the merchant vessel. In: Clausen, Birthe L. (ed.) *Viking Voyages to North America.* Roskilde, 95–108.

6 The Hanseatic cog

Before 1962 the medieval cog was known only from seals and other contemporary illustrations. Yet, since then, some eighteen wrecks have been found and several replicas built. The latter were based on the 1380 cog of Bremen, Germany, the 1354 Baltic cog found off the coast of Poel Island near Wismar, Germany, and lastly on a smaller example from Kampen, the Netherlands, wrecked near Nijkerk. Today, this small fleet of replica cogs sails in company, just as the ships would have done more than 600 years ago.

The First Replica: Hanse Kogge of Kiel

It was a sensation: in October 1962, during a dredging operation in the port of Bremen on Germany's North Sea coast, the wreck of a medieval Hanseatic cog was uncovered. Dated to 1380 by dendrochronology, it was the first discovery of its type and would open the door on an ancient world previously known only through iconography and contemporary writings. The Hanseatic League was a trading organisation that grew up in the twelfth century linking cities along the Baltic and North Sea coasts, and their ships carried goods as far north as Bergen in Norway and south even to the Mediterranean. Of all the League's ships the cog was the most common – straight keeled, high-sided with high, steeply raked stem and sternpost, they were strong, sturdy and stable and their cargoes were as diverse as fish, beer, salt, grain, cloth

and weapons, most of which was stored in barrels.

Salvage of the Bremen wreck began immediately and by December 1962 nearly all the timbers had been saved, with the rest being recovered through the following summer. The waterlogged timbers were stored in water-filled tanks for more than ten years until, in November 1972, the keel was laid for the second time.

Over the course of the next eight years the wreck was carefully reconstructed and exact drawings were made of all the pieces and finally of the ship itself. By the end of the project historians and archaeologists knew a great deal about cog construction in the 1300s, but they had gleaned no new information concerning the type's sailing properties. Following the completion of the wreck's reconstruction in 1980, the project

FIGURE 1
The Seal of Stralsund, showing a contemporary depiction of a Hanseatic cog, 1329.

FIGURE 3
The reassembled Cog of Bremen, 1380, looking from the bow.
(Deutsches Schiffahrts Museum)

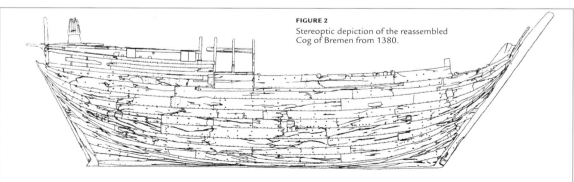

FIGURE 2
Stereoptic depiction of the reassembled Cog of Bremen from 1380.

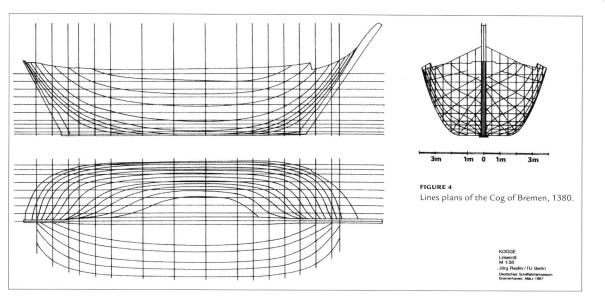

KOGGE
Linienriß
M 1:50
Jörg Redlin / TU Berlin
Deutsches Schiffahrtsmuseum
Bremerhaven, März 1987

FIGURE 4
Lines plans of the Cog of Bremen, 1380.

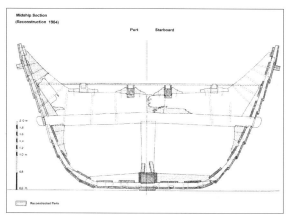

Midship Section
(Reconstruction 1984)

Port   Starboard

Reconstructed Parts

FIGURE 6
A scale model was used to test the rudder in a flow tank at the Kiel Highschool.

FIGURE 5
Midship section of the Cog of Bremen, 1380.

team embarked on its preservation. A stainless-steel tank was built around the ship and filled with 800m³ of water with 40 per cent PEG (Polyethylene Glycol). The cog remained in this solution until all her timbers were fully saturated; the tank was removed in 2000.

It was this frustrating gap in the historians' knowledge that first gave birth to an ambitious idea: a full-scale replica would be built to learn how a cog would have been sailed. The first step was to draw a lines projection of the original hull, averaging out its deformities. Computerised lines drawings were based on the measurements of the original frames and showed the ideal shape of the ship – starting at the midships section the shape of each frame was calculated by following the contour of the inner face of the bottom carvel strakes and the contour of the inside face at the upper edge, of the lapped topside strakes. The weight of the ship's hull, rig and ballast were calculated. Five drawings of cross-sections – in way of the hull's five principal beams – were made based on the measurements of the extant original timbers. In order to check the computed results the plank lines were drawn and found to be correct and smooth. Stability calculations were carried out to estimate the centre of gravity and ballast requirement. Since neither rudder, mast, nor yard were ever found, assumptions had to be made based on seal depictions and new calculations. The rudder, as built, was less slender than seen on contemporary seals and was lengthened to stand above the sternpost so that the tiller could be attached. Its thickness was the same as that of the sternpost. The mast was fashioned from a single trunk, its proportions estimated from the position of the maststep on the keelson of the wreck and the spacing between the longitudinal deck beams. The yard was built in two pieces according to the 1897 rules of the classification society, 'Germanischer Lloyd'. To estimate the weight and centre of gravity of the cargo we assumed

FIGURE 7
A second model was used to test the projected rig in a wind tunnel at Hamburg University.

FIGURE 8
Launching the replica of the 1380 Cog of Bremen.

FIGURE 9
The replica under full sail.

FIGURE 10
Tacking took about 1 minute.

FIGURE 11
Bending the strakes for both sides of the
Ubena von Bremen over an open fire.
(Uwe Peterson)

FIGURE 12
Ubena von Bremen under full sail. When
launched the cog had simple striped
sails but they were later adorned with
the Bremen coat of arms.
(Uwe Peterson)

FIGURE 13
Seal of Kiel, 1365.

that the in-hold barrels were filled with rye. We derived the size of the barrels from medieval custom records. The result was that the cog has 0.22m more draught astern than forward. This was probably correct and intentional as we assume that a pump was installed in the stern and, if you were sailing with a following wind, the pressure on the sail would press the bow down.

Another calculation was made for the ship sailing 'light' – in ballast but without cargo. In 1976 a cog wreck dating from 1375 (five years earlier than the estimated date of the Bremen cog) was discovered near Vejby in Denmark – unlike all the previous wreck finds this one was discovered with its ballast and so gave researchers a clear 'weight of ballast to length of keel' ratio. The ballast requirement for the Bremen cog replica was thus calculated to be about 26 tonnes.

Subsequent trials would show that in all conditions the stability is sufficient with one exception: if the mast is stepped in an unballasted hull, the stability is negative. It is possible that this is why the cog of Bremen sank – no ballast stones were found, either in the hull or on the riverbed nearby.

The next problem was the design of the rig. As well as medieval town seals, which show cogs as one-masted ships setting a single

square sail, we have the 1444 writings of Timbotta. Giorgio Timbotta da Moda was a Venetian merchant who recorded the measurements and proportions of the Italian version of the cog (the *cochce*); he mentions that the height of a cog's mast should be four times the beam at deck level, and the yard should be four-fifths as long as the mast. The height of the mainsail should be half the length of the yard and may be increased by two or three bonnets that can be joined to the sail by a system of loops and eyelets.

To investigate the rig we started with the following measurements: length of mast 24m; length of yard 16m; sail area 210m³. This proposed rig was tested in a wind tunnel with a 1:25 model. The results showed that the sail was of acceptable size and would enable the cog to reach hull speed. It was also proved that with such a sail the cog could go to windward.

Armed with this new knowledge we started our project to build a full-scale cog at the Rathje shipyard in Kiel in June 1987. The aim was to build as faithful a copy of the original Bremen cog as was possible. Together with the association 'Youth in Work' the new cog was built and commissioned within four years.

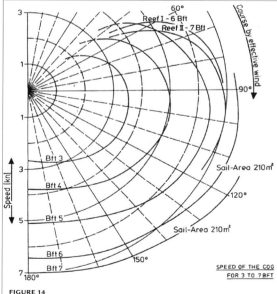

FIGURE 14
Results of the wind-tunnel tests, showing the estimated speed of the cog on various points of sail.

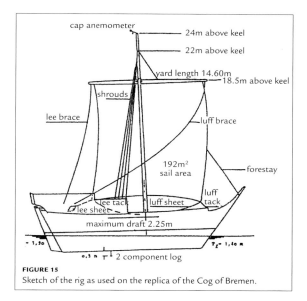

cap anemometer

24m above keel

22m above keel

yard length 14.60m

18.5m above keel

shrouds

lee brace

luff brace

192m² sail area

forestay

luff tack

lee tack

luff sheet

lee sheet

maximum draft 2.25m

2 component log

FIGURE 15
Sketch of the rig as used on the replica of the Cog of Bremen.

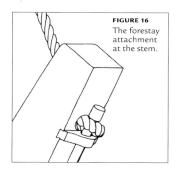

FIGURE 16
The forestay attachment at the stem.

The keel was laid in February 1988 and young trainees worked under the direction of master shipwright Uwe Baykowski until October 1989, when the hull was launched. It was built as a stressed-shell structure – the shape of the hull is determined by the length of the keel, the rake of the stem and sternpost and the dimensions of the strakes; all transverse timbers, such as floors and futtocks, as well as the keelson and inner planking, are calculated, one at a time, beginning with the fifth strake; to achieve the correct form, moulds were used.

The entire structure was built of best-quality oak – about 120m³ in all. After laying the keel (15.9m × 40cm × 12.5cm, made in three parts) the stem and sternpost were fitted to the knees at both ends of the flat keel. The lowest four strakes of the hull planking were carvel laid while the upper nine were lapped as were those of the original – only the Baltic cogs did not have this carvel/clinker construction but were, rather, clinker-built with narrow planks. The thickness of the original handsawn planks varied from 38mm to 55mm, but for the replica all planks were of 45mm with the exception of the strake at the turn of the bilge, which was 55mm. The planks were steam-bent in a box – in the Middle Ages, bending would have been done over an open fire. In the box it took two and a half hours of steaming to achieve sufficient flexibility to twist the ends of the bottom planks from horizontal amidships to vertical at stem and stern (over a fire the process would have taken about an hour more).

The clinker planks were fastened with about 10,000 forged nails – of stainless steel instead of iron because of the greater resistance to corrosion. All the clinker seams were caulked from inside; oakum was used rather the medieval concoction of moss and animal hair. After caulking the seams were further secured internally with slats of oak held by stainless-steel cramps. The carvel bottom was also caulked but from outside. Once plank No 8 on each side had been fitted, work began on installing the keelson, futtocks, five breast hooks in the bow and stern, and the ceiling planks, which were fastened with conical, wedged trunnels – all the breast hooks and knees were of grown crooks. At plank 8 four large crossbeams were installed – their ends extending out beyond the hull, their heads notched to fit overlapping planks that were cut to let them in. (It is not known exactly why the beams were built overlong: one theory is that it may have been to offer protection to the topsides; another is that it offered greater transverse strength to the hull structure.) On top of these crossbeams large grown knees were placed to bear the four longitudinal deck beams (21 × 17cm). On the medieval cog the deck planks were laid loose between these beams so that they could be easily lifted when loading or discharging cargo. However, for the replica we chose to build a watertight deck and so laid plywood beneath the oak deck planks, which were between 1.2m and 1.3m long, 40cm and 57cm wide, and 3.5cm and 4cm thick – both elements were through-fastened to the beams with forged nails.

After the hull was launched in October 1989 the cog was finished afloat. A sterncastle was built with two small cabins below deck. Between these cabins – on deck – was located a large windlass, while atop the sterncastle itself a capstan was mounted for hauling braces and sheets. The mast – total length 24m, final diameter 66cm at the foot, 20cm at the head – was hewn from a single Danish larch. The standing rigging consists of four pairs of shrouds fabricated from

FIGURE 17
The bottom of the *Wissemara* during construction; note the moulds that clearly show the U-shaped cross section.

FIGURE 18
The *Wissemara* just prior to launching.

36mm-diameter hemp-coloured synthetic line, reinforced with stainless-steel wire. Each shroud is tightened by a lanyard and a pair of three-hole deadeyes – examples of such deadeyes were found inside the original cog. A pair of adjustable shrouds was also rigged to lend support to the single forestay – the latter being of 45mm rope of the same type as that used for the shrouds. The bottom of the forestay is bent to a rope eye led through an 85mm hole in the stem – it can be tightened or loosened by turning the eye with a peg.

Following the advice of Ole Crumlin Pedersen (a leading expert in naval architecture and marine archaeology from Denmark whom we consulted many times during the project – (see Chapter 5), we decided to shorten the yard and sail by about 1m, resulting in a sail 13.34 × 7.2m (96m²) that can be reefed to 83m² or 70m². The area of the mainsail can also be increased by attaching bonnets to the footrope – there are three bonnets in all, each measuring 13.34 × 2.4m (32m²), giving a total sail area of 192m², twice the size of the original sail. The sail is made of Duradon. Together, sail and yard weigh 600kg.

When lowered the yard can lie along the length of the deck. To hoist yard and sail eight crewmembers are needed at the windlass; we measured a tension force of more than 2 tonnes. When sail is due to be taken in it is brailed up to the yard with the buntlines and the yard is then easily and quickly lowered by using a downhaul, which runs around the windlass in the opposite direction to the halyard.

The first sailing trials were held in June 1991. The cog was initially sailed with ballast but without cargo. Thus, the fully equipped ship has a displacement of 91 tonnes, a mean draught of 1.65m and a stern trim of 0.5m. The initial stability was measured by running a heeling experiment. The transverse metacentric height of 0.72m over the centre of gravity is sufficient, providing the sail is reefed in good time in wind speeds of Force 5 and higher. Up to Force 5 we sailed with the full sail (192m²) and attained a speed of 5 knots. With five-sixths of the sail (160m²) we reached a speed of 7 knots in Force 6–7. Sailing on a reach in Force 7, the cog attained 8 knots for a

short period. We were able to sail up to about 70° off the wind and the cog was surprisingly simple and quick to tack. With the helm laid hard to leeward the ship turns into the wind and begins to luff. As the sail is backed against the stay, the bowlines are tightened. In this position the cog still has steerage but moves slightly astern. She continues through the wind all the way on to a beam reach and then the yard is braced around. Four crew members work the bowlines and tacks, while four others work the sheets and braces – bowlines, sheets and tacks are eased and the yard comes around. Then the new weather tack is hauled along with the leeward sheet and brace. Tacking takes about one minute to complete. On all courses the tack of the sail had to be hauled as close as possible.

Response to the helm was satisfactory, indicating that the size and shape of the rudder are appropriate. In a seaway of about 0.75m wave height, rudder deflections of 6° to 7° were required to hold a course. With increasing draught and strong wind this angle increased up to 15°. The cog proved to be a stable sailing vessel. Even in rough weather she takes no water on deck because the bulwarks are high and closed. The greatest heeling angle was found to be less than 20° on a beam reach with full sail in more than a Force 7. Leeway was about 10° to 15°.

However, because of the hull's compact shape and lack of deep keel, the cog's sea-keeping is extremely rough. Fully laden the roll motions last 5.4 seconds while the pitch motions last only 4.5 seconds. In an unfavour-able seaway amplitudes of 10° were measured for pitch and roll angle, causing considerable physical strain and often sickness for the crew. But, in general, her manoeuvring characteristics under sail are convincing. The cog's average statistical speed for all courses calculated from all readings were: Force 3, 3.4 knots; Force 4, 4 knots; Force 5, 5.1 knots; Force 6, 6 knots.

After the sailing trials two diesel engines of 159kw each were installed in the aft section with two pump jet-propulsion plants amidships – thrust can be turned through 360° and so the cog can be easily turned and manoeuvred; she can be run under engine at 7 knots in calm waters.

FIGURE 19
The *Wissemara* sailing under main and two bonnets

Bremen Cog (Hanse Kogge)

LOA	23.27m
LOD	22.65m
LO Keel	15.60m
Stem rake	4.81m
Sternpost rake	2.25m
Maximum beam	7.26m
Beam on deck	6.45m
Depth (from bottom of keel to top of bulwark amidships)	4.26m
Draught unladen, ballasted	1.65m
Draught laden	2.07m
Hull weight	55.80 tonnes
Weight with rig and ballast	91.10 tonnes
Weight fully laden	140 tonnes
Length of mast	24.00m
Total sail area	192.00m²
Crew	14

    1 master
    4 at the weather tack
    4 on the sterncastle to handle braces and sheets
    1 at the buntlines
    2 at the ripcords
    1 at the helm
    1 at the downhaul

The second replica: *Ubena von Bremen*

At the same time as the project in Kiel was realised a group of enthusiasts started to build another replica of the cog in Bremerhaven. Here the aim was to reconstruct and build a ship with the lines and measurements of the historical find but under the supervision of the classification society 'Germanischer Lloyd' – the result is a replica that can be sailed by a small crew.

First the lines of the original cog were lofted full size. Using these mould drawings all frames and strakes could be designed. The hull was built frame first. Web frames were erected in way of the five crossbeams. All strakes were bent over an open fire, steaming planks for both sides at the same time. The after part of the hull was changed from the medieval because the cog would have an engine and single-screw propeller from new. Thus, a deadwood was attached to the sternpost and the rudder shape was altered considerably. All fastenings were of stainless steel. The hollow mast has a length of only 21m and the yard is 18m. The sail is thus

rectangular in shape – 17.3 × 6m (103.8m²). This can be enlarged by two bonnets – 17.3 × 3m (51.9m² each) and, if necessary, can be reefed down to 25m². With 36 tonnes of ballast, *Ubena von Bremen* has a very good stability but a greater draught than the aforementioned 'Hanse Kogge' built in Kiel. A 280kw diesel engine was fitted, as was electric and hydraulic power for the winches and steering gear. Speed under engine is about 7 knots, while under sail 6 to 7 knots can be achieved. Beneath the sterncastle are small cabins for the master, restroom and shower, galley and navigation room; the crew's accommodation is beneath the main deck.

In August 1991 *Ubena von Bremen* set out on her maiden voyage, tracing the trading voyages of the Hanseatic League and visiting Lübeck, Wismar, Stralsund, Greifswald, Stettin and Danzig. Since then she has represented Bremerhaven on several occasions and at tallship events; her sterncastle has been decorated with the coats of arms of the Hanseatic towns.

The third replica: *Roland von Bremen*

This near copy of the Hanse Kogge was built in Bremen. She has some slight alterations in the rig: a hinged mast was mounted instead of a pole mast and the yard is hoisted by lifts – ropes fastened at both ends of the yard and led through two blocks at the top of the mast and thence down to the deck; their function is to keep the yard horizontal as it is being raised and lowered. I have no proof, either on seals or in other illustrations, that lifts were used in medieval times. *Roland von Bremen* also has a diesel engine – of 279kw – and two Schottel pump jets, one forward to starboard, the other in the stern to port. The speeds of *Roland von Bremen* compare closely to those of the Hanse Kogge of Kiel.

Kampen Kogge

This replica, built in Kampen, the Netherlands, is the most authentic of all the cogs now sailing in the North Sea. She was based on a wreck found near Nijkerk, the Netherlands. She is somewhat smaller than the cog of Bremen: LOA 21.58m, beam 7.56m, draught 1.9m, sail area 144m². Hull and deck were built in the same way as all the aforementioned replicas, but in the open air using green oakwood as would have been done in the Middle Ages. The sterncastle is mounted above the deck on pillars, so the helmsman has a better view in all directions. Sail, shrouds and ropes are made of hemp rather than synthetic materials.

The Poeler Kogge and the replica *Wissemara*, the Baltic version of a medieval cog

In 1997–8 the wreck of a medieval cog was discovered in the Baltic near the island of Poel. She was built of pine and dated to 1354 by means of dendrochronological analysis. That part of the hull that could be saved consists of fifteen strakes of 11m in length and a cross-section of 40 × 8cm. The seams were nailed and fastened with trunnels to about fifty floor timbers. The keel, 18 × 0.6m, was saved as were the stem and sternpost. It was therefore possible to design a 1:10 scale model, which was used to generate the lines and to develop construction drawings for a 1:1 scale replica. The missing parts of the hull and superstructure were reconstructed following the design of the Bremen cog.

What are the differences between the Baltic type and the North Sea type? First it is U-shaped in cross-section instead of trapezoid. The keel is upright and the stem slightly rounded, while the sternpost is straight but with less rake. The hull, of twenty-five narrow strakes, is clinker-built throughout. The timbers were larger throughout as pine was used rather than oak, which is an inherently stronger wood. Draught and depth are smaller, while the cargo-carrying capacity is greater than that of the Bremen cog – about 200 tonnes total insteard of 87 tonnes.

The keel was laid in March 2001 and the cog was launched in May 2004. Construction was completed afloat with rig and machinery installed. A 255kw diesel engine and single propeller was installed. The mast is 32m long, the yard 16m. Total sail area is 276m², divided between a mainsail and three bonnets. The successful maiden voyage was made in August 2006. Since then *Wissemara* has joined the company of medieval sailing vessels.

Wissemara

LOA	31.5m
Beam	8.5m
Draught	2.6m
Depth	3.65m
Length of mast	32m
Sail area	276m²
Crew	10

Conclusion

All the described replicas of the North Sea and Baltic cog, with their different shapes and sail areas, have clearly demonstrated that the shipwrights of the Middle Ages built quality vessels while knowing nothing of the theory of stability or righting arms. This was proved by scientific tests in the wind tunnel of the University of Hamburg, in the flow canal at the technical high school of Kiel, and through sea trials of the full-scale Hanse Kogge replica carried out by the Institute of Naval Architecture of the Technical University of Berlin. It is hoped that research work will continue to determine which of the natural materials available in medieval times is most suited for the sails.

WOLF-DIETER HOHEISEL

BIBLIOGRAPHY

Baumann, Peter: 'Abenteuer Hanse-Kogge, Logbuch einer Seereise' in *Die Geschichte*, Deutsche Verlags-Anstalt GmbH, Stuttgart 1992.

Baykowski, *Uwe Hansekogge – Der Nachbau eines historischen Segelschiffes von 1380*, RKE-Verlag, Kiel, 1991.

Brandt, Hartmut and Karsten Hochkirch, 'The sailing Properties of the Hanse Cog in Comparison with other Cargo Sail Ships', *Ship Technology Research*, Vol. 42, 1995.

Hoffmann, Gabriele und Uwe Schnall, *Die Kogge – Sternstunde der deutschen Schiffsarchäologie*, Schriften des Deutschen Schiffahrtsmuseums Band 60, Convent Verlag, Hamburg 2003.

Hoheisel, Wolf-Dieter and Uwe Baykowski, 'A full-Scale Replica of the Hanse Cog of 1380', in *Crossroads in Ancient Shipbuilding*, ISBA 6, Oxbow Monograph 40, 1994.

7 the caravel

More than any other ship type, the caravel is associated with the Iberian explorations that led to the opening of the sea route around the horn of Africa to the East Indies and with the discovery of the Americas. The Portuguese lateen caravel sailed close to the wind, mounted a stern rudder and was altogether a fine sailing ship, though perhaps not ideally suited to long downwind passages. Its use, however, extended well beyond these overseas voyages, and outside Portugal square-rigged caravels, with square mainsail and foresail and lateen mizzen, became popular as cargo carriers and warships. In northern Europe, in the late fifteenth century, they were adapted by every maritime region and it is to Germany that we look for an example of a modern replica of this type.

The 36m *Lisa von Lübeck*, three-masted replica of a Hanseatic caravel, has been sailing the old Baltic and North Sea Hanseatic routes since 2004.

When the *Gesellschaft Weltkulturgut Hansestadt Lübeck e.V.* was founded in 1991 its members set themselves a great task. Several replicas of a fifteenth-century cog had already been seen in Hanseatic waters (Chapter 6), but never a full-scale reproduction of the caravel, its successor. Even the term 'caravel' was little known in the city of Lübeck, former Queen of the Hansa – all Hanseatic-era ships were termed *kogn* (cogs). Indeed, the contemporary chroniclers of the period did not offer any great detail about the various types, and that is how it remained into modern times.

Caravel – named for its hull planking

The word 'caravel' is of Lusitanian origin. Its etymology is the Portuguese word *caravela*. Today, boatbuilders rarely think of 'caravel' or

FIGURE 1
The *Niña*. The replica of a *caravela Redonda*, with square sails on her main- and foremasts and lateen sails on her mizzen masts, a ship type always associated with Portuguese and Spanish exploration. No wreck has survived and, like the Hanseatic caravel, the reconstruction of the *Niña* falls into the category of experimental archaeology.

FIGURE 2
A votive picture hung in the Church of St Marien, Lübeck. It was painted by an unknown artist in 1489 and clearly shows multiple caravels, both at dock (in the foreground) and underway in the distance (see detail right).

'carvel' as referring to a type of vessel, but rather to a method of building a wooden ship where the planks of the outer hull are fixed to a frame so that they butt up against each other edge to edge, giving support to the frame and forming a smooth hull. The method provides a wooden hull with greater strength than that of the clinker-built cog, and is one of the reasons why the cog was superseded by the caravel in the second half of the fifteenth century.

The carvel building method has been used for at least 4,600 years. In 1952 a boat – 1,224 component parts – was found in the funeral chamber of the pyramid of Keops. When the parts were assembled a 43.4m caravel was revealed. But it had little in common with the Hansa caravel of the late fifteenth century.

The caravel replaces the cog

While carvel construction dominated in the Mediterranean region for several thousands of years, clinker construction was preferred in

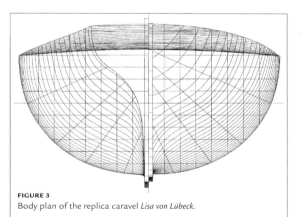

FIGURE 3
Body plan of the replica caravel *Lisa von Lübeck.*

Northern Europe for seagoing vessels. Here, the planks overlap, like the tiling of a roof, and in the time of the Vikings resulted in extremely seaworthy, fast vessels (Chapter 5). Well into the fifteenth century, the vessels of the Hansa shipping companies along the North Sea and Baltic coasts were clinker-built, but the demand for larger ships brought the trend to an end.

Especially in heavy seas, strong torsional forces work on the longitudinal joints of a

ship's hull, particularly when both the fore- and sterncastle are on the crest of a wave while the hull's centre section is in the trough between. In the clinker-built hull these sheering forces are borne solely by the bolts (typically iron or wood in early vessels) binding the overlapping planks; the planks do not give each other mutual support. In an extreme case one plank will ride over another, opening the hull to the sea, and the ensuing leak can cause the vessel to founder.

As ship size and the commensurate load-bearing capacity increased, so did the stress on the bolts. Technical knowledge at the time allowed for the load limit of a clinker-built ship of about 200 tonnes – the 'Poel cog', found in 1997 off the German Baltic island of Poel near Wismar, is this size and is currently the largest known ship from the Hansa period.

The Hansa caravels operated in the same waters as the cogs, including both the North and Baltic Seas as well as along the Atlantic coasts between Britain and Portugal. Occasionally they sailed to Iceland. They carried all kinds of general cargo: salt from Biscay to the Baltic countries, wheat from Prussia to the European Atlantic coast. From the Baltic, too, came honey, wax, jute and hemp; from Sweden iron ore, fats, tallow, skins and butter; Novgorod in Russia exported furs; the Hanseatic cities of Hamburg, Lübeck, Bremen, Wismar and Rostock shipped beer and imported coal from Newcastle in England.

But the caravels were not only used as a merchant vessel. As the following example of the *Peter von Danzig* reveals, they were also employed as corsairs or warships. Even though not built for the purpose, they could be converted to carry breech-loading cannon and, indeed, all merchant ships of the time carried arms as a protection against pirates.

The caravel *Peter von Danzig* (ex-*von Rossel*)

The first mention of a caravel in the Hansa region occurs in 1462. She was the *Peter von Rossel*. There is a report of a *Kraffel* (huge ship) arriving at Danzig from La Rochelle with a cargo of salt. The vessel was of such enormous size for the time that she would have been seen as the *QM2* of her day.

FIG 4

FIG 6

FIGURE 4
The skeleton frame of the *Lisa von Lübeck* looking aft from the stem.

FIGURE 5
Looking through the skeleton frame to the stern of the replica. Above the frame the builders erected a working platform (seen here from beneath, and 1m above that was the deck.

FIGURE 6
Steel bolts (more than 4,000, hand-forged at the Hanseschiff yard) are hammered through, fastening the planking to the internal frames.

FIGURE 7
The main deck prior to planking and the construction of the fore and stern castles.

In the mid-twentieth century Danzig naval architect Professor Otto Lienau drew up plans for the ship and estimated that she could carry 833 tonnes of cargo, which would give her a draught of 5.33m. The hull was 45.4m long and 12.2m in the beam. In his 1942 book, however, Lienau speaks expressly of 'an *attempt* [my italics] to draw up the plans' – he was basing his work primarily on the pre-served catalogued inventory annexed to a 1464 garnishee order (a legal procedure by which a creditor can collect what is owed to him by reaching the debtor's property even when it is in the hands of someone else). At

FIG 5

FIG 7

the time the great ship was in the yard at Danzig with her mainmast destroyed by lightning. In order to secure the costs of repair, the ship had been mortgaged by two local businessmen, but the 1,000 Marks were never repaid by the French. While the ship languished the investors recovered the loan by laying claim to the cargo. The doomed caravel was to have been scrapped, but in the autumn of 1469, considering possible hostilities against the English, the Danzig fathers decided to convert her to a warship. It took until 1471 for the work to be done but when at last she was recommissioned it was as *Peter von Danzig*. After trials in the North Sea – in the early weeks of 1472 – the ship operated as a corsair in the English Channel. Her size alone was enough to put enemy vessels to flight. After a second cruise as corsair in April 1473 off the Thames estuary, she returned to the Elbe estuary with rich pickings and thence continued on to Danzig. The three-master made her last voyage in 1475 when she was wrecked off Brittany. The wheel had come full circle – the unique ship had been built in Brittany and she was scrapped there. Nothing of the vessel or her fittings was preserved for posterity.

Caravel building at Lübeck

A 1477 contract between the city of Lübeck and shipbuilder 'Bartolomeus' is preserved in the Lübeck city archive. The document was subjected to scientific study by historian Andreas Kammler. Unfortunately the dimensions of the ship are not specified because she was to be a sister to an existing vessel. However, of great interest is the use of the Middle Low German phrase *umme dat kraveel anders genomet den vawiker te bouwen*, 'to build a new caravel also known as the *vawiker*'. (Kammler believes that the word 'vawiker' means a caravel built in the southwest-England port of Fowey.) The contract clearly reveals that caravels not only sailed in the fifteenth-century Baltic but also that they were built there. Moreover, the mariners of Lübeck seem to have had some experience with the type. What remains unclear is why they wanted the vawiker design.

Experimental nautical archaeology

No caravel of the Hanseatic period has survived, nor has any wreck been discovered. Accordingly the 'reconstruction' of the Lübeck Hansa ship falls into the field of experimental nautical archaeology. The entire project had to be created, as it were, from parts of a jigsaw – probabilities, logical inferences and other fragmentary evidence. Individual caravel parts have been found in houses, fountains and roadworks – when a wooden ship was wrecked during the Middle Ages, useful parts were appropriated to build wooden pathways, to protect a fountain or for housebuilding. Such parts were often purpose-shaped and maritime experts have been able to determine which part of the ship they were from and approximately how large the ship must have been. Contemporary artwork depicting caravels is to be found, predominantly in churches. In the Marienkirche at Lübeck, for example, hangs a Bergen maritime painting by an *exvoto* – an oil painting dated 1489, it commemorates a disaster along the Norwegian skerries. The ship in the fore-ground is strongly stylised, as was the tradition of the time, but the ships in the background are authentic in their propor-tions. This has provided important infor-mation about rigging, tackle and the hull form above the waterline. Neither caravel models nor technical sketches were known in the fifteenth century when shipwrights tended to work by 'rule of thumb' and ships were built not to a plan but on the basis of tradition and experience.

In 1920 a caravel model was built for the German Museum at Munich based on the work of Kiel-based naval architect Carl Busley. In 1962 Busley's concept, and two other works by Walter Vogel and Paul Heinsius, influenced the designs of Heinrich Winter, on sale since then to model builders. In the 1990s these four pieces of twentieth-century research – Busley, Vogel, Heinsius and Winter – formed the platform for discussion regarding the planned reconstruction of a full-sized Hansa caravel of the later fifteenth century.

The Weltkulturgut society built a 1:10 scale model from the Winter blueprints in 1994. The hull was constructed using a skeletal framework as dictated by the rules of naval architecture, but the realisation of a full-scale replica needed much more research. In 1995 a scientific-technical council was founded. It was headed by Professor Eike Lehmann (board member of Germanischer Lloyd and chairman of the Technical Shipbuilding Society); engineer Wolf-Dieter Hoheisel, former technical director of the German Shipping Museum at Bremerhaven; Professor Peter Tamm, former chairman of the Springer publishing board; and Professor Hartmut Brandt of Berlin University. This working group collated all available knowledge for the project.

In order to determine the shape of the ship's hull – particularly below the waterline – scientific staff at the Technical University of Berlin, led by Professor Hartmut Brandt, evaluated the evidence for hull form over the last thousand years. Comparing ships from either side of the caravel age enabled an approximate hull form to be established. The principal guide in this was the *Mary Rose*. This warship, built in England between 1509 and 1511, sank in 1545 and was lifted in 1967. Because the wreck has not been preserved in its entirety – and has been dated to a quarter of a century later than the Hansa caravel – it gave rise to much further speculation about the possible caravel hull shape. For example, with regard to the sterncastle it is still not known when the changeover from a rounded stern to a transom stern occurred. Building foreman of the *Lisa von Lübeck*, master shipwright Heino Schmarje, settled the matter with the following observation: 'For the proposed shape of the ship's hull, from the point of view of the wooden-ship builder, it is almost impossible to build a rounded stern. The planks require severe bending, which results in their constantly splitting. Why would the shipbuilders of that time have wanted to make life so difficult for themselves?' Thus, after much argument, for and against, the decision was taken for the transom stern.

The experimental archaelogy was greatly helped by considerations regarding the *Lisa von Lübeck*'s loading hatch. Shipbuilders are always anxious to avoid weakening decks by introducing unnecessarily large holes. Every seaman shudders at the sight of huge hatches – which are difficult to make watertight with traditional means. On the other hand, shipping companies and stevedores like large hatches; they simplify loading and unloading and cleaning procedures. The compromise has ever been to build a hatch opening just large enough to accept the biggest expected item of cargo.

It was therefore necessary to establish what goods and containers would have been stored below decks in the Hanseatic period. The first to be considered was the barrel. Barrels were the forerunners of the modern container; all liquids and any goods sensitive to damp were shipped in barrels (or relatively small stone jugs). The barrel had to be transported between ship and shore and was probably no heavier than 2 tonnes laden. A beer or wine barrel would have been 1.6m tall and 1.3m diameter, barrels of wheat an extra 0.3m in diameter. Since horses were also transported – and these were larger than the barrels – the breadth of the main hatch must have been approximately 2.8m to accommodate the greatest length of a horse.

And so the research continued. Indeed, there were many examples of individual items being inferred during the building phase and then included in the design and subsequently built-in after due investigation of the technical possibilities of the time.

Determining the dimensions of the replica

As no particular ship was to be copied, but only a type, it was down to those charged with the design to decide the ship's size. The dimensions of the *Peter von Danzig* did not correspond to the average Hanseatic caravel. Indeed, it was so large that, almost certainly, it could not have entered any of the ports of the Baltic or southern North Sea with cargo. The river Trave, for example, which leads to the port of Lübeck, was never deeper than 2.6m in the estuary until 1815 – indeed, not until 1883, 400 years after the arrival of *Peter von Danzig*, was the depth of the channel increased to 5.3m.

Literary sources on commercial shipping and shipbuilding prior to the seventeenth century do not provide satisfactory

information on the average size of seagoing vessels in the Hanseatic period and the conclusions of researchers are diverse and lack a reliable basis. What is known is that in 1412 the Hanseatic Council decided against building larger ships. Even in the era of the cog, harbour installations had not kept up with ship size; cargo had to be discharged in the roadstead into lighters. It was difficult to accommodate ships of more than 25m length in the harbour at Lübeck. Thus, 'giants' such as *Peter von Danzig* or the 1565-built *Adler*

von Lübeck must have been exceptional along the North Sea and Baltic coasts.

Lisa von Lübeck is, perhaps, an average-sized caravel. Her principal measurements are based on the designs of Heinrich Winter and approximately correspond with the ships depicted in the Bergen commemmorative painting.

Building the *Lisa von Lübeck*
Lisa von Lübeck was built outside Lübeck old town. The yard on the Wall Peninsula is a site

The *Lisa von Lübeck* was planked
using the 'French planking' system.
Every fourth plank is nailed to the
plank above and below. Between
each group of planks a space is left
for the stopper plank, which is
fitted last and very precisely shaped.

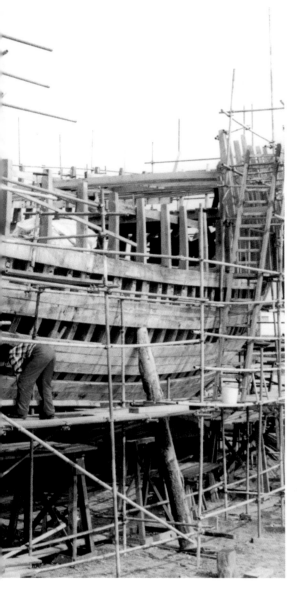

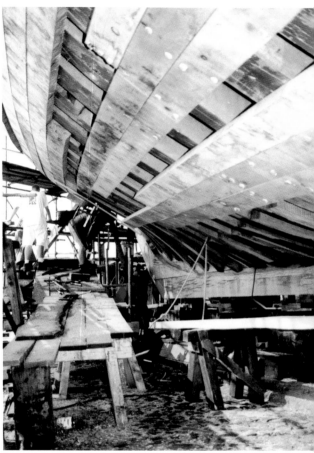

rich with history. The Lübeck boatyards were
located there until the introduction of iron
shipbuilding in the 1880s. Cogs, then caravels,
and finally, in 1566, the superlative *Adler von
Lübeck*, a galleon displacing 2,000 tons, were
built on the peninsula. (In its turn the galleon
was the successor to the caravel.) For the past
hundred years the Wall Peninsula has served
as a harbour defence.

The city gave the *Gesellschaft Weltkulturgut*
a vacant shed and waterside yard in which to
build the replica. Workshops and offices were

set up in the shed, while wood for the replica
was stored in the open and staging was built
for the caravel. A classic launching from the
stocks would not be possible instead the ship
would have to be lifted into the water by a
floating crane.

Besides building the caravel, one of the
reasons the *Gesellschaft Weltkulturgut* wanted
its own shipyard was to provide
apprenticeships for unemployed people, aged
eighteen to twenty-five, who lacked any
formal trade training. The apprentices were

joined by previously unemployed or retired craftsmen who passed on their knowledge and expertise in wood- and metalworking. Watching the vessel take shape in the yard served as an incentive for the workers – more than 300 collaborated on the construction over the five-year period; after two years the workers were all gradually replaced; only project leader Heino Schmarje was present throughout the entire project and was often the only qualified shipbuilder in the yard.

The hull of *Lisa von Lübeck* is of oak; 170 oak trees – 800m³ of wood – were selected by Heino Schmarje and foresters from the Lübeck city forest. They were between 150 and 300 years old and had been planted specifically to supply timber for shipbuilding. The use of oak was determined by the avail-ability of wood in the Hanseatic era; unlike Scandinavia and the Eastern Baltic, northwest Germany had almost no coniferous trees and into the fourteenth century the oak was the dominant tree in the region known today as Schleswig-Holstein. As the result of climate change, oak was gradually replaced by beech but because beech, is not suitable for shipbuilding, in the Middle Ages the Lübeck planners began to plant oak trees. However, oak is not appropriate for masts because it is too heavy and insufficiently flexible. In earlier times the well-known Riga pine was imported by sea for mast construction. Coniferous trees were first planted in Lübeck in 1610, and so it was not until the end of the seventeenth century that wood from the local forest became available for masts and spars. The masts of *Lisa von Lübeck*, however, are from the Lübeck forest. The foremast is larch, the main and mizzen Douglas fir – the latter grown in Lübeck for about a century. Since it is possible that some conifers were grown in the Hansa period, it was considered accept-able to use conifers from the local forest.

Lisa von Lübeck's keel was laid on 31 May 1999. It consists of three oak beams 8m long, 300mm wide and 400mm deep, secured by hook joints to make an overall keel length of 20m. Forty-two frames are bedded on the keel; each is in seven parts. Sawn from grown branches, each frame is 170mm thick and all are sistered. After the framework, stem and

sternpost had been assembled, in the autumn of 2001 the builders strengthened the skeleton with 80mm-thick oak ceiling planks fastened to the inner face of the frames. The uppermost of these support the deck beams, which are up to 8m long and 260 × 280mm thick – after being steamed for seven hours these could be bent to give the deck a slight camber. The deck beams and other wood were sawn to size with a marquetry saw which, of course, would not have existed 500 years ago then ship's carpenters would have cut sections from tree trunks and branches with an adze or axe. Today, one finds few craftsmen competent in this work – it is physically demanding and dangerous, and in the twenty-first century unnecessary. In Hanseatic times the deck beams would not have been steambent. Rather, there were considerably more free-standing oaks, which often had a crooked trunk from which excellent beams could be hewn. The oak used in the building of the *Lisa von Lübeck* all came from the Lübeck forest. Here the trees are planted in close proximity to each other and grow straight and slender. The only excep-tions were the two crooked oaks harvested from the edge of the forest; these were used for the stem.

Since no original caravel has been found, the contemporaneous dimensions of the various components are unknown. For this reason the volume *Germanischer Lloyd Guidelines for the Construction of Wooden Seagoing Ships*, last edition 1964, was used as the manual. This book of tables and formulae relies on many centuries of experience. The smallest plank thickness – 65mm – is to the *Germanischer Lloyd* guidelines. The wood for the oak planks was sawn to 80mm. Having been stored for two years, it was introduced to the construction from the spring of 2002 onwards.

The hull has twenty-eight planks to a side – if laid end to end, they would measure 1,400m. The employed method of construction is known as 'French planking' – every fourth plank is nailed to the plank above and below. Thus, between each group of three there is one plank space left for the stopper planks, which are inserted last and are shaped very precisely.

The planks were secured with 210mm-long, 14mm-diameter steel bolts. More than 4,000 of these were hand-forged at the Hanseschiff Yard. Oak contains tannic acid, which is very quick to act on naked steel, so all the bolts were zinc-coated. This would not have been done on the original caravels, but today's builders wanted the *Lisa* to have a much longer life than would have been typical for the ships of the Hanseatic period.

At either end of the superstructure are the 'forecastle' and 'sterncastle'. The word 'castle' originates from the original purpose of these raised fighting platforms, which made it easier to defend the ship but were obviously a target for the attacker. They are built of oak formed by an extension of the framework and supported by underlying beams or deckhead planks, on which rest the castle deck beams. To save weight the two castles are decked with larch, which was also used for the main decks. In contrast to the practice on the cogs, caravel decks were fixed to protect the cargo from water ingress. The longitudinal planking was caulked with tarred hemp.

Before being launched, the hull below the waterline was copper sheathed against 'shipworm' – the *teredo navalis*. This saltwater clam nests as larvae in wood and bores finger-sized burrows, which in favourable conditions can destroy a wooden hull within a few months. The original habitat of this parasite was the tropics, but during the exploration of the New World, ships returning to Europe were infested. Thus, to protect their planking, hulls of ocean-going ships were given a protective layer of lead, copper or metal. It is unknown when this procedure was introduced into the Hanseatic region, but since the *teredo navalis* has become very common in the Baltic over recent decades, the *Lisa von Lübeck* was given a sheath of 0.8mm copper plate with a tarred underlay nailed to the oak planks – copper also reduces the growth of algae and barnacles on the hull.

The christening ceremony was performed on 27 March 2003 by local entrepreneur Lisa Dräger who, in 1991, had first had the idea for the replica. She named the caravel *Lisa von Lübeck*. A floating crane lowered the 190-tonne vessel into the Trave river. Rigging work began in the summer of 2003. The shrouds and stays are of artificial fibre reinforced with steel wire; outwardly the material resembles classic hemp rope. All the *Lisa*'s rope and cordage is of man-made fibre for its better resistance to weather.

She sails better than expected

On 1 December 2004 *Lisa von Lübeck* sailed on her maiden voyage in Lübeck Bay and so began a long learning period. Few of the crew had ever sailed a square-rigger. The caravel was rigged with square sails on fore and main, and a lateen on the mizzen –something new for everybody. The honorary crew is made up of members of the *Gesellschaft Weltkulturgut Hansestadt Lübeck e.V.* – the society had now evolved from being a shipyard operator to a shipping concern.

The most intriguing question for historians and shipbuilders alike was: does the caravel sail better than her predecessor, the cog? To begin with it must be remarked that there were many pessimists in shipping circles. 'She'll bob about like a cork,' was just one of the predictions. The full bow above the waterline does seem to promise poor performance but underwater the hull is remarkably streamlined. The assumption that the rounded mainframe would be too flexible and lack stiffness was unfounded.

Forty-five tonnes of fixed lead ballast provide a metacentric height of 116.5cm. Even in a Force 7 with the wind abeam the caravel sails relatively upright under the 181m² mainsail. Under just the 58m² foresail the caravel makes 9 knots in a Force 9 with a following wind and, despite having 30 per cent less sail area per tonne displacement, she is as fast as a replica cog.

However, there was a less pleasant surprise during the scientific sail trials. *Lisa von Lübeck* was driven 1.8 miles to leeward in the most favourable case as she came up to the wind. The first attempt to turn her failed completely. As soon as the wind backed the mainsail, the caravel drifted uncontrollably to leeward and was finally driven sternwards. Accordingly, a technique was developed which made it possible to turn the ship almost on the mark.

FIG 10

FIG 11

FIG 12

The lateen is backed and the helm is put over to the lee side; the combined effect brings the ship into the wind. As soon as the mainsail begins to luff it is lowered. As the ship turns through the wind the foresail backs and the lateen fills, favouring the turning movement. Once the ship is on the new tack, the foresail is braced around and the ship stops while the mainsail is rehoisted. Sixteen crewmen are required for this manoeuvre.

Despite her turning issues, the caravel is better on the wind than the cog because the sail surface is divided between three sails. This gives a better trim and the ship is easier to steer and hold on course. The *Lisa von Lübeck* can sail 60° off the wind without serious reduction in speed; the drift is then around 15°.

How the ship sails fully laden has not yet been determined. At 200 tonnes she has a draught of 2.9m unladen. It is assumed that in Hanseatic times she would have carried up

FIG 13

FIG 15

FIGURE 15

Despite the use of modern materials for longevity and strength, considerable care was taken with the traditional appearance of the *Lisa von Lübeck* replica. Thus, shrouds and stays are all of artifical fibre reinforced with steel wire but they resemble classic hemp. Note the Hanseatic crest of the town of Lübeck on the mainsail.

FIGURE 10

Below the waterline the hull was entirely sheathed in copper. It is not known if this practice would have been employed in Hanseatic times but was thought expedient for the replica, which would be sailing in waters now plagued by shipworms.

FIGURES 11 AND 12

Lisa von Lübeck on the hard prior to launching. The rounded carvel-planked underwater hull and substantial overhang of the forecastle are clearly evident. Note the transom-hung, shallow-draught rudder and, below the stem, the mechanism for the modern addition of the bow rudder, which greatly improves the caravel's manoeuvrability.

FIGURE 13

The mainmast's forestay is tensioned via a series of deadeyes in the traditional manner. Note the stays going forward and aft to fore and mizzen masts.

FIGURE 14

Lisa von Lübeck sailing under full sail in the Baltic.

FIG 14

to 300 tonnes of cargo in good summer weather; this would increase the draught to 3.6m leaving a freeboard of just 0.5m.

Sailing into the past

Between May and October each year, *Lisa von Lübeck* sails the old Hanseatic routes as a floating ambassador for Lübeck. Danzig, Copenhagen, Malmö, Stettin, Rostock, Wismar and Stralsund were Baltic ports with which Lübeck had commercial ties in the Hanseatic era. She also makes regular visits to Hanseatic cities such as Bremen and Hamburg on the North Sea coast and in 2009 made calls at Kampen, the Netherlands, and King's Lynn, England, amongst other places.

On board the 200-tonne three-master passengers and crew do experience how it must have been to sail in Hanseatic times, but they also have the benefit of some modern technology: if the wind is not from the right quarter, the 347hp diesel engine is called upon. The motor is a standby to ensure voyage safety in some of the most crowded waters of the world – today the caravel encounters many more larger and, above all, faster ships than she would have done in the Hansa era. In calm or fog, seafaring goes on and, again for reasons of safety, the *Lisa von Lübeck* is fitted with radar, an automatic identification system, GPS and VHF radio. Below the stem is a bow rudder, which eases the difficulty of manouevring in narrow harbours.

The designers attempted to make the caravel as authentic as possible based on the available knowledge, but the inclusion of twenty-first-century technology and the partial use of modern materials was unavoidable. It is not intended that the *Lisa von Lübeck* should languish ashore as a static monument. The aim of the project – besides being an experiment in nautical archaeology of which the scientific sail trials form a part – is to experience living history. As many people as possible should have the opportunity to admire the Hansa ship at port celebrations and sailing institutions. But it is surely better to sail aboard the *Lisa von Lübeck*, even if the changed circumstances of the twenty-first century have resulted in some modifications.

Lisa von Lübeck

LOA	35.90m
LOD	30.12m
Beam	8.30m
Beam across yardarms	9.30m
Designed draught	2.86m
Gross registered tonnage	164 RT
Nett registered tonnage	49 RT
Total sail area	277m²
Mainsail	181m²
Foresail	58m²
Mizzen	38m²
Spars	
Main mast (height above keel)	24m
Main yard (length)	15m
Foremast (height above keel)	18m
Foremast yard (length)	8.5m
Mizzenmast (height above keel)	12m
Mizzen yard (length)	10.5m
Main engine	255kW
Speed, maximum (under motor)	8.5 knots
Speed, maximum (under sail)	9 knots
Ballast (lead bars)	45 tons

BURKHARD BANGE

BIBLIOGRAPHY

Bange, Burkhard: *Lisa von Lübeck, Das Hanseschiff des 15. Jahrhunderts*, Hamburg, 2005
Busley, Carl: *Die Entwicklung des Segelschiffes, an 16 Modellen des Deutschen Museums in München*, Berlin, 1920
Heinsius, Paul: *Das Schiff der hansischen Frühzeit*, Köln 1986
Hoffmann, Gabriele und Schnall, *Uwe: Die Kogge*, Bremerhaven, 2003
Kammler, Andreas: 'Schiffbau in Lübeck 1477', *Zeitschrift des Vereins für Lübeckische Geschichte und Altertumskunde*, Band 86, Lübeck, 2006

Lienau, Otto: *Geschichte und Aussehen des Großen Kraweels Peter von Danzig*, Berlin, 1942
Rehder, Peter: *Die Gewässer im ganzen Umfange des Niederschlagsgebietes der Trave, unter besonderer Berücksichtigung der schiffahrtlichen Verhältnisse*, Lübeck, 1890
Vogel, Walter: *Geschichte der deutschen Seeschiffahrt*, Berlin, 1915
Winter, Heinrich: *Das Hanseschiff im ausgehenden 15. Jahrhundert*, Bielefeld, 1975
Wolf, Thomas: *Tragfähigkeiten, Ladungen und Maße im Schiffsverkehr der Hanse*, Köln, 1986

PART II

THE AGE OF DISCOVERY, 1600—1750

8 early seventeenth-century ships

In this chapter we look at replicas of ships from northern Europe, whose originals were built during the first half of the seventeenth century, when Dutch shipping was pre-eminent. Turkish pirates, Portuguese administrators, English merchants – almost everyone agreed that Dutch ships were superior because they sailed well, took ground safely in drying harbours, were seaworthy, and required fewer men, and their design as efficient bulk carriers made them cheap relative to their cargo capacity.

FIGURE 1
The *Kalmar Nyckel* replica under full sail including spritsail topsail on a beam reach.

The early 1600s can be regarded as the final phase of the great European Age of Discovery. In 1606 the United Dutch East Indies Company *(Vereenigde Oost-Indies Compagnie* or VOC) sent the *jacht, Duyfken,* on a voyage of exploration 'to Nova Guinea and other east and south lands'. It was to be the first historically recorded voyage to Australia – for the first time all the populated continents of the world were known to geographers. At this same time Henry Hudson, commanding *Halve Maen* (*Half Moon*), was also making voyages of exploration on behalf of the VOC, and successful colonial enterprises of settlers from northern Europe were beginning in North America, as was large-scale seaborne trade with Asia. But Dutch maritime exploration, colonial ventures and empire-building were just a small fraction of Dutch shipping operations. Since the late Middle Ages Dutch fleets had increasingly dominated the growing freight of bulk cargoes such as grain, salt and timber within Europe.

The first replica of an early-seventeenth-century ship (Figure 4) was built in the Netherlands in the opening decade of the twentieth century, to commemorate the 300th anniversary of Hudson's exploration of what is now the New York area, but the vessel discussed here is the second *Halve Maen* replica, built in Albany, New York, in 1989. The original *Halve Maen* was a small jacht – a relatively fast type of armed vessel – built in 1608.

FIGURE 2

Midsection drawn using a three-sweep tangent-arc system. Each sweep is an arc: part of the circumference of a circle. Where two sweeps meet or reconcile their tangents must coincide. A-B is the height of breadth; B-C is the main breadth; B-H, the half breadth, is fourteen-fifteenths of the height of breadth. G-F, which is the breadth of the flat of the floor, is one-sixth of the main breadth; J is the centre of the wronghead or floor sweep, it is vertically above F and the sweep's radius is two-sevenths of the breadth. The futtock sweep centred at K has a radius seven-eighths of the breadth. The breadth sweep centred in the height of breadth line at L has a radius four-ninths of the height of breadth. The line J-K runs through L (with a little fudging) but this is not necessary. The proportions for the radii are arbitrary (and slightly inaccurate) but cannot be varied greatly if the arcs are to reconcile. In most English designs A-B was greater than A-G. However, if A-G was too small in proportion to A-B, in an attempt to provide broad floors, the radius of the futtock sweep would be too great or would have its centre below the height of breadth, which was impossible. Therefore the breadth of the flat of floors was necessarily small in deep-hulled ships. Ships designed in this way could not have the broad floors and large cargo capacity that merchants desired.

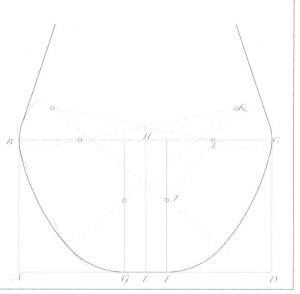

FIGURE 3

Morphometric analysis of the sheer. In this example the length from the bow to the lowest point of the sheer is measured and can be calculated as a fraction of the total bow-to-stern length to give a ratio of proportions.

FIGURE 7

Kalmar Nyckel. This more recent photograph shows the addition of a fore topgallant sail, something that might have been added during the career of the original ship.

FIGURES 8 AND 9

Plank-first construction of the *Duyfken* replica. The planks are temporarily held together by small cleats. In places the planks show slight charring having been bent to shape over an open fire.

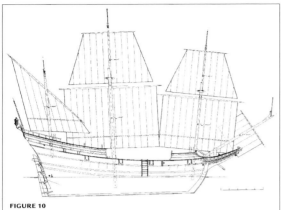

FIGURE 10
The *Duyfken* replica's sail plan. The lower sails, or courses, are large while the topsails are relatively small.

FIGURE 11
1989 *Halve Maen* replica's sail plan, very similar to *Duyfken*'s.

FIGURE 12
Seventeenth-century ship with half-masted topsail. The ship is sailing close hauled. The main tack has been taken inboard to allow the ship to lie closer to the wind. Although the main topsail yard is half-masted the topsail is not luffing.

Mayflower was a modest-sized English merchantman built *c*1610; her replica was built in Brixham, England, and was launched in September 1956.

Batavia was a large VOC *retourschip* – a heavily-armed merchant ship – built in 1628; the replica was launched in the Netherlands in April 1995.

Built in 1625, *Kalmar Nyckel* was a medium-sized, Dutch-built, armed merchantman, a *pinas*, which carried Swedish settlers to North America; the replica was built in Wilmington, Delaware, and was launched in September 1997 (Figure 1).

Duyfken was another small jacht built *c*1600 and was used in the Netherlands' initial incursion into the East Indies spice trade before making her voyage of exploration and reaching Australia; the replica was launched in Fremantle, Western Australia, in January 1999 (Figures 14 and 15).

All are three-masted, square-rigged vessels with square-tuck sterns surmounted by high aftercastles.

Replicas of early-seventeenth-century ships are necessarily speculative, particularly in their underwater hull form. Very few

contemporary shipwrights built from plans drawn on paper and there are no surviving plans that can be safely said to represent ships as they were actually built. Indeed, the Dutch built the lower hull plank-first, inserting the frame timbers into a plank shell that had been sculpted by eye. The technique allowed shipwrights to experiment and modify design to suit changing circumstances in trade, and this they did very successfully – but it was a

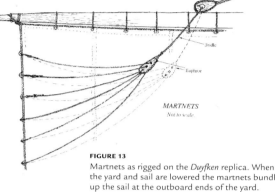

MARTNETS
Not to scale

FIGURE 13

Martnets as rigged on the *Duyfken* replica. When the yard and sail are lowered the martnets bundle up the sail at the outboard ends of the yard. Because there are no footropes it would be difficult to furl the sails at the ends of the yards, below.

FIGURE 14
Duyfken with topsails
half masted off the
Cape of Good Hope.
(Michael Redding –
viewfinder.com.au)

technique in which the design existed in the shipwright's mind rather than on paper. There has been a tendency to assume that early-seventeenth-century Dutch ships were similar in hull form to later examples for which better evidence exists. Furthermore, it might be argued that there has been a tendency to see 'Age of Discovery' ships as clumsy, high-sided versions of later designs.

In recent times nautical archaeology has discovered a few shipwrecks with sufficient intact hull structure to provide some evidence of hull form. Of particular interest is a late-sixteenth-century Dutch merchantman excavated from the Waddensee in the Netherlands in the 1990s and known from its site location as *Scheurrak S01*. There is also the magnificent *Vasa* preserved in Stockholm, Sweden. *Vasa* was a very large warship built by a Dutch master shipwright, but she cannot be regarded as typical because her short history indicates a design that had been stretched to disastrous effect, probably through regal interference.

In the absence of plans, ships were built to

FIGURE 15

Duyfken close-hauled in a stiff breeze with the main topsail half masted and the fore topsail furled.
(Michael Redding – viewfinder.com.au)

detailed specifications set out in contracts, a good number of which are preserved in Dutch archives. In some, deadrise is specified, giving evidence that jachts could be quite sharp-bottomed. However, such contracts and other archived data must be read with caution. For example, beam as recorded in the seventeenth century is rarely, if ever, the extreme beam as we understand it today. Rather it was the beam measured *inside* the ceiling, often at an arbitrary height and arbitrary position along the ship's length –

frequently no one could say how a particular ship had been measured.

This was not just a Dutch problem. In England Samuel Pepys, secretary to the Admiralty, noted in his diary for 16 January 1668:

My work this night with my clerks till midnight at the office was to examine my list of ships I am making for myself, and their dimensions, and to see how it agrees or differs from other lists; and I do find so great a difference between them all that I am at a loss which to take; and therefore think mine to be as much depended upon as any I can make out of them all.

Researchers should attempt to achieve performance equivalence: a replica ought to have carrying capacity equal to the original; should not need excessive ballasting; should be able to make passages at similar average speeds; should be reasonably manoeuvrable; and should have some ability to make ground to windward.

The below-water hull form – very important to a ship's performance – is inferred from incomplete shipwrecks, information in contracts, treatises on shipbuilding from later in the seventeenth century, and a small number of models that are clearly not scale models.

Above the waterline the picture is clearer. At the end of the sixteenth century the Dutch invented marine art as a significant genre of fine art. Prior to that, representations of ships by accomplished artists are very rare, but researchers reconstructing the design of Dutch ships from the early seventeenth century, and thereafter, have access to such a wealth of iconography that statistical techniques should be used in the analysis. To give one example, it is possible to measure where the lowest point of the sheer occurs and demonstrate that, in the great majority of examples, it is well forward of midships – there was little rise forward but considerable rise towards the stern (Figure 3).

The replicas considered in this chapter show significantly different hull forms. They represent changes in form that occurred through the seventeenth century, differences between Dutch and English naval architecture, and also different research strategies.

The *Halve Maen* and *Kalmar Nyckel* were Dutch vessels (a jacht and a pinas, but the terms were often used interchangeably) built just 16 years apart. Yet their replicas are radically different in appearance. At the beginning of the seventeenth century, ships retained some of the characteristics of the sixteenth century as evidenced in the *Mary Rose* and the *Scheurrak S01* shipwrecks. Hulls were relatively broad-beamed, but narrow at bow and stern, and the midships section – or

point of maximum girth – was either halfway between stem and sternpost or a little aft of that. This can be clearly seen in contemporary iconography (Figures 5 & 6) but was not properly understood until shipwreck archaeology alerted us to the hull form. However, within two or three decades a hull form that is familiar to us from later ships had emerged: it was less beamy but much of that beam was carried into broad bows and sterns, and the point of maximum girth had moved further forward. (These changes can be seen as responses to the way ships were measured and taxed or levied, rather than a desire to improve sailing characteristics or capacity relative to the bulk of the ships' structure. There was, however, an increase in capacity relative to registered dimensions.)

The *Halve Maen* replica has a midsection with broad flat floors and a sharp turn to the bilge: a hull form known from shipwreck archaeology and well suited to navigating the shallow Waddenzee and Zuiderzee of the Netherlands. It is said to have been designed using a tangent-arc system, Joseph Furttenbach's 1629 *Architecture Navalis*, and the archived specifications of the original ship (the tangent-arc system is further explained in Figure 2). The replica is high-sided and heavy in appearance. Dimensions are: 65ft length on deck (19.8m), 14ft 9in beam (4.50m), 7ft 5in depth of hold (18.84m); her designer and builder was Nicholas Benton.

The *Kalmar Nyckel* replica, designed by Thomas Wilmer and Iver C. Franzen, has moderate deadrise, the turn of the bilge starts close to the keel and continues till maximum beam is reached above the waterline, but the turn of the bilge does not start with a small-radius sweep as it would if a seventeenth-century tangent-arc system were used. (The basis of the research for this replica has not been published.) The lowest point of the sheer is surprisingly close to midships and the rise of the sheer to the bow is probably greater than would have been typical in 1625. The ship appears much lower and sleeker than the *Halve Maen* replica. Dimensions are 97ft length on deck (29.57m), 25ft beam (7.62m), 12ft draught (3.66m).

The *Batavia* replica's midsection has some

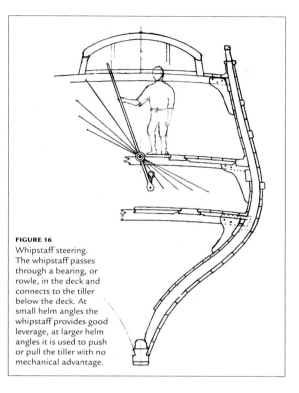

FIGURE 16

Whipstaff steering. The whipstaff passes through a bearing, or rowle, in the deck and connects to the tiller below the deck. At small helm angles the whipstaff provides good leverage, at larger helm angles it is used to push or pull the tiller with no mechanical advantage.

narrow. The width at the break of the forecastle is half the width at the break of the aftercastle. The width at the wing transom is half the maximum beam, and the high stern rises to a very narrow apex. Below the waterline the bow and stern are moderately sharp and hollow. Although the sheer is pronounced, the main deck follows its line; much of the height of the stern is created by the sheer. Ships of other European nations generally had flatter sheer and their aftercastles were more built up. This can be clearly seen by comparing the *Duyfken* and *Mayflower* replicas.

The original *Duyfken* was known to outsail the larger ships that she sometimes accompanied, and she was used to explore dangerous lee shores. The replica's design is intended to produce sailing characteristics consistent with the original's achievements. *Duyfken*'s dimensions are: 19.9m length on deck (65ft 3in), 6m beam (19ft 7in), 3m depth in hold (9ft 10in). The replica was designed by this author and Adriaan de Jong.

The *Mayflower* replica was designed by William Baker using an English tangent-arc system demonstrated in Matthew Baker's *c*1600 manuscript. The replica's dimensions are: 84ft length on deck (25.6m), 22ft beam (6.71m), 12ft 6in depth of hold (3.81m).

The hull form created using a three- or four-sweep tangent-arc system is very interesting and raises important questions. The tangent-arc system necessarily produces a midsection with narrow floors and little initial stability – the arcs will not reconcile except when the floors are very narrow (Figure 2). Indeed, ships built using such a system cannot stand up without ballast and could not safely take ground in drying harbours: the *Mayflower* replica was floated from the dry dock in which she was completed with 68 tons of ballast – it was only just adequate. She eventually sailed with 133 tons of ballast plus stores and gear – so heavily ballasted that the main deck was at the waterline and the gun ports were too close to the waterline to be opened at sea. The tangent-arc system is known to have been used for designing successful warships, but its application to English merchant ships is puzzling. Merchants and administrators

hollow at the garboards but very little deadrise and a sharp turn to the bilge. It is a type of midsection exposited in van Yk and Witsen's books about shipbuilding published later in the seventeenth century, and is similar to the midsection of the *Vasa*. Maximum beam is forward of the midpoint between stem and sternpost and the bows are fairly bluff and broad; the ship has considerable sheer. Dimensions are: 45.3m length on deck (148ft 6in), 10.5m beam (34ft 6in), 5.1m draught (16ft 9in). The replica was designed by Willem Voss and Robert Parthesius.

Duyfken's midsection shows moderate and hollow deadrise, broad floors, and a moderately firm turn to the bilge – it is copied from that of the *Scheurrak S01* wreck; a jacht of the day might well have had more deadrise. The maximum beam is at the waterline in way of the mainmast, which puts it a little aft of the midpoint between stem and sternpost. With a length:beam ratio of 3.315:1 *Duyfken* is a broad-beamed ship. Her bows are rounded rather than sharp at the waterline, but are fairly

certainly complained that English merchant
ships were designed like warships and were
thus greatly flawed. On the other hand,
Samuel Pepys noted that the commercial
master shipwrights – who were sometimes
contracted to build naval vessels when there
was too much work for the Navy's own yards
– could scarcely count, let alone draw a ship's
draft (plan), and yet they produced hull forms
'so as best to take in all the variety of uses we
are led to desire in a ship'. We do not know
how they designed their ships.

Construction

While much of Europe had changed from
plank-first to frame-first construction by the
early sixteenth century, the Dutch continued
to build the lower hull plank-first through the
seventeenth century. The excavation of the
Batavia shipwreck in 1972–6 on Australia's
west coast drew attention to that largely
forgotten aspect of Dutch shipwrightery
apparently at odds with the current understanding of the frame-first construction's
place in the development of naval architecture

FIGURE 18
The *Duyfken* replica during initial sailing trials, July 1999.

and European dominance of the seas.

Dutch ships were built with carvel or flush planking. Temporary cleats were used to hold the planks together until frame timbers were fitted (Figure 8). The planks were bent to the required shapes by heating them over open fires until they became slightly plastic. In forming the tight bends in the bow, significant charring on the inside of the planking was inevitable. Large ships, such as *Batavia*, were built with two layers of planking, presumably because of the

difficulty of bending planks thick enough for a single layer of planking and because the plank shell, rather than the frames, was conceptually the essence of the ship's structure. Animal hair and tar were spread between the layers and in the plank seams.

Frame timbers – floors, futtocks and top timbers – were not scarphed together to form complete frames. Many trunnels were used for fastening, along with iron spikes and bolts. Deck beams were not dovetailed into the beam shelf but were secured by large hanging knees. Few lodging knees were fitted.

The *Duyfken* replica was built plank-first as an exercise of experimental archaeology. Oak was sourced from Latvia. The Duyfken Foundation's master shipwright, Bill Leonard, had previously built the *Endeavour* replica (Chapter 12), but building plank-first was a courageous leap in the dark. Initially, progress was slow. Some shipwrights were good at bending and twisting planks to shape over open fires, others had real difficulty visualising the required shapes. Progress improved when it was recognised that tending the fires was a specialist, full-time under-taking in itself, and that fires should burn good-quality hardwood, chopped to approximately uniform size. In the end construction went well and proved that 'plank-first' can be not only efficient but also requires little infrastructure because full frames do not have to be lifted and erected. As built the ship was not identical to the ship as designed on paper, although three temporary moulds were used to help visualise the shape (the moulds were not left in position during construction); there is some asymmetry, but the lines are fair and pleasing.

The *Batavia* replica was built using oak from Denmark and employed direct heat to bend planks, but she was built frame-first with a single layer of planking. Gas torches were used for plank bending. However, shipwrights who worked on *Batavia* and went on to build other replicas including the Kampen kogge. Page 82 reported better results using wood fires – advice taken by the Duyfken Foundation.

Halve Maen, *Kalmar Nyckel* and *Mayflower* were also built frame-first and their planks were steamed.

Rig

Dutch marine artists were consistent in their depiction of lead of rigging – it can be inferred that they had good understanding of rigging and its use.

Duyfken's rig is the standard basic rig for sea-going ships of the seventeenth century: three-masted with square lower sails and topsails on the fore and main masts, a steeply steeved bowsprit with a square spritsail set below it, and a lateen mizzen, which is the only fore-and-aft sail. *Batavia* and *Kalmar Nyckel* both have vertical bowsprit topmasts on which they can carry spritsail topsails, and they carry square mizzen topsails over their lateen sails. *Batavia* has small topgallants on both fore and mainmast; *Kalmar Nyckel* now has a fore topgallant (Figure 7).

Duyfken's topmasts are scarphed to the lowermasts. The scarph is so devised that it is theoretically possible to send down the topmasts with the lowermast standing rigging in place. Fidded topmasts were unusual before the third decade of the century. The lower masts of the fore and mainmasts are relatively tall so the courses are deep. Her topsails are also deep and have much taper. The topsail yards are half the length of the respective course yards.

The rigging is relatively simple. There are braces and lifts, sheets and tacks; the foresail and mainsail are hoist by halyards and double halyard tyes. Topsail halyards are rove through a single block on the halyard tye and can be shifted to the windward side for tradewind sailing. There are running parrels on the lower sails, no parrel on the spritsail, and the topsails have iron-hoop parrels that can either be seized to the halyards, or used

Table 1.   Materials used when replica was first commissioned.

Ship	Principal timber	Cordage	Sails
Mayflower	Oak	Manila	Flax
Halve Maen	White oak	Synthetic, steel wire standing rigging	Synthetic: *Duradon*
Batavia	Oak	Hemp	Flax
Kalmar Nyckel	Courbaril planking, purpleheart frames	Synthetic	Polyester
Duyfken	Oak	Hemp	Flax

with the halyard running through them, with downhauls bent, to allow the topsails to be lowered into the lee of the courses 'poleacre' fashion.

Main tacks are rove through fairleads in the rail and belayed to large kevels. Because the foremast is right up in the bow, stepped over the stem, the fore tacks are rove through a short spar (*botteloef* or outlicker) run out below the beakhead. The tacks are belayed at the forward rail of the focsle: the starboard tack belays to port and vice versa.

There are no buntlines, slablines or leechlines. There are clewlines on the topsails and spritsail, and a single clewline on the mizzen, but there were originally no clew garnets because they were not used before about the middle of the seventeenth century. Topsails were furled aloft but courses were furled with the yards lowered to the rail or just above it. Martnets bundle up the outboard parts of the courses towards the yardarms, which cannot be easily reached and furled in the absence of footropes (Figure 13).

Duyfken's topsails are fairly easily furled aloft although there are no footropes because the main topsail yard is only 6m long (19ft 7in). All square sails are furled with a glut in the bunt – bundled to the centre of the yard.

There is no reefing but there are bonnets latched to the foot of the foresail, mainsail and mizzen. Removal of the bonnets is a final sail reduction in heavy weather rather than a first reef.

Clew garnets were later rigged on the *Duyfken* replica because of difficulty keeping the clews out of the water and lifting them to the deck when lowering the sails. However, it was later realised that the tacks could be used to keep the clews out of the water when lowering and hoisting.

There are bowlines on the leeches of all the square sails except the spritsail.

Duyfken was rigged with hemp rope for standing and running rigging. Sails are hand-sewn flax canvas, with details such as grommets taken from the spare sails that survived on *Vasa*.

The other replicas discussed here have also rigged clew garnets. In some cases other gear, such as buntlines – unknown in the

early seventeenth century – has also been rigged. The two larger replicas, *Batavia* and *Kalmar Nyckel*, have fitted footropes to facilitate furling sails aloft. Even on little *Duyfken*, raising and lowering the mainyard and foreyard every time sails are furled can be heavy work. It is almost always an 'all hands' call.

Sailing the replicas

All the replicas discussed in this chapter have been sailed, although *Batavia*, which has no motor, has only been allowed to set sail running downwind with a line to a tug ahead. In all cases reasonable sailing performance has been reported.

The *Duyfken* replica has made the most extensive voyages, including a voyage from the east coast of Australia to the Netherlands by way of Indonesia, Sri Lanka and South Africa. On that voyage the motors were only used for entering and leaving port when conditions made that necessary, and at the end of the voyage to comply with a tightly scheduled arrival ceremony. The author sailed before the mast on *Duyfken* May–August 2000 and April–December 2001.

Duyfken's initial sailing trials were made before auxiliary mechanical power was fitted. At that time the ship was ballasted rather too much by the stern but nevertheless tacked and manoeuvred handily. In order to comply with survey requirements for commercial operations, more ballast was added, including an external shoe on the keel containing 7 tonnes of lead, giving righting moment even at very high angles of heel. Two diesel engines were installed to drive feathering screws; enough fuel can be carried to give a range of about 300 nautical miles when motoring against a moderate headwind. The replica is more heavily ballasted than the original was ever likely to have been; she is therefore stiffer and must put more load on her rig, which also comes under significant load when motoring into a steep head sea.

Before *Duyfken* was first sailed, extensive *c*1600 iconography was investigated to assess which combinations of sails were most commonly used (see Table 2).

Table 2

Sail configuration	Total number of examples (number of examples sailing on the wind)
Fore course and both topsails	30 (8)
Fore course and main topsail	19 (9)
Fore course, both topsails and mizzen	18 (3)
Courses	17 (2)
Courses and main topsail	9 (6)
Fore course, main topsail and mizzen	7 (3)
Courses and fore topsail	6 (1)
Fore course	4 (0)
Fore course and fore topsail	4 (0)
Courses, both topsails and mizzen	4 (1)
Courses, no bonnets	3 (1)
Courses and mizzen	3 (1)
Courses and both topsails	3 (2)
Topsails only (in battle)	3 (2)
All sail	2 (1)
Fore course and fore topsail and mizzen	2 (0)
Fore course and mizzen	2 (0)
Fore course, both topsails and spritsail	1 (0)
Courses and spritsail	1 (0)
Courses and mizzen	1 (1)
Courses, both topsails and spritsail	1 (1)

The rarity of ships depicted under full sail probably reflects the situations depicted – manoeuvring in harbour or in battle, clawing to windward, or running before a storm. There are no depictions of ships simply sailing the open ocean in good weather.

Because many of the pictures are harbour scenes and others are battle scenes – both with large numbers of vessels depicted – many vessels are shown manoeuvring under reduced canvas – fore course and both topsails is the most frequently seen arrangement for manoeuvring, with fore course and main topsail, and fore course, both topsails, and mizzen also popular arrangements. Almost every practical configuration is shown.

The relative numbers depicted sailing on and off the wind for a particular configuration are probably not significant except in showing that the artists preferred to depict vessels sailing before the wind. Most configurations are seen both on and off the wind. Those configurations that are only depicted sailing off the wind – such as fore course and fore topsail only – are not suitable for sailing on the wind.

Some, but not all, vessels setting courses but no topsails are depicted in heavy weather. Small ships, which have relatively deep courses and small topsails, are seen to manoeuvre in harbour under courses only.

The spritsail is rarely set and the mizzen is not frequently set, even on vessels going to windward.

Before sea trials we were surprised to note that the lateen mizzen was not often shown set, but in practice *Duyfken*'s mizzen has been useful so infrequently that it has ended up being stowed in a chest in the hold on long open-ocean passages. In the seventeenth century the lateen mizzen was probably used largely for manoeuvring in battle and confined waters; when making a straight course the ship steers more easily with the mizzen furled. In most circumstances, *Duyfken* will tack reliably without the mizzen set.

In contemporary iconography European ships of *Duyfken*'s time are never shown with any reefing system although medieval European ships had reef points and some sixteenth-century Asian ships are shown with square sails and reef points. There are only four significant working sails in *Duyfken*'s rig: the two topsails and two courses. When sailing close-hauled it was found that the topmasts bowed to leeward in breezes of about 15–20 knots. If the topsails were handed in that wind strength the ship tended to wallow and could not make any ground to windward – she was under-canvassed. The iconography suggested a solution to the problem: ships are often shown with their topsail yards half-masted and the topsails billowing with a great curve in the leech (Figure 12). This would effectively depower the sails and reduce the load on the topmasts. Before we experimented with this we believed that the sails would flog or slat if half-masted while sailing close-hauled. In fact the topsails continued to set and behave perfectly even before the bowlines were hauled taut and there was no need to control the yards with the lifts. Once half-masting was understood it was possible to carry the topsails in significantly stronger winds. It was also possible to hand the fore topsail and continue to carry a half-masted main topsail over the

FIGURE 19
The *Duyfken* replica with topsails half masted for a squall in the Banda Sea.
(Robert Garvey)

courses when close-hauled if the wind further increased in strength (Figure 15).

The iconography suggests that topsails were sometimes cut so deep in the hoist that even with the yard mastheaded the sail would still hang with a bight or a billow in the leech. Unless the iconography is consistently misleading, mariners of *Duyfken*'s time were not concerned with setting sails with the leech taut – they may even have regarded it as a bad idea, putting unnecessary load on the rig. It is important to note that when sailing close-hauled *Duyfken*'s main course is the first sail to lift or luff if she is steered too close to the wind. This continues to be the case when the topsails are half-masted. It is not necessary to brace the half-masted topsails more sharply and there is no detriment to the ability to steer a course close to the wind.

Half-masting is an imprecise description. The topsails can be set at any height between full hoist and the lowermast head (there is no lowermast cap) depending on wind strength. The only obvious disadvantage is that when the wind does reach a strength that makes furling the topsails necessary the whole deep sail has to be furled, and in the absence of buntlines this can be difficult (seventeenth-century ships sailed with courses rather than topsails set in heavy weather). On a significantly larger ship, furling the topsails in heavy weather must have been a difficult and dangerous undertaking. In some cases they were furled by bundling them to the mast at the doubling rather than up to the yard.

Setting the spritsail when sailing downwind presents no problems. How to trim the sail when close-hauled was less obvious. The simplest and most effective way of trimming the spritsail is suggested by observing the nomenclature of the gear used to trim the yard and regarding the bowsprit as a mast. The lifts lead from the yard arms to blocks near the end of the bowsprit and back to a pinrail in the beakhead. The braces lead from the yard arms to blocks about halfway up the forestay, back to blocks on the bowsprit, and then to the pinrail. As with other square sails, the lifts can be used to prevent the yard cockbilling and there is no need to tend them when tacking or changing course relative to

wind direction. The spritsail yard is left square on its lifts when sailing both on and off the wind. When sailing close-hauled the lee brace is hauled until the yard stands more or less vertical when seen from ahead. When going about, the spritsail can be left aback until other sails are braced for the new tack. Then the braces are tended to invert the yard and the sheets are adjusted slightly. When handing the spritsail the yard is squared with the braces and the braces are then made fast; lifts and halyard are cast off, and the clewlines are used to haul the yard and sail aft to the beakhead. The yard hangs from its braces and conveniently swings just above the figurehead. In most circumstances the spritsail sets well and is easy to handle.

Steering

Duyfken is steered with a whipstaff connected to a tiller, which is just below the main deck (Figure 16). The tiller swings about 20° to port or starboard before it comes up against hanging knees. The rudder is small in its moulded dimension but rather thick in its sided dimension. The immersed blade area is only 1.4m² (15.07ft³). In general steering is quite satisfactory but *Duyfken* is sometimes slow to bear away when the helm is put up to wear ship. It is important to trim the sails to help bring her head off. In most circumstances steering is not particularly strenuous work, even in heavy weather if the ship is making good speed. Attempting to run before the wind under bare poles off the south coast of Africa when steep seas were kicked up by the Agulhas current opposing a strong southwesterly gale proved almost impossible. When the ship was allowed to round up she lay with her head well up into the wind but gradually fell off to lie beam on to the wind as the wind strength decreased. The high stern certainly helps the ship to keep her head up into the wind when lying ahull in very strong winds.

Halve Maen, *Kalmar Nyckel* and *Batavia* are also whipstaff-steered. *Kalmar Nyckel* makes offshore passages regularly and is larger than *Duyfken* and *Halve Maen*. The steering is said to be quite satisfactory. Steve Brooks, a volunteer crewmember commented, 'It works well except it can be more difficult in a following sea when the leverage is working against you.'

Duyfken, *Halve Maen* and *Batavia* have low hutches built on the quarterdeck over the whipstaff, open on the forward side. This gives the helmsperson a view of the sails, which is helpful particularly when sailing on the wind. *Kalmar Nyckel* has no hutch so the helmsperson's view is restricted to what can be seen forward below the quarterdeck. Steering full and by it is necessary to watch the sails and this is said to be somewhat awkward.

The *Mayflower* replica was designed with whipstaff steering but no hutch; however, a wheel on the quarterdeck was fitted for her transatlantic voyage.

Findings

What have we learned? A good replica project should make researchers ask questions that might otherwise never be considered. Projects replicating ships from the early seventeenth century can suggest some important ideas about humankind and the development of technology. Some of the lessons about technology have been noted above: plank-first construction can be an efficient way to build a ship with little infrastructure and investment; the rig of early-seventeenth-century ships is effective, and it is possible to design a replica with good sailing characteristics and seaworthiness.

As earlier suggested there has been a tendency to see seventeenth-century ships as clumsy versions of eighteenth-century ships, and sixteenth-century ships as even more clumsy. However, the type of hull form given to the *Duyfken* replica on the basis of shipwreck archaeology and analysis of iconography produced a manoeuvrable ship capable of maintaining a good average speed, little compromised by the high stern. That high stern can be explained as a defensive/offensive feature – not optimal in terms of performance but necessary when one's enemy's ships have high sterns; in short, the product of an arms race.

Perhaps the broadest lesson relates to how technology develops. Technology in terms of naval architecture has certainly developed, probably at an accelerating rate, but it does not follow an inevitable path – it is not unilinear in development. Attempts to explain it as such – with each step necessary to an inevitable outcome – are refuted: contrary to what is often claimed, frame-first ship-building was neither necessary nor even effective in the development of efficient design and construction in the sixteenth and seventeenth centuries, the period when worldwide seafaring and trade took off.

The history of naval architecture, like history in general, has odd turns and contra-dictions that confound neat explanations. Shipwrights of the early seventeenth century employed ingenuity and thought outside of the box to which some histories would confine them.

Nick Burningham

BIBLIOGRAPHY

Babour, V., 1928. Dutch and English merchant Shipping in the Seventeenth Century. *The Economic History Review* 1:261–90. An excellent discussion of the superiority of Dutch ships as perceived by English merchants and others.

Baker, W.A., 1983. *The Mayflower and Other Colonial Vessels*. Conway Maritime Press, London.

Bengtsson, S., 1975. 'The Sails of the *Wasa*'. *International Journal of Nautical Archaeology* 4(1): 27–41.

Burningham, N. and Jong, A. de, 1997. The Duyfken Project: an Age of Discovery ship reconstruction as experimental archaeology. *International Journal of Nautical Archaeology* 26(4):277–92.

Burningham, N., 1999. (Radio script) Australia's First Ship and the Science Of Naval Architecture. *Ockhams Razor*. Australian Broadcasting Corporation, Radio National 1st August, 1999. http://www.abc.net.au/rn/science/ockham/stories/s40144.htm

—, 1999. (Illustrated version of above script) 'The *Duyfken*: an experiment in Maritime Archaeology'. http://abc.net.au/science/slab/duyfken/

—, 2001. Learning to sail the *Duyfken* replica. *International Journal of Nautical Archaeology* 30 (1):74–85.

—, 2001. Traditional Boat Evolution through Selection and Rational Choice. *Maritime Life and Traditions*. 12: 83–4.

Garvey, R., 2001. *To Build a Ship: The VOC Replica Ship* Duyfken. Tuart House, Crawley.

Van Eyck, 1697. *De Nederlandsche Sheepsbouwkonst opengesteld*. Amsterdam.

Winter, W. de, and Burningham, N., 2001. Distinguishing different types of the early seventeenth century Dutch Jacht and Ship through multivariate morphometric analysis of contemporary maritime art. *International Journal of Nautical Archaeology* 30(1):57–73.

Witsen, N., 1671. *Aeloude en Hedendaegse Scheepsbouw en Bestier*, Amsterdam.

9 The Jamestown Replicas

The largest fleet of early seventeenth-century replica vessels is moored on the James River at the Jamestown Settlement in Virginia, USA. Since 1957, the 350th anniversary of the founding of Jamestown as the first permanent English settlement in North America, the Jamestown-Yorktown Foundation has built and sailed eight vessels. Five still exist – four at the Jamestown Settlement and one in England.

FIGURE 1
Godspeed under sail with spritsail successfully set.

They represent the first three English vessels that brought settlers to begin the Virginia Colony at Jamestown in 1607. Over five decades the Foundation built two *Susan Constant*s (1957, 1991), three *Godspeed*s (1957, 1983, 2006) and three *Discovery*s (1957, 1984, 2007). Currently the Jamestown Settlement exhibits and sails *Susan Constant* (1991), *Godspeed* (2006), *Discovery* (2007) and *Elizabeth* (ex *Godspeed*, 1983). The first *Susan Constant* (1957) served for more than thirty years and was then broken up and sold – a traditional end for aged vessels. The first *Godspeed* (1957) and *Discovery* (1957) became schoolships for the Boy Scouts of America and are no longer afloat. *Discovery* (1984) went to London, England, aboard RFA *Fort Rosalie* in 2007 as part of the 400th anniversary of the Jamestown Settlement.

During the last fifty years of building and sailing these seagoing ships, the Foundation has learned much about early-seventeenth-century English vessels. Thames shipwrights built *Susan Constant* in 1605 and probably the *Godspeed* and *Discovery* four to six years earlier, and the latest Jamestown replicas accurately represent the size and types of their original namesakes.

Researching the background

The identification of any vessel depends on documents that may exist in one or more of four general categories: marine documents; commercial documents; voyage documents; illustrations. Marine documents usually record vessels, crews, masters, cargoes and other particulars for an official or necessary purpose. Commercial documents typically relate to business and are generated by owners, masters, companies and contractors; they may include court proceedings on maritime traffic. Voyage documents include logs, journals, letters, accounts and records that document the passage of vessels from one place to another. Illustrations range from plans of vessels to small drawings of vessels in the cartouche of maps – anything that depicts a particular vessel or represents a particular type of vessel at an established time. Such documents should be contemporary to the events they record and are primary sources

for the vessels concerned. Though fragmentary elements of such document types exist from the thirteenth century, it is during the reign of Elizabeth I (1558–1603) that regular methodologies begin to consistently create such documents and all four categories exist for English vessels in the late Elizabethan age and the reign of James I (1603–25). From such documents sufficient evidence exists to locate, identify and describe vessels named *Susan Constant, Godspeed* and *Discovery*.

The Visscher Map of 1616 presents London in the early seventeenth century. It shows the Tower, London Bridge, the Globe Theatre and all the places known to King James I and William Shakespeare. The panorama is from the south looking across the Thames, London's main avenue of traffic. More than 100 vessels crowd the waterway. They range from small river wherries (taxicabs), deal boats (the 'pick-up trucks' of their day) and 'Eel Ships' (speciality-seafood vendors), to huge merchant ships. When maritime historian and naval architect William A. Baker researched his famed 1957 *Mayflower* (still afloat in Plymouth Harbor, Massachusetts) he used the Visscher panorama to better understand the broad range and size of contemporary vessel types. It is still an excellent 'snapshot' of marine traffic in England's largest port *c*1603–16. Portions of this same panorama were used by the Jamestown-Yorktown Foundation as a backdrop for their museum exhibits. There is also a painting (anonymous but identified as being of the Anglo-Dutch School) entitled *London from Southwark* and dated *c*1630, which shows some of the same area as depicted by Visscher but extends to Ratcliff and Blackwall in the distance. (The Jamestown vessels sailed from Blackwall and the area continued to be used by Virginia Company vessels for many years.)

In the mid-1900s historian David B. Quinn scrupulously researched and published voluminous accounts of the early English and European exploration and settlement of North America that covered the North Atlantic regions sailed by the *Godspeed* and *Discovery*. He used one of the few extant lists of London commerce in the 1600–6 period to get 'a good impression of the character of

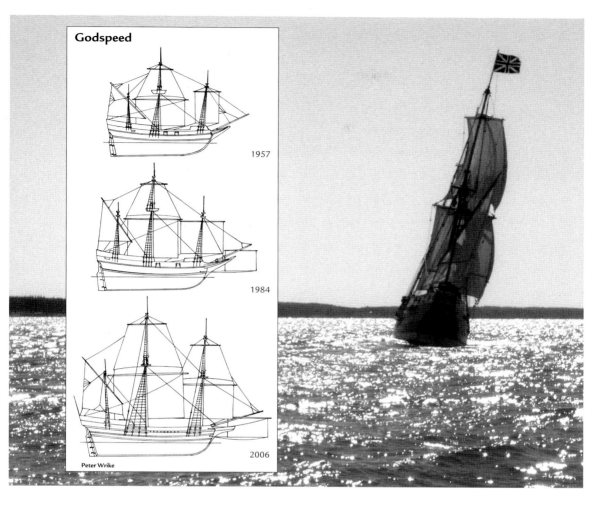

Godspeed

1957

1984

2006

Peter Wrike

FIGURE 2
The 2006 Godspeed replica during sea trials April 2008 (Rick Beyer, courtesy Plate of Peas Productions) and, insert, the three *Godspeed* replicas,

English trade'. In a nine-month period in 1601–2, 714 ships entered London. More than half of these were Dutch, German, French or Scandinavian. Generally English ships were larger than most (average 75 tons). Quinn concluded that 'it is clear that London trade was very active, but that her mercantile marine was at a disadvantage compared with foreigners'. War with Spain (1588–1604) had checked England's commercial shipping growth. But James I's reign saw the end of that war, the rapid rise of the East India Company, the creation of the London Company and the expansion of the

Muscovy Company. The Crown chartered these companies and derived profits from them. They shared governors, had interlocking directorates and the same general pool of investors. The business climate of an ascendant commercial England cared about profit in the early seventeenth century and the Crown exempted Company vessels from entry or clearance documentation. Thus, while in Company use, *Susan Constant, Godspeed* and *Discovery* do not appear in the Port Books.

In April 1606 James I issued a charter for settlement of Virginia. Two companies divided the settlement region between them. The Plymouth Company received rights to territory between present-day Pennsylvania

FIGURE 3

The *Godspeed* replica
under full sail during
sea trials in Penobscot
Bay, Maine
(Rick Beyer, courtesy Plate
of Peas Productions).

and Maine, and the London
Company received rights between
present-day North Carolina and
Maryland. By November 1606 the
London Company had completed
preparations for the settlement of Virginia.
They used a new large vessel, *Susan Constant*,
for their flagship and selected two smaller
East India Company vessels, *Godspeed* and
Discovery, for support. Fewer than sixty
English vessels were in port and most of those
were under contract. The East India, Muscovy,
London and Plymouth Companies operated
more than a third of London's available
shipping. (During James I's reign English
merchant shipping doubled in tonnage due to
these and other companies' overseas ventures.
By the end of his grandson's rule – Charles II
[1630–85] – English tonnage was six times
what it had been eighty years earlier.)

As part of her 1971 PhD dissertation on the
Virginia Company of 1606–22, historian Susan
Hillier prepared a list of known vessels that had
sailed to Virginia from England between 1607
and 1622 – there were seventy-five in all.
Analysis indicates that 43 per cent of these
were less than 100 tons – similar in size to
Godspeed and *Discovery*, while the remaining
57 per cent, were vessels such as *Susan Constant*
– over 100 tons. Hillier used tonnages of 20, 40
and 100 for *Discovery*, *Godspeed* and *Susan
Constant* respectively. She based these on the
contemporaneous writings of explorer, leader
and writer Captain John Smith.

Then, in 1979, while engaged as researchers
in the huge *Virginia Colonial Records Project*
(1952–87) to document all British and
European records relevant to Virginia, Susan
Hillier and fellow historian Alison Quinn
(wife of D.B. Quinn) made an important
discovery. They uncovered a 1606 court case
that gave a figure of 120 tons 'or thereabouts'
for *Susan Constant* – this was used by maritime historian and author Brian Lavery when
designing the 1991 *Susan Constant*. Historian
Brian Dietz researched vessels subsidised by

FIGURES 4, 5 AND 6
The 2006 *Godspeed* replica was built at Rockport Marine,
Maine; framing well underway in December 2004; the
sternpost and transom in frame; planking up in June 2005
(Jacqueline Sheridan, courtesy Plate of Peas Productions).

the Crown from 1558 to 1618. The Crown paid a bounty (5 shillings per ton) to vessel builders and owners provided their vessels be available for use as naval auxiliaries in a national emergency. The bounty applied to measured vessels over 100 tons and included *Susan Constant* at 174 tons (1605). As the bounty measured both burden (weight) and a formula for carrying capacity – tonnage or poundage – the 174 figure is adjusted to 130/131 tons (most recorded tonnages reflect burden only.) A High Court of the Admiralty document from 1615–16 lists *Susan Constant* as 140 tons. A Port of Bristol document lists her as 200 tons in 1618 when she was probably lost to pirates. These differing figures – all contemporary observations within the vessel's lifetime – raise questions.

Tonnage can be used to determine hull size and distinguish contemporary vessels of the same name from one another. The basic 'tun' or 'ton' was the measure of a wine container, usually for tax purposes. Consequently vessels were measured for their carrying capacity. By the late sixteenth century the formula had become more sophisticated and used units other than wine containers. Crown documents stated the earlier and current interpretations of this formula in the Calendar of State Papers (Domestic) in 1626 and 1627 – it used length, depth and breadth of a vessel, or variants thereof, and remained essentially unchanged until the late nineteenth century. Theoretically any one portion of that formula might enable reconstruction of a hull.

Thus, all that is definitively known is that in December 1606 three vessels sailed from Blackwall in London for Virginia. They were *Susan Constant*, *Godspeed* and *Discovery*. *Susan Constant*'s tonnage is variously given as 100, 120, 140, 150, 174 (131) and 200 – clearly she was the largest of the three vessels.

In general, early research on *Godspeed* and *Discovery* was incidental to the search for *Susan Constant*. But in the late sixteenth and seventeenth centuries writer Samuel Purchas (1575–1626) recorded numerous voyages that contain references to the two smaller vessels.

The newly chartered East India Company acquired two vessels – *Godspeed* (60 tons) and

Discovery (70 tons) in 1601. The following year they sailed under Captain George Weymouth to North America to find a Northwest Passage to the Pacific. The two vessels continued in the East India Company's records into late 1603. An unverified personal account states that in '1603 Thomas Weldon of Kingston-upon-Hull owned a 60-ton craft called *Goodspeed*', which he sent to Bear Island (later Cherry Island off the coast of Norway) to 'kill walruses and take a cargo of skins and ivory'. In 1604 Purchas recorded that Weldon, an enterprising twenty-year-old merchant, sailed aboard *Godspeed,* master Stephen Bennett, to Cherry Island for the same cargo as stated in 1603. Later in 1604 Bennett took *Godspeed* to France and brought back 2,031 bottles of wine. This commercial record is in the London Port books. Again in 1605 Weldon sailed with master Bennett to Cherry Island. On this occasion Purchas does not name the 60-ton vessel but the voyage is identical to its predecessors in mission, voyage times, destination, master, owner and vessel tonnage and type.

Sir Francis Cherry governed and invested in the East India and Muscovy Companies. He died in 1605 and in 1606 his executors transferred a number of his assets from the companies to satisfy his debts. *Godspeed* was probably one such asset then acquired by the London Company. One of the purchasers of Cherry's Muscovy Company interests was William Russell of the East India Company.

Russell again sent *Godspeed* and a pinnace to Cherry Island to hunt walruses. They sailed from London in early May 1606 with Stephen Bennett, master of *Godspeed*, and Jonas Poole, master of the pinnace with an eight-man crew. Thomas Weldon again accompanied the expedition. *Godspeed* returned to the Thames on 15 August 1606; the Virginia Company chose her for their expedition later that same year and by 10 December 1606 *Godspeed* was in the service of the London Company. Beyond her service to the Jamestown Settlement in 1606, 1607, 1608, 1609 and possibly 1610, *Godspeed* does not reappear in any known documents.

In the autumn of 1606 the London Company also acquired the pinnace

Discovery. In his definitive 1969 work, *The Jamestown Voyages Under the First Charter 1606–1609*, Philip L. Barbour speculated that the *Godspeed* of the Jamestown Settlement was Weldon's *Godspeed* in 1604, 1605 and 1606 as well as Weymouth's *Godspeed* in 1603. He also states, 'The *Discovery* in turn, less certainly identified than the other two (*Susan Constant* and *Godspeed*) may have been the unnamed pinnace which accompanied Weldon's *Godspeed* in 1606. If so the chief point of interest lies in the fact that the known ship and pinnace were operated by members of the Muscovy and East India Companies…'. *Discovery*'s captain on the Jamestown expedition was Bartholomew Gosnold. Her master was 'Poole'.

It is very probable that *Discovery* was used by the Muscovy Company in its 1604 and 1605 explorations of the Arctic and sub-Arctic regions of the Atlantic, perhaps also in association with Weymouth's 1605 expedition or ventures under Sir Francis Cherry. Admiralty law researcher R.G. Marsden compiled a list of all English vessels mentioned in documents of the reign of James I. His research indicates *Discovery* was renamed *Hopewell* before 1606 and was sailed under master John Knight in an early 1606 attempt to find the Northwest Passage.

In 1610 *Discovery* became Henry Hudson's vessel to the non-existent passage from Hudson Bay to the Pacific. They overwintered in the Bay where the crew mutinied and abandoned Hudson and others in the late spring. *Discovery* returned to London in September 1612 where a trial of the surviving crew was held. The next spring Henry, Prince of Wales, sent Sir Thomas Button with *Discovery*, master Ingram, and *Resolution*, master Nelson, to search again for a Northwest Passage. They overwintered in the Bay and returned to London in late September 1613. In 1614 William Gibbons sailed on *Discovery* for the Northwest Passage but became icebound off the coast of Labrador. He returned in September. In 1615 William Baffin used *Discovery* for his fourth attempt to find the Northwest Passage. Samuel Purchas (1569–1624) recorded and later published Baffin's voyages. He wrote that

Baffin stated that 'his *Discovery* had been [on] the three other voyages (1610, 1612, 1614)'. Master Robert Bylott (on *Discovery* in 1611–12) commanded *Discovery* and her crew of fourteen men and two boys. They sailed in March 1615 and returned in September. In March 1616 Bylott again took *Discovery* west and returned in August. *Discovery* made her last voyage to Virginia in 1621. She then went to the recently established Plymouth Colony in New England. She sailed for England in August 1622 but was driven off course by storms and wrecked in the Azores.

As for *Susan Constant,* she made a voyage to Spain just after her completion in 1605. In November 1606, while being prepared for the Jamestown expedition, she and another vessel collided on the Thames and it was during the subsequent litigation that her tonnage was stated as 120 tons 'or thereabouts'. Repairs were made to three gunports and some planking and she sailed with the Virginia expedition on 20 December under fleet captain Christopher Newport. Upon return to London in 1608 she reverted to command by her former master Coldhurst and continued in the London-to-Europe trade until 1612. Thereafter she was based at Bristol until her loss in *c*1618.

Design and construction

The hulls of late-sixteenth- and early-seventeenth-century seagoing vessels in England were determined by formulae. The formulae applied by Brian Lavery in his 1991 design of *Susan Constant* were principally those of Matthew Baker, Thomas Harriott and an anonymous treatise. They are generally cited as dating from *c*1582, *c*1608/10 and *c*1625 respectively and have been used in the twentieth century for late sixteenth- and early-seventeenth-century vessel designs whether for analysis, illustrations, models or full-sized replicas. Newport News Shipbuilding Company (VA) modelmaker Robert G.C. Fee's designs of the 1957 *Susan Constant*, *Godspeed* and *Discovery* referenced two of these works (Baker's and Harriott's). Naval architect and historian William A. Baker used the formulae for his numerous designs, and naval architect Stanley Potter, who also collaborated on occasion with Baker and worked on the 1983 design of *Elizabeth I*, also used them. However, the formulae are limiting when applied to small vessels. Matthew Baker's formula – the most often cited – was utilised principally for naval vessel design and was applicable to large vessels (100 tons or more) built in England in the Elizabethan and early Stuart reigns; no contemporary vessel designs under 80 tons, based on these formulae, are known to exist.

When designing *Mayflower*, *Deliverance*, *Concord*, *Dove* and other early-seventeenth-century vessels in the mid-1900s, William Baker used traditional formulae. He simply and succinctly defined the then available formulae difficulties as

> …an attempt to apply 'science' to the art of shipbuilding. The method, however, failed to define a fair form at the ends of the

FIGURE 7
Looking up through the rigging from main to foremast on the 2006 *Godspeed* replica
(**Rick Beyer, courtesy Plate of Peas Productions**).

FIGURE 8
The 1991 *Susan Constant* replica alongside in Jamestown, Virginia and, facing, the two twentieth-century replicas

vessel…. At the ends, therefore, the 'art' of the shipwright took over and each shipwright had his own tricks for working from the mathematically defined sections to the stem and sternpost. Two shipwrights working from the same basic data might well have produced two vessels that looked and performed quite differently.

Then, in 1994, historian Richard Barker published 'A Manuscript of Shipbuilding, Circa 1600, Copied by Newton'. It is the first known comprehensive period document that contains tables specifically designed for all vessel types. Generally Newton's formulae do not differ from those of Baker and the others used by Lavery, but his tables allow for the design of relatively small vessels and fill William Baker's void with 'science'. Three tables provided figures for the conventional vessels, 'for a man of war for long voyages'

and 'the first sort for merchantmen which will make them better sailors'. Each table provided keel length, maximum breadth, depth to keel from breadth in the first timber bend breadth at stern, length of higher sweep in maximum breadth, length of fullest sweep, length of wronghead sweep and length of highest sweep in the fashion piece.

In short, the Newton tables provide a variable range for previously unspecified aspects of vessel construction. They generally define that range and reflect the nature of a shipwright's traditional practices around the end of Queen Elizabeth I's reign. Barker stated that the author of the Newton Manuscript 'was clearly literate, and either competent at his own craft or a very well informed observer'.

Particulars for 20+ and 40+ ton vessels are virtually non-existent for the late 1500s and early 1600s. But there survives documentation of two small vessels – *Patience* and *Deliverance* – built in Bermuda in 1610 and sailed from there to Virginia that same year. Their designs were described by historian William Strachey and reveal dimensions that fit within contemporary formulae according to Newton.

Another valuable account of a contemporary vessel comes from the trial of the mutineers on Hudson's 55-ton *Discovery*. Testimony yielded a number of relevant particulars about *Discovery* not found elsewhere and which are also applicable to *Godspeed*. The forward portion of the main deck layout was defined. The galley, gunroom, capstan, pumps and hatch can also be determined. The size of the crew's 'cabins' can be accurately estimated and their spatial arrangement used to compute the distance between the galley and the gunroom. The hatch between these cabins indicates the vessel's maximum breadth. There is a poop deck. The existence of a gunroom reveals *Discovery* was armed, and not merely as an afterthought. Other details refer to cabins, a breadroom, a boat, a shallop, sails, topsails etc.

The first requirement of the merchant vessels *Susan Constant*, *Godspeed* and *Discovery* was to carry cargo. In 1606 that cargo was supplies and settlers across the Atlantic. In the absence of data other than

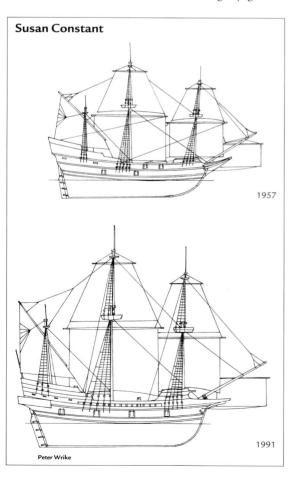

Susan Constant

1957

1991

Peter Wrike

their service to the Virginia Colony, *Susan Constant, Godspeed* and *Discovery* can be assumed to have been typical merchant vessels. Their proportions fell within the limits of such vessels as defined by the Newton tables. Each made multiple successful passages on Hudson Bay and Atlantic waters and their continued employment indicates their seaworthiness and ability to perform. They were not naval vessels but, to be thorough, the researcher examined extant data on any contemporary small vessels. Historian Tom Glasgow looked at proportions of naval vessels and used figures and vessels from 1590–1. These vessels and their tonnages (variously given) were *Advice* 49–50, *Charles* 70–119, *Cygnet* 28–30, *Makeshift* 49, *Moon* 68–85, *Spy* 49 and *Sun/Sonne* 40–5. They all vary from the Newton tables in beam (narrower) and depth (deeper).

Multiple replicas

The early Jamestown replicas were built as part of a massive fiscal and physical effort marking the 350th anniversary of Jamestown's settlement. Together with a replica Indian village and a replica fort the vessels went on permanent display in 1957. The Commonwealth Commission, which authorised construction of the 1957 fleet, chose Robert Fee in 1955 to design the three vessels. They also required him to make the vessels' appearance 'identical to the 1949 painting by Griffith Bailey Coale'.

In 1949 Commander Griffith Bailey Coale, USNR, did a huge and meticulously detailed painting of the arrival of the three vessels off Jamestown Island. He consulted with many persons, including historian R.C. Anderson and Robert Fee. He selected dimensions for each vessel based on the 100-, 40- and 20-ton figures. The rigs he chose included a two-masted *Discovery*. In 1946 Fee had completed a model of *Susan Constant* for the Virginia Historical Society and Coale based his painting on that model. He published an extensive article in *The American Neptune* in which he welcomed corrections to and comments on his depiction – regrettably he died within months of its publication. (In the mid-1950s veteran modelmaker Augustus

Crabtree built models of all three vessels – two of *Susan Constant* at different scales. Crabtree relied on his accumulated experiences to depart from Fee's designs and described his *Susan Constant* models as 120–30 tons; his *Godspeed* and *Discovery* models were also larger than the 1957 replicas.)

By the early 1980s the 1957 replicas were tired and unseaworthy for visitors. The Foundation turned to new designers for replacements. The new *Godspeed* (1983) and *Discovery* (1984) were designed by Newport News Shipbuilding Company's William Boze and Duncan Stewart, using the same dimensions as for the 1957 vessels. They stated 'the authors/designers… will in no way attempt to set the record straight as to what the proper dimensions for the ship(s) should be…'. Fee, Boze and Stewart all carefully recorded their findings in professional journals.

Later, in his 1991 design of *Susan Constant*, Lavery logically and methodically performed his research and presented his findings for a 120-ton vessel. His assumptions and drawings fall within the ranges provided by the Newton tables and his work is a fine example of applied research. His subsequent book on *Susan Constant* in the 'Anatomy of the Ship' series sets a benchmark for early English vessels.

In 1999 the Foundation recognised the need to replace the ageing *Godspeed* and *Discovery*. Captain Eric Speth, fleet manager and chief operational officer, developed a methodology to research, design and construct a new *Godspeed* and a new *Discovery* for the 400th anniversary of the Jamestown Settlement (2007). The Foundation issued RFPs (Requests for Proposals) for a researcher, then for a marine architectural firm, and finally for construction and delivery of the vessels. These phases included all the necessary tasks of bid, review, award, monitoring and funding. During each phase Captain Speth periodically utilised knowledgeable persons to review progress. In 2001 the Foundation selected this author as researcher for *Godspeed* and *Discovery*. Extensive research in the United States and the United Kingdom produced documentation and drawings sufficient to establish the probable appearance of the vessels.

For the new *Godspeed* and *Discovery* all previous research was reviewed and documented. A thorough and careful analysis of more than 280 contemporary records yielded the ownership, operational, commercial, voyage and marine documents relevant to the vessels. A month-by-month chronology on each vessel revealed their uses, location and other particulars. The most vexing challenge was the correct determination of the tonnage and rig. Based on the evidence presented and the previous under-sized replicas, the Foundation selected a more robust tonnage for each vessel. This resulted in a *Godspeed* and *Discovery* that were far more proportionate to the 120-ton *Susan Constant* and significantly larger than the previous replicas from 40 tons and 20 tons to 48 tons and 24 tons. Concept drawings to scale provided hull designs that gave the best appearance and performance potential for the *Godspeed* and *Discovery*.

The sailing rigs chosen for the two vessels represented a synthesis of the traditional

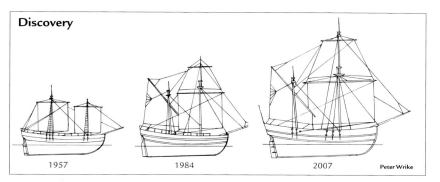

Discovery

1957   1984   2007   Peter Wrike

FIGURE 9
The three *Discovery* replicas and, below, *Discovery* (1957) and *Susan Constant* (1991) alongside in Jamestown, Virginia

visual and written evidence tempered by more than half a century of replica sailing and related experience from the Jamestown-Yorktown Foundation and other organis-ations: Plimoth Plantation (MA), *Mayflower*; New Netherlands Museum (NY), *Half Moon*; Historic St Mary's City (MD), *Dove*; Elizabeth II State Historic Site, *Elizabeth*; Bermuda, *Deliverance*; Great Britain, *Golden Hind*.

While the overwhelming contemporary evidence depicts three-masted vessels as typical, the foundation determined that *Discovery* should be two-masted.

After careful review of the research and additional concept drawings, the Foundation chose Tri-Coastal Marine to do the naval architecture for the new replicas. This produced builder's plans and provided for twenty-first-century standards of propulsion, navigation, safety, power and compliance to State and US Coast Guard licensure. The plans went to Rockport Marine, Maine, for construction of *Godspeed* and *Discovery*. This experienced yard has the training, tools, techniques and suppliers to produce all types and sizes of traditional vessels. They applied twenty-first century standards and proven materials to ensure the designer's expectations were met and the hardwoods used could give the new vessels at least a thirty-year life.

But perhaps the most significant difference between these two replicas and their prede-cessors is in their performance.

There is no evidence of a standard for sailing performance for the 1957 Jamestown fleet. It was a 'fleet in being', designed to be seen and only seldom used. Consequently the vessels deteriorated not only from little use but also from poor materials, lack of main-tenance and a harsh environment. The 1957 fleet appeared 'boxlike' compared to the 1983 and 1984 replicas. The later *Godspeed* and *Discovery* represented improvements to the hull form and appearance. However, *Godspeed* (1983) seldom worked to windward and was described as 'a barrel with a sail' – she was sea*un*kindly. Nevertheless, she received rig and other enhancements, went to England and, in 1987, resailed the original (1606–7) route to Virginia. Her captain on that voyage, George Sally, found her a very unsatisfactory

sailer and her accommodation areas, partic-ularly the 'tween decks', were uninhabitable (they had just 2ft 8in headroom).

Mark Preisser, captain in the Virginia Institute of Marine Sciences fleet and a former first mate on *Susan Constant*, has sailed four of the Jamestown replicas. He rerigged the 1984 *Discovery* with a square sail on the foremast and a topsail and lateen on the main. This measurably improved her performance and she could work to wind-ward even in light winds. The 1991 *Susan Constant*, with sufficient wind, also performs well. Preisser believes the 2006 *Godspeed* has the best handling of all the Jamestown vessels.

In the 1990s the Foundation instituted a scheduled maintenance programme to down rig and renew both standing and running rigging. Permanent crew were assigned to the vessels as working and sailing replicas and a significant corps of volunteers was developed to augment the crew both in port and on voyages. Experience from these people and events, coupled with the shared experience of other replica captains and crews, ensured continuous performance enhancements. Thus, the new *Godspeed* and *Discovery* are superior sailers to their earlier namesakes, thanks to improved hull design, rig and professional crews.

The Foundation's eight vessels have employed whipstaffs, tillers and one ship's wheel (1984 *Discovery*). The 1606–7 fleet had both whipstaff (*Susan Constant*) and tillers (*Godspeed* and *Discovery*). The tiller is very responsive for smaller vessels but diminishes as vessel size increases and as sea conditions worsen. The new *Godspeed* and *Discovery* have tillers. Of necessity the *Susan Constant's* whipstaff requires two persons – one on deck to give commands and at least one below to handle the staff. Preisser commented on *Susan Constant's* whipstaff.

The whipstaff could be handled with ease in light and moderate weather. In heavy weather it lived up to its name and could require numerous persons to steer the ship. The whipstaff was located in the aft cabin. When the command was given to sail 'full and by,' often when the ship was beating to weather, the helmsman, not being able to see ahead of the ship, or much outside at all, would peer through a small port and watch the main course. Since the forecourse could be braced up sharper, due to the geometry of the shrouds, the main course was the first to luff. The helmsman would steer into the wind until the main course luffed, then fall off just enough to fill the sail, thereby keeping all the sails full and steering efficiently close to the wind.

Nonetheless, the whipstaff is a necessary fixture on larger early-seventeenth-century replica vessels; today it is usually augmented by a modern power system below as a supplemental source or secondary method of steering.

Conclusion

The Foundation's latest replica vessels – *Godspeed* and *Discovery* – reflect the greatly enhanced hull configurations made possible by the application of Newton's tables. There are now professional naval architects who have experience designing and adapting replica vessels. Traditional construction methods and materials (often woods from foreign places) provide the most durable vessels. Experience with rig design and ship's furniture have led not only to better performance but to the prevention of accidents that may result in damage or injury. Boatbuilders are available with modern skills, devices and, again, experience to improve replica-vessel production.

In 2006 at the beginning of the new *Godspeed*'s voyage along America's East Coast, the Governor of Virginia and other officials heard Dr Tim Runyon's keynote address. Runyon heads East Carolina University's Maritime Studies programme. Towards his conclusion he asked 'How good is this representation of the *Godspeed*?' He answered from the research reviewer's comments in 2002. '[This] …effort sets a new standard for all replica vessels.'

PETER WRIKE

BIBLIOGRAPHY

Baker, William A. *Colonial Vessels: Some Seventeenth-Century Sailing Craft.* Barre, Massachusetts: Barre Publishing, 1962.

Barbour, Philip L., ed. *The Jamestown voyages under the first charter, 1606–1609: Documents relating to the foundation of Jamestown and the history of the Jamestown colony up to the departure of Captain John Smith, late president of the council in Virginia under the first charter, early in October, 1609.* 2 vols. The Hakluyt Society Press, 2nd ser., Nos. 136–7, 1969.

Barker, Richard. 'A Manuscript on Shipbuilding, Circa 1600, copied by Newton,' *Mariner's Mirror*, Vol. 80, 16–29.

Boze, William and Duncan Stewart. 'The Reproduction of the *Godspeed*,' *Marine Technology*, Vol. 24, No. 2 (April 1987): 115–30.

Coale, Griffith Baily. 'Arrival of the First Permanent English Settlers off Jamestown, Virginia, 13 May 1607', *American Neptune*, Vol. 10, 3–12 + 8 plates.

Dietz, Brian. 'The Royal Bounty and English Merchant Shipping in the Sixteenth and Seventeenth Centuries', *Mariner's Mirror*, Vol. 77, (February 1991), 5–20.

Fawcett, Howard H. Jr. 'Sailing the Jamestown Ships', *Transactions of the Society of Naval Architects and Marine Engineers* (1958), 46–66.

Fee, Robert G.C. 'The Jamestown Fleet', *American Neptune*, Vol. 17, 173–80.

_____. 'Design and Construction of the Jamestown Ships', *Transactions of the Society of Naval Architects and Marine Engineers*, Vol. 66, (1958)

Foster, Sir William, ed. *The Four Voyages of Henry Hudson*, with 'A Discourse Designed to Commemorate the Discovery of New York by Henry Hudson', *Collections of the New York State Historical Society for the Year 1809*, I (1811), 17–40, 61–188.

Hillier, Susan. *A List of Ships Traveling Between England and Virginia, 1607–1630.* Williamsburg, VA: Colonial Williamsburg Foundation, 1970.

Lavery, Brian. *The Colonial Merchantman* Susan Constant *1605*, The Anatomy of the Ship Series. Annapolis, MD: Naval Institute Press, 1988.

Markham, Sir Clements R., ed. *The Voyages of William Baffin, 1612-1622.* Hakluyt Society Publications, 1st ser., No. 63, 1881.

Marsden, R.G. 'English Ships in the Reign of James I', *Transactions of the Royal Historical Society*, new ser., 19 (1905), 309–42.

Massachusetts Institute of Technology, Hart Nautical Collection.

Public Record Office, Kew Gardens, London, UK Reference E.190
Domestic Records Information 9, 2001, 400
Port of London: Mich. 1601–Mich. 1602 12/1
  Mich. 1604–Mich. 1605 12/3
  Jan. 1605–Dec. 1605 12/7
  Xmas 1605–Xmas 1606 13/5
  Xmas 1607–Xmas 1608 14/4
  Xmas 1608–Xmas 1609 14/5
Port of Bristol: East. 1603–Mich. 1603 1133/5
  East. 1605–Xmas 1605 1133/6
  Xmas 1608–Xmas 1609 1133/8
  East. 1611–Mich. 1611 1133/10
  Port of Hull: East. 1602–Mich. 1602 311/10
  Mich. 1602–East. 1603 311/11
Port of Ipswich: East. 1602–Mich. 1604 599/4
  East. 1604–Mich. 1604 599/5
Port of Southampton: Xmas 1604–Xmas 1605 819/4
  East. 1605–Xmas 1605 819/6

Purchas, Samuel. *Hakluytus Posthumus or Purchas His Pilgrims*, Vol 13, 14 and 16. Glasgow: The Hakluyt Society, James MacLehose and Sons, 1906.

Quinn, David Beers, ed., with the assistance of Alison M. Quinn and Susan Hillier. *New American World: A Documentary History of North America to 1612.* Vol. I: *America From Concept to Discovery: Early Expeditions to North America*; Vol. III: *English Plans for North America. The Roanoke Voyage. New England Ventures*; Vol. IV: *Newfoundland from Fishery to Colony. Northwest Passage Searches*; Vol. V: *Extension of Settlement in Florida, Virginia, and the Spanish Southwest.* New York, NY: Arno Press and Hector Bye, 1979.

St. Mary's City (MD) Commission, *The Maryland Dove.* Maryland Department of Economic and Community Development, 1984.

Wellsman, J.S. *London Before the Fire, A Grand Panorama.* London: pub for Sidgwick and Jackson, Ltd. by Wood Westwood & Co. Ltd., 1973.

Wrike, Peter J. *The* Godspeed *and* Discovery *of London and Virginia, 1606–7.* Final Report and Drawings, 2002. This 217 page report includes 415 pages of Appendices and 418 pages of selected bibliographical sources. Copies are at the Jamestown Yorktown Foundation (VA), East Carolina's Maritime Studies Program (NC) and the Mariners' Museum (VA).

10 Bezaisen, Japan's coastal sailing Traders

In western maritime histories, Japan is not generally viewed as a major seafaring power. The criteria for pre-eminence in this regard are usually measured by the reach of a country's exploration and trade, or its naval might. Japan's problem is largely one of timing; it did not become a naval power until the twentieth century, and most western scholars have interpreted Japan's maritime importance in light of its reclusiveness, a perception magnified by the timing of European contact. The West's great era of exploration encircled the globe just as Japan entered its famous 250-year period of exclusion – known as the Edo era – in which foreign travel by Japanese was banned, and contact with foreigners strictly controlled. It has often been written that to enforce these restrictions, Japanese shipwrights were required to build vessels that were inherently unseaworthy, yet another blow to Japan's maritime reputation. Japan's four most significant replica ships emerge from this introspective period of the country's history. They were never intended to sail out of sight of Japan's shores; instead, they sailed through a political and maritime era that looked only inward, ignoring the horizon.

FIGURE 1

Running downwind on Aomori Bay, the summer of 2006. Of four replica bezaisen in Japan only *Michinoku-maru* and *Kesen-maru* are in the water, and the former is the only one actively sailed. She is owned and operated by the Michinoku Traditional Wooden Boat Museum in Aomori City.

(Douglas Brooks)

Japan was an important maritime power in Asia before the Edo era. Although the Tokugawa shogunate did begin to adopt laws restricting sailing vessels from foreign voyages in the early 1600s, there were no actual ship-building restrictions. Japanese vessels had, before that time, carried on extensive trade with the Ryukyu Kingdom (modern-day Okinawa) and kingdoms in present-day Korea, China, Thailand and Vietnam. The ships that carried out this trade reflected technological influences from Japan's Asian neighbours, as well as the influence of the Portuguese and Dutch, who had been sailing to Japan since 1543.

The Edo era (1603–1868) began with the consolidation of government power under the Tokugawa shogun and ended with Japan's forced opening to western diplomatic missions and trade. The shogunate's decision to cut itself off from the outside world was, in many ways, just an extension of its domestic policy: namely, limiting any influences that might threaten the shogun's absolute control. The greatest threat from the outside world was Catholic Christianity, which the shogun feared could subvert loyalty to the emperor and thus Japan's political and social structure. By 1600 the Portuguese and Dutch had established trade in southern Japan on the island of Kyushu, particularly in the port city of Nagasaki, and as a result the region had become the centre of Japanese Christianity. The shogunate's first edicts involving trade were to forbid commerce with Kyushu as a way of limiting the power of that region in favour of Edo (present-day Tokyo) where the shogun ruled.

The subsequent series of edicts on trade – known collectively as *Sakoku* – eventually culminated in 1641 with an absolute ban on all foreign travel. Strictly controlled trade contacts with the Dutch, Koreans, Chinese and Ainu (Japan's aboriginal population, living mainly in Hokkaido) were established, but Japan's own overseas maritime activities were suspended.

Japan's geography, however, would ensure that the country would necessarily maintain and develop its shipbuilding traditions. The Japanese archipelago is essentially a line of

mountains, with a relatively limited amount of arable land around the margins. Travel through the country was difficult but a few major rivers and Japan's inland waters offered limited trade routes to the steep slopes and thick forests of the interior. But, in seeking to restrict the military power of its vassals, the shogunate placed restrictions on the use of carriages and the construction of large bridges. The seas surrounding Japan were the most viable highway for goods and so the maritime history of the Edo era is represented by the thousands of coastal traders that moved goods around the country.

There are several terms used to describe Edo-era coastal traders, the most generic being *bezaisen*. This was the term that seamen and shipowners tended to use. The literal origins of the name are vague but probably refer to vessel type – *sen*, as a word ending, means 'ship' – and sometimes the word is

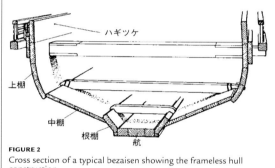

FIGURE 2
Cross section of a typical bezaisen showing the frameless hull construction.
(From *Zusetsu Wasen Shiwa* (Historical Japanese Ship Drawings), by Ishii Kenji, Shiseido Books, 1983. Reproduced from *Nihon no Fune - Wasen Hen* (Ships of Japan - Indigenous Designs), published by the Museum of Maritime Science, Tokyo, March 1998)

romanised as *benzaisen*. More specific terms for the coastal traders include *kitamaesen* – best translated as 'northern coastal trader' – the type that sailed along the Sea of Japan coast to Hokkaido. From the north the most common cargo was herring, salmon and kelp in trade for rice, salt, cotton, cloth and *sake* (rice wine) from the mainland. It has been said that the term kitamaesen was used by Pacific-coast sailors and was a derogatory reference to the ships of the Japan Sea. This Japan Sea coast is more rural than other parts of the country and, hence, sometimes seen as

FIGURE 3

Yahata-maru was owned by Gonzaemon Ukon of Fukui Prefecture and represents a typical kitamaesen type that sailed in the Sea of Japan. She is shown fully loaded, with her peculiar cargo fence and her deck piled high. Two *tenma* small craft lie alongside. Her raised rudderpost and tiller are clearly visible, as are her foremast and gaff-rigged mizzen. Her capacity is over 2000 koku (300 tons) yet she was registered as a smaller vessel (1,357 koku) to avoid the Meiji government's 1887 restrictions on the construction of large, Japanese-style ships.
(Reproduced from *Nihon no Fune - Wasen Hen* (Ships of Japan - Indigenous Designs), published by the Museum of Maritime Science, Tokyo, March, 1998)

a more backward region. The trading vessels that sailed between Osaka and Edo were called *higakkikaisen*. The general public tended to refer to these vessels as *sengokubune*, literally 'one thousand koku ship' – the koku being a traditional volume measurement: one koku of rice is the amount required to feed one person for one year.

Bezaisen developed during the Edo era and one major misconception about them is that shipbuilding rules put in place by the shogunate forced shipwrights to build vessels that were inherently unseaworthy in order to enforce Japan's isolation. Scholars have long pointed out that the rudders on these ships were not hung on gudgeons but instead had a rudder stock that passed through a beam – an arrangement inherently weak – and it has often been written that this type of rudder construction was mandated by the shogunate. In fact, there were no actual shipbuilding restrictions under the shogunate; bezaisen were simply never designed for offshore sailing.

Japan's earlier Asian trading ships were heavily influenced by foreign technologies, and paintings and other illustrations of the fleet show round-hulled, carvel-planked ships,

often using fully battened, junk-type rigs. By contrast, bezaisen were built with methods similar to those found in Japanese small craft. Throughout Japan the majority of small craft feature a horizontal plank keel, generally twice as thick as the planking, with a hard-chine hull composed of two strakes, the top strake nearly vertical over most of its length. Where strakes are built up of several planks these are edge-fastened to each other. In some parts of Japan sawn frames are installed, but largely the strength of this type of construction rests in the hull itself. In lieu of frames, horizontal beams cross the hull at the chine and sheer. The beam ends are either tenoned through the hull and wedged from the outside or locked in place with shouldered keys. Another feature is the side planking aft, which often runs past the transom to form a chamber that protects the rudder.

The bezaisen reflected this same monocoque construction but started with a boxed keel, the sides of which gave the vessel some lateral resistance when sailing to windward and also reduced the overall draught. There were no curved frames within the hull; instead it was strengthened by floor timbers and massive athwartship beams at the chine and sheer. The deck planking was entirely unfastened, which facilitated the loading and unloading of cargo. The large rudder, set within the protective overhang of the stern planking, extended several feet below the bottom of the hull and also contributed to the lateral resistance of the hull. The rudder could be raised or lowered using a windlass, facilitating shoal-draught sailing. The single mast could be lowered and the rectangular sail could be handled by a small crew. Often a ship's boat, or *tenma*, was carried on deck. All in all, the bezaisen's design and hull shape lent itself to efficient construction, a relatively shallow draught that could easily enter small harbours and estuaries and rest upright when beached, and a rig that could be easily worked.

To date, four replicas of bezaisen have been built in Japan since 1990. The story of their construction is the story of one man, Mr Niinuma Tomenoshin (in keeping with Japanese protocol I use the family name first, followed by the given name), one of nine children born to a rural family in the coastal town of Ofunato in Iwate Prefecture. Iwate is a rugged, isolated region situated on the northeastern coast of Japan's main island of Honshu. In post-war rural Japan there were very few opportunities and Niinuma followed his father into the boatbuilding trade, beginning his apprenticeship at age fifteen. Ofunato is today a busy port, being one of the best protected natural harbours along this stretch of Japan's Pacific coast, and locally there has always been a demand for fishing vessels of all sizes as well as a tradition of shipbuilding.

By the 1980s Niinuma realised, however, that his generation would be the last trained in traditional Japanese wooden boat construction and he began to dream of building a sailing ship from Japan's Edo era. At that time maritime scholarship on the subject was limited and reference materials practically non-existent. To this day traditional boatbuilders in Japan (as well as some house and temple carpenters) draw their plans on a plank of wood. Such plank drawings are durable and many drawings from the days of original bezaisen still exist. Unfortunately, the shipwright and, indeed, today's boatbuilders, drew just a profile of the vessel; the half-breadth dimensions were either memorised or derived from formulae, and there were no construction details drawn. Such secrecy was pervasive and has left Japan with very little detailed or complete documentation about the design or construction of bezaisen. In his research, Niinuma relied on old paintings. Another source of information are old models, which shipowners often commissioned for Shinto shrines and Buddhist temples as offerings for the protection of their fleets.

Niinuma began building models himself to

FIGURE 4
Painting on wood, showing the fully loaded bezaisen *Hôfuku-maru.*
(Painting in the collection of the Awagasaki Hachiman Shrine, Reproduced from *Nihon no Fune - Wasen Hen* (Ships of Japan - Indigenous Designs), published by the Museum of Maritime Science, Tokyo, March, 1998)

FIGURE 5
This painting, dated 1861, from Awagasaki Hachiman Shrine, purports to show one bezaisen (foreground) preparing to transfer cargo to another. Note the ship's boat ready to be launched through the railing.
(Reproduced from *Nihon no Fune - Wasen Hen* (Ships of Japan - Indigenous Designs), published by the Museum of Maritime Science, Tokyo, March, 1998)

work out an accurate design. He also began to assemble materials from the region and from a group of about thirty shipwrights who still possessed the necessary skills to build an authentic replica. Eventually a local newspaper editor took up the cause and the project began to take shape in the late 1980s. In 1991 the Prefecture of Iwate decided to underwrite the project as part of Japan Expo. The replica was launched in 1992 and has been home-ported in Ofunato ever since. She is not actively sailed, however, and is only taken off her mooring once a year for a local festival.

Initially this project was greeted with widespread scepticism and even Niinuma admits that he had no idea whether the vessel would work. Like his forebears, he drew the lines and construction details on wood. He was the sole designer – no naval architects were involved and there was no modern analysis of the lines before construction commenced.

This first vessel, named *Kesen-maru*, is 62ft overall and displaces 30 tons. Her mainsail is 460 square feet and she also flies a small sail on a foremast. Niinuma built her entirely of local materials: cedar for the hull, red pine for the deck, beams and floorboards, oak for the rudder. The 56ft mast came from a single cedar tree. Her fastenings were all hand-forged nails, and nail heads exposed on the exterior of her hull were covered with copper plates, a technique widespread in Japanese boatbuilding.

Although *Kesen-maru* ultimately proved to be a positive sensation and at least vindicated Niinuma's design work, she came under criticism from scholars who claimed that she was not an absolutely faithful replica. Niinuma's second ship, launched in 1997, was designed with help from a Tokyo research institute and built for the Ogi Folklore Museum on Sado, an island in the Sea of Japan and part of Niigata Prefecture. The museum is located just above the sleepy fishing village of Shukunegi, a port that, during the Edo era, was an important shipbuilding town.

Niinuma brought his team of shipbuilders from northern Japan to Sado and built the bezaisen in just over a year. Local carpenters built a structure to house it, as there was never any intention to launch this second ship. Sado Island is known for its fine cedar forests and all the materials for the ship were furnished by local loggers. An island blacksmith even made the fastenings and all the ironwork. This time Niinuma used a 200-year-old plank drawing from the late Edo period for the design and he describes the Sado vessel as the most authentic, in terms of materials, of his four ships. The ship's cradle rides on tracks and in fine weather the museum rolls her outside and raises the sail. The ship has also frequently served as a set for television historical dramas.

FIGURES 6 AND 7
Master Shipwright Mr Niinuma Tomenoshin, at his home in Ofunato, Japan, along with some examples of his woodworking skills, including a wooden marquetry valise, and a wooden vase.
(Douglas Brooks)

The largest of Niinuma's four replicas are his two most recent: *Naniwa-maru*, launched in 1999 and built for the Osaka Maritime Museum, and *Michinoku-maru*, launched in 2005 by the Michinoku Traditional Wooden Boat Museum in Aomori, Japan. Both vessels are roughly the same size but *Naniwa-maru* was a collaboration between the shipwright Niinuma and a team of maritime scholars.

Naniwa-maru is the centrepiece, literally and figuratively, of the Osaka Maritime Museum. The vessel, fully rigged, rests in a giant glass geodesic dome set in Osaka harbour, accessible to visitors via an undersea tunnel. The ship is encircled by four floors of exhibits that recount the history of Osaka, its art and the development of trading ships known as *higakkikaisen* (the name may refer to the lattice-like construction of these ships' bulwarks – *higakki* means lattice – and the lattice was also the symbol of Osaka's merchants' guild). Higakkikaisen specifically refers to those traders that sailed the route between Osaka and Edo – the most important trade route in Japan and the means by which Osaka rose to become the mercantile centre of the country.

Naniwa-maru was built by Niinuma's crew at the Hitachi shipyard in Osaka, and the funding for both project and museum came from the Port of Osaka. Some of the construction methods were modern, such as using a steambox and bending the planking around steel moulds set on the keel. Traditionally planks were bent over an open fire, a process called *yakimage* and widespread in Asia; Niinuma confessed that steam is a superior technique, as it heats the wood more deeply and makes it more elastic.

In the original concept *Naniwa-maru* was to be finished and immediately placed inside the maritime museum's dome, but as she came closer to completion a number of sailors, naval architects and researchers began to insist that she should be sailed. With no one alive with any first-hand knowledge of how these vessels were handled, she represented an unprecedented opportunity to explore the capabilities of the type. Historically, one of the most famous voyages of higakkikaisen was the annual 'race' from Osaka to Edo. Like the 'races' of the square-rigged ships of the Australian wheat trade, the Osaka-to-Edo race was about commerce and being the first to get a product – in this case cotton and sake – to market. Records show that the first ships reached Edo from Osaka (a distance of 362 nautical miles) in forty-five hours, sailing at a 7–8 knot average, but it remained a mystery how these ships handled, particularly upwind. One of Japan's largest foundations came forward to underwrite the extra costs of launching and conducting sailing trials.

The team that studied the sailing qualities of *Naniwa-maru* consisted of Professor Emeritus Nomoto Kensaku of Osaka

FIGURE 8
View below decks on *Michinoku-maru*. The two fixed blocks are part of her rigging for the braces, which run to the captstans below decks. The opening in her stern looks out on the rudderpost and the capstan in the centre is for raising the rudder.
(Douglas Brooks)

FIGURE 9
A shrine model built by Mr Niinuma Tomenoshin whose grandfather was a temple carpenter.
(Douglas Brooks)

University, Professor Masuyama Yutaka of the Kanazawa Institute of Technology and Professor Sakurai Akira of Kyushu University. The single square sail is a well understood technology, but in the case of *Naniwa-maru*'s sea trials, the major question was determining how this type of rig and hull shape performed when reaching and whether it could successfully sail upwind. At the time of the tests *Naniwa-maru*'s principal dimensions were as follows:

Length overall:	29.9m / 98ft 1in
Breadth moulded:	7.4m / 24ft 3in
Depth moulded:	2.4m / 7ft 10in
Light weight (hull, rig and rudder):	88 tons
Ballast:	56 tons
Crew, instrumentation, etc:	3 tons
Total displacement:	147 tons
Waterline length:	23m / 75ft 5in
Draught forward:	2.0m / 6ft 7in
Draught aft:	2.2m / 7ft 3in

Before sea trials, the researchers conducted towing tests on a hull model (1/20 scale) and wind-tunnel tests on an above-waterline model (1/30 scale). Both sets of tests were done in an attempt to develop predictions of the replica's eventual performance, as well as to study potential sail trim positions and the amount of drive force they created. The Port of Osaka – owners of the ship – had provided a limited window of opportunity in which to sail *Naniwa-maru*, so the model testing was also designed to take at least some of the guesswork out of the full-size ship trials. As a corollary, the researchers also wanted to see if tank and wind-tunnel modelling could accurately predict the sailing qualities of a historic vessel for which there was no other documentation.

The sail trim study had to take into account some unique features of the bezaisen mainsail. The massive masts of these ships were only stayed fore and aft. The lack of shrouds gave the yard much more freedom of

FIG 11

FIG 12

FIGURE 11

Michinoku-maru's stern, showing the space which allowed the rudder to be raised when beaching or navigating shallows. The tackle used to raise the rudder is just visible on the rudder stock. The large, deep rudder also provided some resistance to leeway when sailing upwind.

(Douglas Brooks)

FIGURE 12

Japan's traditional ships were capable of standing upright on their narrow plank keels, so they could be beached at low tide to work on the hulls. The sides of the box keel also provided some lateral resistance when sailing upwind. The mortises, visible in the chine rubstrake, have copper covers that protect the heads of the fasteners, a technique common to traditional Japanese vessels, large and small.

(Douglas Brooks)

FIG 10

FIG 15

FIGURE 10

Michinoku-maru under construction. She was built by a crew of about a dozen shipwrights who worked seasonally for two years. The total building time was just eleven months. The head shipwright and the nucleus of this crew come mainly from the Tohoku region of northern Japan and have built all four of Japan's replica bezaisen.

(Mr Kon Masaaki)

FIGURE 15

The stern in profile, showing the sweep of the planking. Traditional Japanese boat builders bend planking over an open fire, a technique widespread across Asia. *Michinoku maru's* builders, however, used a steambox, a technique borrowed from the West that the head shipwright believes is more effective. The topsides are left unpainted, a practice common in Japan for wooden boats until the late twentieth century.

(Douglas Brooks)

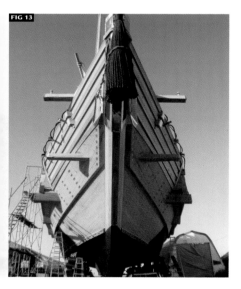

FIG 13

FIG 14

FIGURE 13

Michinoku-maru, built by Niinuma Tomenoshin at the shipyard of the Michinoku Traditional Wooden Boat Museum in Aomori, Japan, just a month prior to her launch in November, 2005. Her backbone and framework are Douglas fir from North America while her planking is Japanese cedar. Essentially a frameless hull with the planks' edges nailed to each other, the beams that strengthen the hull are clearly visible.

(Douglas Brooks)

FIGURE 14

Michinoku-maru, at 100ft and 100 tons, is the most recent of four replica bezaisen built in Japan. Her mast is made of a single cedar tree from the forests of northern Japan where she was built. All fastening heads are covered with copper plates, which is also used to protect seams and beam ends, as well as an ornate decoration on the stem head.

(Douglas Brooks)

movement; it was braced to a pair of windlasses located below the poop deck. Perhaps most unusual was the lack of a footrope in the sail; instead, the foot of the bezaisen sail had many pendants attached to a massive line that lay athwartships on deck just behind the mast. A series of bowlines (usually three or four) ran from the leech of the sail forward. As the researchers surmised, the rope-and-pendant arrangement was primarily for downwind sailing, while the bowlines came into play when reaching. Historically, shortening sail was done by gathering the foot of the sail and tying it around the base of the mast, or lowering the yard, or a combination of the two.

The sailing trials took place in August 1999 in Osaka harbour, a generally sheltered body of water, with wind speeds of between 10 and 20 knots. The ship was accompanied by a 10m (33ft) sailing yacht motoring under bare poles. The speed and direction of the wind were measured at the yacht's masthead, as it was felt that no accurate readings could be measured from the replica itself, due to the turbulence created by the large sail. Speed of the ship was measured on board the chase boat and then corrected by employing a pair of highly accurate GPS devices, one mounted on each vessel, which compared their locations relative to each other.

Running downwind it seems as if the arrangement of multiple pendants controlling the shape of the sail's foot can have a marked effect on performance. In the trials the ship ran downwind rigged two ways: firstly, drawing only the clews at either end of the foot, the way a western square-rigger does; secondly, using the pendants. On average the latter method yielded a 10 per cent higher speed. This experiment in rigging the ship's square sail in both western and Japanese ways was also tried on a beam reach, but the researchers found that drawing in the foot using the pendants was no advantage on this point of sail. They did conclude, however, that the pendants were useful off the wind to a quartering reach.

Naniwa-maru's fastest point of sail was on a beam to broad reach, which surprised no one. The great mystery, however, was her windward ability. Among the few historic accounts of how these ships sailed was a statement by a master mariner that he often sailed with the wind four points off the bow. Of course this is apparent wind in the mariner's face and, as the researchers had already found, the layout of these vessels on deck coupled with down-wash windflow from the single sail made any apparent-wind readings suspect. Another historic document recorded a bezai ship gaining four miles to windward on a close-hauled tack of twenty miles. Although current and leeway were unknown for this event, it does correspond to a tack angle of 156°, which is about what the researchers were able to perform in the sailing trials. Speed obtained was 25 per cent to 30 per cent of actual wind speed.

Tacking *Naniwa-maru* involved wearing her around from one tack to another. This particular manoeuvre requires precise sail handling and rudder control, so it was the most suspect part of the sea trials given an inexperienced crew. Although the sail itself is simple, the running rigging is quite complicated. Proficiency in co-ordinating changes in sail trim while wearing the ship around was more than could be expected of the research crew. Unfortunately it is impossible to know how the original crews handled bezaisen. However, the results obtained tacking in the sea trials were surprisingly similar to the computer modelling, thus proving that tank and wind-tunnel testing can be an effective predictor of such vessels.

Finally, the researchers reported that *Naniwa-maru*'s bottom was quite fouled with barnacles by the time of the test period (10mm or about ⅜in thick). To calculate the resulting effects on performance, they assumed a clean bottom and calculated that the ship could reach an angle of 70 degrees to windward with a speed 30 per cent of true wind speed, with 40 per cent of wind speed possible from a beam to broad reach, and slightly less than that sailing downwind.

The most recently built replica bezaisen was launched in 2005 in the northern Japanese city of Aomori. *Michinoku-maru* was commissioned by the Michinoku Traditional

Wooden Boat Museum, an institution with the largest collection of historic boats in Japan – primarily regional small craft, along with a number of other large vessels from throughout Asia. Niinuma had complete freedom in designing and constructing *Michinoku-maru*, a freedom he relished after collaborating with historians and engineers in the construction of his second and third ships. In Japan, craftsmen are regarded as aloof and prickly personalities, and often with good reason. Even today the very mention of a traditional apprenticeship will make people shudder. The traditions, secrecy and strictness of artisan crafts in Japan, especially today, seem to belong to another era. While the historians debated whether Niinuma's bezaisen were authentic replicas, and scoured manuscripts for 'proof', Niinuma regarded his own experience as just another link in a chain of craftsmen. He says that while the professor may discover evidence in his research, these are just pinpoints in the vast, historical darkness. In his view, his own instincts were probably no different from the Edo-era shipwrights. Such, he said, is the difference between the professor and the carpenter.

Niinuma calls *Michinoku-maru* the culmination of his experience. As such, he says she is the best sailing and most useful of his four ships. Her construction, however, was carried out under a strict budget, and much of Niinuma's design work involved cutting building costs. Her wood comes from a number of sources: Japanese cedar for the

FIGURE 16
View on deck showing the vessel under sail. The multiple sheets are clearly visible, as are the opens seams between the sail panels, which automatically spill air as the wind increases. The sheets fasten to a large line running across the deck. The tiller is also visible. The after deck planks are not fastened, but just rest in rabbets on the supporting beams. Historically these vessels sailed with just a handful of crew.
(Mr Kon Masaaki)

FIG 17

FIG 18

FIGURE 17

Michinoku-maru sailing close hauled, the main line receiving her sheets is rigged nearly fore and aft on her deck. Researchers who sailed an earlier replica bezaisen in Osaka were surprised by this type's windward performance.
(Mr Kon Masaaki)

FIGURE 18

Running downwind, *Naniwa-maru* shows the multiple lines used to control sail shape in these vessels. Her latticework bulwark construction provided resistance to hogging in these vessels.
(Professor Masuyama Yutaka)

FIGURE 19

Close view of *Michinoku-maru* running downwind. Her sail construction, with vertical panels loosely laced together, is clearly visible. Note the multiple sheets along the foot of the sail.
(Mr Kon Masaaki)

Amazingly, the sole drawing used for the construction was a 1/10 scale plan that Niinuma drew on a sheet of plywood. It is no different from the drawings used in the Edo era. Niinuma and his men worked using the traditional Japanese measuring system of *shaku*. Despite the widespread use of the metric system throughout Japan, carpenters, boatbuilders and many other traditional craftsmen still use shaku. It is a decimal-based system: one shaku is divided into ten *sun*, one sun into ten *bu*, and one bu into ten *rin*. The smallest dimension a carpenter typically uses is 5 rin (1.5mm or $\frac{1}{16}$in). The conversions are:

$$1 \text{ shaku} = 30.3\text{cm} = 11^{11}\!/_{16}\text{in}$$
$$1 \text{ sun} = 30.3\text{mm} = 1^3\!/_{16}\text{in}$$
$$1 \text{ bu} = 3.03\text{mm} = \frac{1}{8}\text{in}$$

Principal dimensions and scantlings of *Michinoku-maru* are as follows:

Length:	104.7 shaku	34.55m (113ft 4¼in)
Beam:	29 shaku	9.57m (31ft 4¾in)
Plank keel thickness:	1 shaku	30cm (11¾in) thick
Upper planking:	6 sun	18cm (7in) thick
Stem:	39 × 2 × 3 shaku	12.87m × 61cm × 91.5cm (42ft 2¾in × 24in × 36in)
Rudder post:	1 shaku	30.3cm (12in) in diameter
Deck planking:	2 sun	6cm (2⅜in) thick
Mast height:	92.3 shaku	30.46m (99ft 11¼in)
Mast at deck:	2.5 shaku	75.56cm (2ft 5¾in) square

Niinuma believes that *Naniwa-maru* and *Michinoku-maru* are capable of carrying 150 tons, equivalent to a 1,000-koku ship. Historically, bezaisen were built to carry twice this amount.

Michinoku-maru was built in a small shipyard in Aomori city owned by the maritime museum, and Niinuma's crew lived in a house at the shipyard. They were paid a daily rate, which is typical for carpenters in Japan, who work eight-hour days but can be obligated to work longer (for the same daily rate) as the deadline for completion approaches. Cutting expenses as much as

FIGURE 20

Michinoku-maru in her berth at the Michinoku Traditional Wooden Boat Museum in Aomori City, Aomori, Japan.
(Mr Kon Masaaki)

planking, Douglas fir from Oregon for her backbone, and various woods from China; the one-piece cedar mast came from the forests of Iwate Prefecture. The traditional nails used in the other three ships were all blacksmith-made and represented a large percentage of construction costs. To edge-fasten the hull and cut costs on *Michinoku-maru*, Niinuma used 15mm (⅝in) galvanized lag bolts approximately 1ft long. These bolts were driven at a very acute angle between adjacent planks. Otherwise the construction was traditional. Niinuma calls the frameless hull of traditional Japanese boat construction *zentai hantai*, which means, literally, 'whole resistance'. Although he built large, wooden plank-on-frame fishing vessels in his career, he still considers this traditional method 'reasonable', especially when one considers ease of construction and overall costs. It certainly is efficient: at over 100ft, *Michinoku-maru* was built by Niinuma and his fifteen-man crew in just eleven months, spread out over two years.

FIGURE 21
Naniwamaru sailing
a beam reach on
Osaka Bay.
(Professor Masuyama
Yutaka)

possible, the final cost for *Michinoku-maru* was about 200 million yen (about $1.8 million in US dollars – at 110 yen to the dollar, the exchange rate in November 2007). Material costs represented three-quarters of that total with labour costs accounting for the balance. A steam box was used for bending planking but there were no building moulds; the floors and beams were fitted to hold the planks as they were bent to shape.

Since the launching the museum has sailed *Michinoku-maru* in summer months in the enormous bay at Aomori where she is homeported, moored in front of the maritime museum. Niinuma says that he would like to build more of these ships but he and his crew are getting older and quality materials become harder to find.

The construction of replica bezaisen coincided with a flurry of museum construction in Japan through the 1990s. Many of the projects were justified as infrastructure developments for rural regions; the hope was that they would boost tourism and rural economies. But by 2000 the

Japanese economy had failed to recover and many of the projects faced serious financial shortfalls and, as of this writing, it seems unlikely that any more will be undertaken.

Despite the practical experience, research and strenuous analysis, replicas of Japan's coastal trading ships labour under the same question asked of all reconstructions: How accurate are they? The unknowns surrounding them – how they were built and sailed – far outweigh what we know with certainty. But it is hard to place these particular ships in any larger context. Bezaisen bear almost no relation to the pre-Edo-era Asian traders that preceded them, and Japan's modernisation in the Meiji period was so rapid that they disappeared without a trace. Except for some photographs from the late 1800s and early 1900s showing bezaisen with gaff-rigged mizzens, after contact with the West there was no real development of the type. Bezaisen are a fitting symbol of the withdrawn and xenophobic Edo era, existing in a period of feudal reclusiveness. Less than a decade after Commodore Perry brought his fleet of iron-hulled steamships into Tokyo Bay in the 1860s, forcing Japan to open up to the West, the Meiji government enacted restrictions forbidding the construction of Japanese-style ships over 500 koku – it was an effort to encourage the development of a western-style merchant fleet. Almost overnight bezaisen – along with sword-wielding samurai, shoguns and the tradition-bound world that they inhabited – had become anachronistic.

DOUGLAS BROOKS

BIBLIOGRAPHY
Adachi Hiroyuki, *Nihon no Fune – Wasen Hen (Ships of Japan – Indigenous Designs)*, published by the Museum of Maritime Science (Tokyo), March, 1997.
Marc Bauer, naval architect, Tri-Coastal Marine, author interview, August 2007.
Masuyama Yutaka, Nomoto Kensaku, Sakurai Akira, *Numerical Simulation of Maneuvering of 'Naniwa-maru,' A Full-scale Reconstruction of Sailing Trader of Japanese Heritage*, paper delivered at The 16th Chesapeake Sailing Yacht Symposium, Annapolis, Maryland, March 2003.
Niinuma Tomenoshin, author interviews, Aomori, Japan, 2003, and Ofunato, Japan, 2005.
Wasen (Japanese Ships), exhibition catalogue published by the Museum of Maritime Science (Tokyo), 1990. Captions translated for the author by Taoka Shunji.
Yamamoto Shunichi, 'Kesen-maru; A Sengokubune Replica From Japan', *WoodenBoat* 110, January/February, 1993.
———, letter to the editor, *WoodenBoat* 114, September/October 1993.

11 the schooner sultana

On 8 March 1768 His Majesty's Royal Navy purchased what would prove to be the smallest schooner ever to see active service in the Royal Navy. At just 52 64/92 tons burthen, the schooner *Sultana* was the unlikeliest of warships. Built by American shipwrights at Benjamin Hallowell's South Boston shipyard, she had been conceived as a coastal merchant schooner.

FIGURE 1

Sultana, a reproduction of a 1768 Royal Navy revenue schooner, under sail on the Chesapeake Bay off Annapolis, Maryland. Built in 2001 from a 1768 Royal Navy survey of the original schooner, *Sultana* is considered one of the most accurate eighteenth-century reproductions in the world.

(Drew McMullen)

Destined for a life of hard work in relative obscurity, her fate changed forever when the British Parliament enacted the notorious Townsend Acts, or 'Tea Taxes', just as *Sultana* was being framed up in the Hallowell yard in the summer of 1767.

The burden of enforcing the new Townsend Acts fell to a reluctant Royal Navy. The largest and most professional navy in the world at the time, the Royal Navy did not particularly relish its new role as customs collector. Nonetheless it was the only arm of the British Empire that possessed the experience and resources required to enforce the wide array of taxes that Parliament had levied on the American colonies.

Initially the most significant challenge facing the Admiralty was a compete lack of suitable patrol vessels. Having just vanquished the French in the Seven Years War, the Royal Navy had no shortage of large and powerful warships, but it lacked the smaller and nimbler vessels that would be required to patrol colonial merchant ships and

smugglers in the shallow and constricted waters off the North American coast. Ironically, the solution would be found not in the great shipyards of the British Isles, but rather in the upstart yards of their North American cousins.

In 1768 the Royal Navy faced a challenge that has been chronic throughout its existence – a shortage of funding. This particular shortfall was precipitated by the enormous debts amassed in the course of the Seven Years War. In an effort to fulfil its new customs mission while expending a minimum amount of resources, the navy chose to expand its fleet by purchasing existing American vessels rather than building anew. The approach had several advantages – chief among them being that it was cost-effective. Labour and materials were far less expensive in the Americas and a vessel of *Sultana*'s size could be obtained 'as-is' for a fraction of the cost required to build it from scratch in Britain.

Furthermore, American-built vessels were, by design, well suited for service along the North American coast. In the mid 1760s American shipwrights were well on their way

FIGURE 2
Original draught of the schooner *Sultana* recorded on 21 June 1768 at the Royal Navy Yard in Deptford. The original 1768 lines and construction details recorded in this draught were reproduced without alteration in the modern *Sultana*.
(© National Maritime Museum, Greenwich, London)

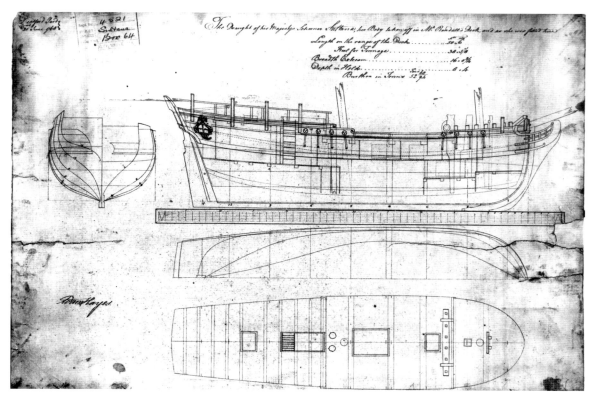

to perfecting what would become the quint-essential American design – the schooner. Nimble, well adapted for sailing upwind and easily managed by a relatively small crew the schooner's characteristics fit the Royal Navy's needs to a tee.

Sultana was the smallest of a handful of American schooners acquired for the Royal Navy in the 1760s. Upon her purchase she was brought to England to be rerigged, refitted and re-armed to make her suitable for her new duties. Then *Sultana* was returned to North America and spent the period from 1768 to 1772 patrolling for smugglers along the Colonial coast from Halifax, Nova Scotia, to Cape Fear, North Carolina. During this time she stopped, rummaged and searched more than 1,000 individual merchant vessels voyaging to and from ports all around the Atlantic.

The activities of *Sultana* and her fellow Royal Navy revenue cutters so infuriated the Americans that these small and relatively defenceless schooners soon became a favourite target for the colonists' anger. In 1773 Benjamin Franklin even went so far as to target his ire towards the Royal Navy's patrol boats in a piece entitled, 'Rules by Which a Great Empire May be Reduced to a Small One':

Convert the brave, honest officers of your navy into pimping tide-waiters and colony officers of the customs. Let those who in time of war fought gallantly in defense of their countrymen, in peace be taught to prey upon it. Let them learn to be corrupted by great and real smugglers; but (to show their diligence) scour with armed boates every bay, harbor, river, creek, cove, or nook throughout the coast of your colonies; stop and detain every coaster, every wood boat, every fisherman; tumble their cargoes and even their ballast inside out and upside down; and, if a penn'orth of pins is found unentered, let the whole be seized and confiscated. Thus shall the trade of your colonists suffer more from their friends in time of peace than it did from their enemies in time of war. Then let those boats' crews land upon every farm in their way, rob the orchards, steal the pigs and the poultry, and insult the inhabitants. If the injured and exasperated farmers unable to produce other justice should attack the aggressors, drub them, and burn their boats, you are to call this high treason and rebellion, order fleets and armies into their country, and threaten to carry all of the offenders three thousand miles to be hanged, drawn and quartered. Oh, this will work admirably!

Sultana narrowly escaped destruction at the hands of angry colonists in Newport, Rhode Island, in 1771 and again off New Castle, Delaware, in 1772. Finally, when her sister-schooner, HMS *Gaspee*, was captured and burned by rebellious colonists near Providence, Rhode Island, the Admiralty concluded that conditions in the colonies had become too dangerous for such vessels. In the autumn of 1772 *Sultana* was ordered to sail for England, where her crew was paid off, the vessel was decommissioned and finally, on 10 December 1772, she was sold for £85 at public auction.

A new *Sultana* is conceived

In 1997, 225 years after the original *Sultana* disappeared from historic record, a handful of people in Chestertown, Maryland, decided to dedicate themselves to building a full-scale reproduction of the Royal Navy's tiniest schooner. At face value, the concept was quixotic. Though small by eighteenth-century standards, the prospect of authentically replicating a 100ft, 50-ton wooden schooner in a town with a population of only 4,500 (and virtually no maritime infrastructure) was daunting. Not surprisingly, the initial plan was greeted with some well-deserved scepticism. Where would the millions of dollars of funding come from? What would be done with the completed vessel? Why pick *Sultana* – a vessel that had never even visited Chestertown?

The challenges are significant for any group that sets out to build and maintain a replica sailing ship, and it was no different for the group from Chestertown. There are few more daunting or less profitable business models than the operation of a large, traditional, wooden sailing vessel and there is

no shortage of 'tall ship' projects that have set
out with grand ambitions only to encounter
insurmountable obstacles along the way.
Fortunately for the Chestertown group, they
had four key advantages that would serve their
project well as it moved from concept to reality.

Without question, *Sultana*'s greatest initial
asset was the involvement of John E. Swain,
the project's innovator and a master shipwright with over thirty years of invaluable
experience. While the services of a master
shipwright are obviously central to the construction of any reproduction vessel, this
individual is generally hired as a contractor
only after much of the design planning is
complete. The inclusion of Swain from the
outset served to guide and ground the effort
while establishing an aura of credibility that
proved critical in attracting support. To the
lasting benefit of the project, Swain was
committed to the long-term success of the
endeavour and worked hard not only to build
an able reproduction of *Sultana* but also to
cement the group of supporters who would

FIGURE 4
The modern *Sultana* requires a crew of six to operate her full set of sails, while the original sailed with a complement of twenty-five men who handled and maintained her more extensive rig under sail for weeks at a time without interruption.
(Drew McMullen)

keep her afloat for the duration of her sailing life.

Ironically, the group's second great asset was that, with the exception of Swain, most of the others who guided the project's initial progress and who would eventually come to compose its Board of Directors, had little or no maritime experience. Rather than a team of sailing buffs, the *Sultana* group included bank and college presidents, businessmen and non-profit professionals. While it might sound odd to cite the *lack* of expertise as an asset for a shipbuilding project, the professionalism and detachment that this

group brought to the project proved enormously helpful. If, at the outset, some of the *Sultana* team couldn't tell a sheet from a halyard, in the long run it was much more valuable that they could read a balance sheet and determine a liability from an asset.

The Chestertown group's third strength was the early definition of a single, clear, credible mission for the new *Sultana* – education. While building and sailing a wooden schooner are vastly enjoyable activities, they alone are rarely reason enough to justify an enormous investment of time and resources. By establishing, at the outset, that any replica vessel it built would ultimately be used as a 'floating classroom', the Chestertown group was able to quickly construct a rational set of criteria by which all of its decisions could be guided. These criteria were important in making even the most fundamental of decisions – including the selection of *Sultana* herself. At 52ft on deck, *Sultana* was large enough to accommodate educational day-trips for a single classroom of students, while not being so enormous that she became unwieldy when underway. Additionally, *Sultana*'s history, steeped in the story of the American Revolution, would allow her to easily integrate into a subject matter that was required in almost every school in the United States.

The final asset was Chestertown itself. Established by the King of England in 1706 as one of seven international shipping ports in the province of Maryland, Chestertown had grown by the mid eighteenth century to become one of the larger ports on the mid-Atlantic coast, a commercial rival for cities

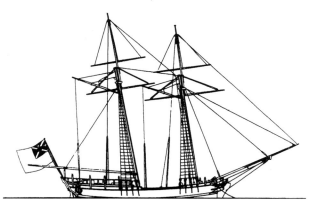

FIGURE 6
Line drawing of *Sultana*'s rig based on spar measurements recorded during her 1768 survey at the Deptford Yard.
(Drawing by John Poicus)

such as Annapolis, Baltimore and Norfolk. Though it faded as a seaport following the American Revolution, by the middle of the twentieth century Chestertown had begun to gain new recognition as one of the United States' best preserved colonial towns. Drawn by the town's history, the surrounding region's pastoral landscape and the unique tidewater culture of Maryland's Eastern Shore, new residents were soon arriving from across the United States and beyond. By 1997, when the

effort to rebuild *Sultana* was initiated, Chestertown boasted a small but incredibly talented population that included international financiers, engineers, authors, artists, entrepreneurs and, yes, shipwrights. Ultimately, the citizens of Chestertown would contribute more than 250,000 volunteer hours and $2 million to the construction of the new *Sultana*.

Building the reconstruction
Less than a year after the original vision for *Sultana* had been conceived, sufficient funds had been raised to begin moving forward with the schooner's construction. As with any multi-million-dollar project there was no shortage of decisions to be made. Generally, these fell into two categories – what was the best way to construct the vessel for safety, longevity, historic accuracy and utility for its future life as a school ship; how could the organisation best take advantage of the construction of *Sultana* to further its mission?

One of the most exciting aspects of *Sultana*'s construction was the wealth of preserved historic documentation about the original vessel. Prior to her purchase by the Royal Navy in 1768, the Admiralty ordered a complete survey to be performed on the schooner to ensure that she was fit for service as a revenue cutter. The results of this survey included a lengthy written technical description of *Sultana*'s construction as well as an exquisite and precise lines plan of the schooner. Amazingly, the Royal Navy and Public Records Office in London has preserved *Sultana*'s 1768 survey for more than 200 years along with the official logbooks of the schooner's Captain, Lieutenant John Inglis, and her master David Bruce. Together, these documents contained more than 2,000 hand-written pages, offering amazing insights into the vessel's design, construction and sailing characteristics.

The task of interpreting these historic documents and transforming them into a modern-day reproduction fell, in large part, to John Swain. While the *Sultana* team consulted with scores of historians, naval architects, engineers, archaeologists, riggers and sailors in North America and Great Britain, it was ultimately Swain's vision that guided the schooner's construction.

Swain's first, and perhaps most significant, decision was that *Sultana*'s reproduction be constructed using the traditional double-sawn framing and carvel planking techniques that would have been used in the original 1768 vessel. While more modern, cost-effective methods of construction, such as 'cold moulding', could have been effectively employed, Swain and the *Sultana* team never seriously considered deviating from the eighteenth-century techniques. Swain was confident that he could use traditional building techniques without breaking the budget and all involved agreed that replicating the 1768 *Sultana* as closely as possible was important for the mission and integrity of the project.

While the basic design and construction of the new *Sultana* would thus be faithful to her eighteenth-century namesake, the new vessel would by no means be a completely authentic replica. The 1768 *Sultana* was probably built to last no more than a decade, all the while being maintained by a full crew of sailors in an era of relatively cheap labour. By contrast, the new *Sultana* was envisioned to have a life span of no less than fifty years and to sail in a world of modern Coast Guard regulations and high labour costs. In order to make the new *Sultana* a practical school-ship for the twenty-first century, Swain and the *Sultana* team elected to employ a variety of more durable materials in the vessel's construction. For the hull, this meant framing in Osage orange – a dense and rot-resistant hardwood – and the limited use of long-lasting, naval-grade silicon-bronze fastenings. In the rig, hemp rope was replaced with Dacron and polypropylene, canvas sails with synthetic, durable proxies and wooden block 'shives' with bronze.

In addition to upgrading to more durable materials, Swain and his team also took the time to add several modern steps to the traditional construction process. Whenever two pieces of wood were joined, the facing surface of each was painted with anti-fungal primer and the joint was bedded in a thin layer of asphalt-based roofing tar. As construction progressed, the completed portions of the vessel were regularly soaked in a solution of dissolved sodium borate, another anti-fungal compound. These simple but important steps would help to slow the eventual intrusion of rot and prolong the life of the new *Sultana* by many decades.

If some non-traditional methods and materials were employed to lengthen *Sultana*'s life span, Swain chose to stick with several eighteenth century construction techniques that, while time consuming, were difficult to improve upon. Perhaps the best example of this was the extensive use of wooden trunnels. Of the approximately 15,000 fastenings that held together the schooner's frames, planks, knees and beams, fully 75 per cent were Osage orange or black locust trunnels (the remainder being silicon-bronze bolts and rods). Swain recognised that, properly employed, wooden fastenings could have the same holding power as metal but would avoid the corrosion and electrolytic problems that even the best metals ultimately present.

While the construction techniques for *Sultana* were mostly updated variations of traditional methods, the pace at which the schooner was built and the type of labour employed were radically different from anything that might have been seen in the 1700s. Typically, the finances and carpentry of large wooden shipbuilding projects put a premium on getting the project done quickly (the 1768 *Sultana* appears to have been built in about six months). For the building of the new *Sultana*, however, Swain and the Chestertown group took the exact opposite approach, electing to construct the schooner at a virtual snail's pace. There were many reasons behind this approach but chief among them were that the ongoing construction of the schooner was seen as a valuable activity in and of itself.

By prolonging the building phase, the Chestertown group gained precious time to develop the organisation and expand its network of supporters – aspects further enhanced by the enormous numbers of volunteers who worked on the schooner's construction. During the three and a half years that *Sultana* was being built, there were never more than four professional shipwrights on the project; working alongside them were more than 100 volunteers who ultimately contributed over 200,000 man-hours to the project.

A successful launching

On 24 March 2001, thirty months after the laying of her keel, the new *Sultana* was launched into the waters of the Chester River

in Chestertown. The launching marked the culmination of more than four years' work on the part of the building crew and thousands of supporters throughout the mid-Atlantic region of the United States.

Following three additional months of rigging and outfitting, the vessel was appropriately commissioned on 4 July, the anniversary of America's declaration of independence from Great Britain – an event that was brought on in no small measure by the controversial activities of British vessels like *Sultana*.

The end of construction marked the beginning of an exciting, yet uncertain, time

for the *Sultana* group. *Sultana* was the only reproduction of a two-masted, double square-topsail, 'Marblehead' schooner sailing anywhere in the world. While great efforts had been made during the planning phase to ensure that *Sultana*'s 200-year-old design would be suitable for her new life as a school ship, at the time of her launching all that Swain and the *Sultana* group had to go on was the informed guesswork of a team of naval architects and consultants. While these modern sources were invaluable, the best indicator of what to expect from the completed vessel came from the historic documents preserved by the Royal Navy – most importantly the logbook entries of *Sultana*'s Captain, John Inglis.

Based on the survey performed by the Royal Navy in 1768, the original *Sultana*, as outfitted in Boston, was a simple merchant schooner, carrying no more than five sails, including a gaff-rigged mainsail, a loose-footed gaff-rigged foresail, two headsails and, perhaps, a single square course on the fore-mast. When the Royal Navy purchased *Sultana* in 1768, she was delivered from Boston to the Deptford Naval Yard outside London to undergo a complete refit. Central to this was a major expansion of the rig from its original five-sail, 'bare-poled', merchantman rig to a much more complex and ambitious rig featuring two topmasts and numerous new sails. Examination of Inglis's logbooks reveals that the Royal Navy version of *Sultana* had as many as thirteen sails including:

1   Main Sail

2   Fore Sail (loose footed)

3   Inner Stay Sail (stay sail)

4   Outer Stay Sail (jib or flying jib)

5   Fore Top Sail

6   Main Top Sail

7   Fore Course

8   Main Course

9   Water Sail
    (probably flown under the bowsprit)

10 & 11   Stunsails (flown off the Fore Top Sail)

12   Stay Sail (fore and aft, flown between the Main and Fore Topmasts)

13   Square Sail (flown from the lower Fore Mast on a dedicated spar).

This expanded rig was only possible with a corresponding expansion of the crew. Based on a standard merchant-ship tonnage-to-crew ratio of 10:1, the 52-ton *Sultana* would probably have sailed with no more than five crew in her original Boston merchant ship configuration; when she departed the Deptford Yard following her refit, she carried a complement of twenty-five sailors, an increase of 400 per cent. This larger crew was essential not only for the operation of the new rig but also to provide the additional manpower needed to search and seize smugglers.

Inglis and the *Sultana* crew quickly learned about some of the unique characteristics of the Marblehead schooner. Originally developed in Massachusetts and greater New England, the Marblehead was designed to be a simple, flexible merchant vessel capable of both coastal and oceanic sailing with a minimum number of crew. The Marblehead hull is characterised by a broad, bluff bow (sometimes referred to as a 'cod head') trailing to a narrow and shapely stern (referred to as a 'mackerel tail'). These aspects of the hull shape produced a schooner with considerable capacity for cargo but one that could also suffer pronounced weather helm when the schooner's sails were not properly balanced. Amidships, the Marblehead design, and particularly the design of *Sultana*, featured a rounded hull that made her tender in a breeze until she was healed sufficiently to bring the ballast into play. Indeed, on their first trip across the Atlantic, Inglis and his crew realised how tender the design could be when they encountered a significant storm just after leaving England. Inglis recorded *Sultana*'s performance in his logbooks:

> September 12, 1768 – Strong gales and squally with rain – brought too under the foresail. Shipped a great deal of sea. Obliged to heave overboard into the sea 12 half-hogsheads of beer to save the schooner from foundering.

Upon reaching Halifax at the conclusion of this crossing, Inglis immediately had an additional 10,000lb of ballast placed in the schooner's hold. Based on this, it seems plausible that during its refit, the Royal Navy failed to add sufficient ballast to compensate for the enormous expansion of sail area.

One of the more interesting facts to be gleaned from Inglis's logbooks is the regularity and rapidity with which the topmasts, sails and yards (both main and fore) were struck and brought to deck. When Inglis encountered or anticipated windy conditions, he clearly

had no hesitation in ordering the entire upper portion of the rig to be brought down, a process that – judging by the logbooks –*Sultana*'s twenty-five-man crew could accomplish in less than an hour. There are numerous instances recorded in the logbooks when the schooner's topmasts and yards were struck and reset multiple times in the course of a week, and on several occasions the task was accomplished twice in a single day!

FIGURE 8
Sultana lies peacefully to her anchor in Commegy's Bight, just south of her home port of Chestertown, Maryland.
(Drew McMullen)

Inglis's need for making such rapid and significant changes to the rig probably springs from two characteristics of the original vessel: her susceptibility to being laid on her side in a good breeze due to the more aggressive rig, and the relative light weight and strength of the topmasts, topsails, yards and associated rigging. Experience with the modern *Sultana* has shown that 20 knots is the upper end of the wind spectrum where the topsails can be prudently flown. In a true gale it is easy to imagine that the 1768 vessel's furled topsails and rig would quickly become an enormous liability. This conclusion is borne out in Inglis's logs, which document two episodes between 1768 and 1772 when the schooner's topsails, topmasts and yards are blown off and lost during unexpectedly strong storms.

A modern performance

While designed and built to stand up to the rigours of transatlantic travel, it is unlikely that the new *Sultana* will ever have the opportunity to make such a voyage or encounter the types of conditions regularly experienced by the original. Still, in her first years of operation, *Sultana*'s reproduction has had numerous opportunities to be tested while sailing the waters of North America's largest estuary, the Chesapeake Bay. In large part, the experience of sailing the modern *Sultana* has confirmed much of what Lieutenant John Inglis recorded in his logbooks.

Like the 1768 *Sultana*, the modern reproduction requires the captain to pay close attention to the balance of the fore-and-aft sails to avoid pronounced weather helm. The forward-most staysail, or flying jib, can be particularly important to balancing the rig when the schooner is sailed close to the wind. When not balanced properly, the helmsman at *Sultana*'s 7ft tiller must use all his strength to keep the schooner from rounding up into the wind. However, with the sails properly set and trimmed, handling the tiller can be a breeze.

Unlike the original *Sultana*, the repro-duction is limited by United States Coast Guard regulations to sailing with only six of the thirteen sails featured in the 1768 Royal Navy rig (the sails featured on the modern vessel include the main, fore, inner stay sail, outer stay sail, fore top sail and main topsail). While this reduced rig functions more than adequately for the vessel's normal sailing routes on the Chesapeake Bay, it is easy to see

how the additional sails would have greatly aided Captain Inglis and his crew in balancing the rig and maximising the vessel's speed under a wide variety of conditions. If there is a particular point of sail where the compara-tive limitations of the modern vessel's reduced rig are most apparent, it is downwind. There is no question that the large square courses flown beneath the fore and main course yards on the 1768 rig would have made the original *Sultana* much more able off the wind.

On rare occasions the modern *Sultana* has reached speeds approaching 10 knots but generally seems most comfortable in the 7- to 8-knot speed range when fully powered in 20–25 knots of wind. These figures match closely with the top speeds recorded by Inglis. While *Sultana*'s reproduction has certain performance advantages – she's coated with modern bottom paint and receives regular hull cleanings – these are almost completely cancelled out by the burden of dragging a single 32in bronze propeller off her sternpost.

One of the most distinctive features of sailing *Sultana* is that, as the vessel approaches hull speed, the fore and aft trim noticeably changes. At speeds above 5 knots, *Sultana*'s bow lowers itself as much as 1ft into the water while the stern rises a corresponding amount. This is almost certainly one of the reasons that Captain Inglis regarded the 1768 *Sultana* as a very 'wet' vessel. Rather than 'slicing' through the water as you might experience on a modern sailboat, the most appropriate verb to describe *Sultana*'s progress through the water, might be 'plough.' The combination of the schooner's bluff eighteenth-century bow and reduced freeboard forward as she approaches hull speed results in a vessel covered with spray in a moderate chop and, at times, awash with up to 6in of blue water amidships when making way through heavier seas – the experience is foreign to many modern sailors but exhilarating nonetheless.

While the reproduction *Sultana* precisely replicates the size, lines and basic rig of the original, there are two aspects of her construction that unquestionably alter her sailing qualities. To conform to US Coast Guard stability requirements for passenger-carrying vessels, *Sultana*'s reproduction is much more conservatively ballasted than was the original.

We know from Inglis's logs that the 1768 vessel was ballasted principally with 'shingle ballast', or medium-sized, rounded stone placed as low in the cargo hold as possible. On the new *Sultana* shingle ballast has been replaced with the combination of an 11,500lb lead shoe bolted to the underside of the schooner's keel and an additional 38,500lb of internal ballast in the form of 75lb lead ingots. While this ballast configuration makes the new vessel far safer than the original, it also results in a vessel that is stiffer in a breeze and quicker to snap back to vertical in a lull or when tacking.

The other modern alteration that impacts the new *Sultana*'s sailing characteristics is the use of modern materials for her standing rigging, running rigging and sails. The natural-fibre shrouds, stays and lines of the 1768 *Sultana* were replaced with galvanised-wire-rope standing rigging (served and parcelled for an authentic appearance) and synthetic polypropylene running rigging. The contemporary rigging materials make the new rig stronger and easier to maintain, but also stiffer, with both standing and running rigging less prone to stretching. Because of the strength of the modern materials, there is both the ability and temptation to push today's *Sultana* further than Lieutenant Inglis might have pushed the 1768 schooner. In this sense, the modern rig (and the modern rigs of many traditional sailing replicas) trades one category of risk for another – while it is less likely that an individual line or component of the rig might fail, the fact that the entire rig can operate in higher winds can actually increase the risk of a truly catastrophic rig failure, including the failure of spars, masts, blocks and metal fittings. Because of this, the captain must be a prudent sailor and resist the urge to push the modern materials to their limit.

Thanks to careful planning and conservative seamanship, the new *Sultana* has sailed with more than 40,000 students in her first decade and, thus far, avoided the perilous sailing experiences of her eighteenth-century namesake. As the vessel and the group of people who guided her creation age, *Sultana* will continue to face new challenges. The maintenance burden for her 185,000lb wooden hull will grow with each passing year and new generations of stewards will need to be identified to shepherd the schooner through her anticipated 100-year lifespan. Though sailing the modern *Sultana* is a different experience from that encountered by Lieutenant Inglis in 1768, the challenges of operating an eighteenth-century vessel in the twenty-first century require many of the same qualities demanded of sailors through the centuries: ambition, organisation and the prudent management of risk. With a little luck these qualities will continue to guide the new *Sultana* as she sails into her future.

Sultana 2001 General Specification

LOS	97ft
LOA	59ft
LOD	52ft
LWL	51ft 3in
LBP	50ft 6in
Draught	8ft
Beam	16ft 8in
Height of rig	67ft
Sail area (excluding main topsail and fore course)	1,830ft^2
Weight	68.05 tons (152,432lb)
Engine	225hp

DREW McMULLEN *with*
CAPTAIN ROBERT BRITTAIN

SULTANA'S PRIMARY DOCUMENTS
'The Draught of His Majesty's Schooner Sultana… 21 June 1768.' Drawing. Negatives 4521–2, collection of the National Maritime Museum: London.
United Kingdom, Public Record Office. *The Logbook of Lieutenant John Inglis, Commander of Sultana, 13 July 1768 to 7 December, 1772*. PRO, Adm. 51/4358: 5,6,7,8,9.
——. *The Logbook of David Bruce, Master of Sultana, 19 July 1768 to 7 December 1772*. PRO, Adm. 52/1455.
——. *Muster tables of His Majesty's schooner Sultana, 1768–1772* (crew lists). PRO, Adm. 36/7269.
——. *Admiralty board orders to survey Sultana, 12 February 1768*. PRO, Adm. 2/237:425.
——. *Survey results of Sultana from the Navy Board, 2 March 1768*. PRO, Adm. 106/3315.
——. *Admiralty Board orders to Navy Board for purchase of Sultana,*

9 March 1768. PRO, Adm. 2/237: 494-5.
——. *Navy Board notice of Sultana's purchase and recommendations for manning and arming, 3 May 1768*. PRO, Adm. 106/2199:40.
——. *Admiralty orders for manning and arming, 4 May 1768*. PRO. Adm. 2/238:5.
——. *Letter from Deptford Yard to Navy Board indicating Sultana ready to receive men, June 1768*. PRO, Adm. 106/3315.
——. *Admiralty Board letter directing Sultana to be put into service, 13 July 1768*. PRO, Adm. 2/238:69.
——. *Admiralty instructions for Sultana's provisioning, 13 July 1768*. PRO, Adm. 2/238: 68.
——. *Admiralty instructions to supply Sultana with brandy, 27 July 1768*. PRO, Adm. 2/238:88.
——. *Letter from Rear Admiral Montagu regarding Sultana's return to England, 8 October 1772*. PRO, Adm. 1/484.

12 HM Bark *Endeavour*

In October 1987 journalist Bruce Stannard, a member of the new Australian National Maritime Museum (ANMM) board, approached Bond Corporation Holdings (BCH) to ask if they would sponsor the construction of a replica of HM Bark *Endeavour*. This was to be a full-size sailing ship and the centrepiece of a proposed floating fleet when the museum was completed in Darling Harbour, Sydney. *Endeavour* was the natural choice: in 1771, James Cook had sailed her along the uncharted east coast of the continent, leading directly to British settlement of Australia seventeen years later.

FIGURE 1
With topsails and topgallants furled, *Endeavour* is comfortable running before a gale.
(Photograph taken for the HM Bark *Endeavour* Foundation, photographer unknown)

Alan Bond, director of BCH, had just won the America's Cup with *Australia II,* built in Fremantle, Western Australia, so he already had the facilities and workforce needed to build a large vessel. He agreed to build *Endeavour* as a gift to the nation to celebrate Australia's bicentennial year in 1988. The Endeavour Project was formed in October 1987, under general manager John Longley, with a proposed delivery date to the ANMM of November 1990. However, what started as a three-year plan turned into seven challenging years at a cost of AU$17 million. Two years into the project BCH was mired in financial and legal problems and on 9 December 1989, the proposed launching date, all building stopped. The workforce of thirty-five was laid off and the builder had unpaid debts of $200,000. Through the following eighteen months, as the challenges grew, so did the commitment, passion and dedication of the Fremantle building team and its many supporters. Many came back to work for free on weekends and in their spare time, and volunteers opened the shipyard to visitors and tourists, keeping alive the ship's motto 'Be excellent to each other'. Yoshiya Corporation of Japan offered to complete the ship but then had to withdraw. Success finally came in August 1991 with the formation of the HM Bark Endeavour Foundation, under the chairmanship of Sir Arthur Weller CBE, with patron HRH Duke of Edinburgh and historical support from the National Maritime Museum, Greenwich. Breathing a huge sigh of relief, the Fremantle team set to work to finish the ship.

As *Endeavour* progressed it became obvious that, although her long-term future lay in education and tourism at the ANMM, she had a vital role to play as an expedition ship. First she should fly Australia's flag on a four-year circumnavigation of the world. Commissioned on 16 April 1994, she departed Fremantle in October for her maiden voyage to Sydney. Over the next eleven years the *Endeavour* replica would sail more than 168,500 nautical miles – she went twice around the world, doubled the Horn and circumnavigated New Zealand and Australia before being handed over to the Australian government and into the care of the ANMM on 17 April 2005.

History

In 1769, a year after His Majesty's Bark *Endeavour* had set sail under the command of Lieutenant James Cook, William Falconer published his first marine dictionary. In it he defined a bark as 'a general name given to small ships, of one or three masts without a mizzen topsail'. He added that the British coal trade applied the term to broad-sterned ships without any ornamental figure on the stern or prow, which 'owe much to the Dutch ships design'.[1]

The sixteenth and seventeenth centuries were a Golden Age for the Dutch. For 100 years their East India Company (VOC) dominated the lucrative Far Eastern spice trade and, closer to home, they held a monopoly on trade with the Baltic countries. All goods in or out of the Netherlands were subject to Dutch taxes that had to be cleared through Amsterdam, making it the shipping, warehousing and financial centre of Europe. As Dutch merchants and shipbuilders grew rich, they wisely invested some of the profits into improving their ships. Over the following years, working through a number of design changes, they produced the *fluyt*[2] – a ship that could carry the maximum cargo on a given length of keel while employing the smallest crew: in modern terms, a bulk carrier.

Fluyts were practical rather than beautiful. Squat, flat-bottomed, rectangular in shape and full-bodied, they were built by the Dutch from light, cheap timbers to be sailed with shorter masts and smaller crews. During the same period the British were building large, heavy oak ships and were frustrated enough to record: 'The Fleming have eaten us out, by reason that they carry halfe as cheape againe as we can, in regard that their fashioned shippes sail with so few men.'[3] It was the Anglo-Dutch wars (1652–72) that eventually broke the Dutch monopolies and, at the same time, provided the British navy with a steady supply of fluyts taken as prizes. Of the estimated 1,200 to 1,500 ships captured, the majority were sold to British shipowners and merchants. But by the end of the war the British had to look again to their own ship-designing skills.

The discovery of coal in the English

FIGURE 2
Volunteer crew working a sail. Despite *Endeavour*'s engines and other modern equipment, the ship is still sailed traditionally and crew must go aloft to shorten, furl or set sail.
(Richard Polden)

FIG 4

FIGURE 4
Looking forward along the completed lower/mess deck, showing fore and main mast positions and hatches.
(John Lancaster)

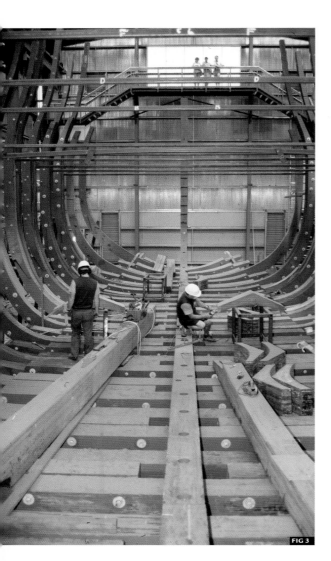

FIG 3

FIG 7

FIGURE 3
Looking forward with the vessel in frame the sheer size of the timbers is visible as is the collier's flat bottom, relatively hard bilge and generous tumblehome.

(John Lancaster)

FIGURE 7
Shipwrights fasten Oregon planks to the starboard side as planking nears completion, April 1992.
(John Lancaster)

FIGURE 5
The 'fashion piece', which joins the side of the ship to the stern, is shaped by a traditional adze.

(John Lancaster)

FIGURE 6
Looking across the starboard quarter towards the bow, the laminated jarrah frames are in place.

(John Lancaster)

Midlands encouraged the development of a northeast shipbuilding industry and the impetus to improve on the fluyt's manoeuvrability and strength. By 1722 the East Coast ports of Whitby, Newcastle, Stockton, Scarborough and Hull were well-established shipbuilding centres, and as the century progressed hundreds of north-country cats shifted coal,[4] alum and local produce south to London, the Channel ports, and across the German Sea (North Sea) to the Baltic countries. Daniel Defoe, visiting Whitby, wrote of the prosperity this had brought to the town where ships were built that 'measure little and stow much…'.[5] Forty-six years later Swedish naval architect Frederick Chapman described these cats as having a narrow stern, projecting quarters, deep waist, no figurehead, being strongly built up to 600 tons, with an average speed of 2.5 knots, very manoeuvrable, with the capacity to sail backwards, and easily handled by a crew of twelve or less. Barks, he said, were similar but had a wider stern.[6] British shipbuilders and merchants had learnt their Dutch lessons well.

During wartime hundreds of colliers were employed by the Admiralty to transport troops, horses, armament and supplies, so it was not just guesswork that prompted the Navy Board to select a Whitby collier for the Royal Society's voyage to the South Pacific. As usual, several of these merchant ships were lying in the Thames in April 1768 and *The Earl of Pembroke,* built by Thomas Fishburn of Whitby, was purchased for £2,307.5s 6d, renamed *Endeavour* and fitted out at Deptford Dockyard where (to the great delight of the Fremantle team 220 years later) her lines were taken off and deck plans were recorded.

Building the replica

A number of the Deptford drawings still exist at the National Maritime Museum, Greenwich and were the basis for drafting the full-size patterns necessary to build the replica. They clearly show the new deck placed on the strengthening beams of the collier, dividing the huge hold in two. This deck provided eighty of Cook's officers and crew with cabins and mess areas and the hold below was big enough to carry all the food

and equipment for ninety-four people on a three-year voyage.[7] The only missing plans were of the stern and rigging.

David Steele's seminal eighteenth-century book, *The Elements and Practice of Rigging and Seamanship,* provided much of the information for the rigging, and two sketches of the stern made by artist Sydney Parkinson during the original voyage gave enough information to extrapolate the stern windows and carvings. Further research into Admiralty archives revealed a 1768 invoice from Deptford shipwrights that corroborated the stern windows and gave further details, including the companion on the quarter deck, the removal and repairs to bulkheads and some cabin fittings.[8]

Many forgotten shipbuilding skills had to be learnt, and when Englishman David White joined the Fremantle team to draft the plans, he brought his extensive knowledge of eighteenth-century ships from twenty years' working in the NMM Draught room.[9]

The Fremantle team agreed that the *Endeavour* replica should be constructed as closely as possible to the original ship but, with modern health and safety requirements and constraints on time and money, they knew that some compromises were inevitable – cutting the timbers in an eighteenth-century sawpit appealed to the purists but not to the accountants.

Building materials represented the first compromise. Many eighteenth-century timbers such as oak, elm and Baltic pine were no longer readily available in the necessary sizes and quantities, nor was iron and flax at a price the project could afford. Jarrah, a West Australian hardwood, was substituted for oak and elm, Douglas fir for Baltic pine. Various other local woods were used including karri, wandoo, blackbutt, tallow wood, tuart and sheoak. Inquiries for suitable grown and recycled woods were made around the country, and a new four-lane highway in New South Wales – on the other side of the country – turned up trumps: numerous big hardwood trees had been felled leaving behind natural curved-grain blackbutt, tallow wood and bloodwood stumps and roots due to be burnt in situ. With the somewhat unusual commission to cut curved-grain timbers in pieces 7ft long, 10in square at each end and shaped like a boomerang,[10] three stout (some said 'mad') volunteers camped out and cut forty natural-grown knees over a period of seven weeks. A large quantity of recycled timber, used for breast hooks and deck fittings, came from various locations, including a redundant timber bridge, an old wheat bin, a defunct wool store, a Second World War munitions factory and a disused nunnery – there would be a lot of Australian history in the new *Endeavour*.

The huge timbers needed for the ribs and large curved wale that runs around the bow, together with the planking immediately above, could not be found, so had to be laminated. Thousands of 1in jarrah boards had to be stacked, then cut to the form of huge wooden patterns. The final shape was then taken apart, each piece being numbered and then glued together in the correct order. It was a laborious and dirty job and for weeks the workshop was covered with a fine red jarrah dust that found its way into everything – eyes, ears, food and drink.

Traditional construction methods soon meshed with modern techniques and safety needs. The floors and bends were fitted and fastened together in the traditional way with chocks and large iron rod riveted over plates at each end – but the iron was galvanised and threaded on one end wherever a really tight joint was required. If the threaded rod was visible then copper rod was riveted over clench plates for an authentic finish, which remained of paramount concern throughout the construction. It was necessary to first heat the thick planking to bend it around the bluff bow, but modern methods failed and the planks kept splitting – when they were heated in a traditional steam box they bent easily into place.

Thousands of trunnels fastened the external and internal timber planking.[11] Iron spikes were used at the end of the planks – except below the waterline, where coach bolts were fitted for added security. Unlike the original, each piece of shaped timber was treated with an epoxy-based preservative and red lead to give extra protection against rot.

Local blacksmith Jan Jansen and his son set up a forge in the workshop and crafted the thousands of traditional iron fittings – bolts, spikes, nails, hooks, plates, mast straps, iron-bound blocks, door hinges, a great cabin-heating stove, the iron firehearth (for cooking), the stern lantern and more than thirty hanging lanterns.

Endeavour, surprisingly, had a considerable amount of carving at the stern. The original Deptford drawings showed an elaborate quarter badge window as well as carrick heads carved in the likeness of a sailor, while Parkinson's sketches indicated further decorative carving on the stern. These drawings were extrapolated and, combined with research into carvings typical of the period, produced the final designs; they were all hand-carved by local artist Jenny Scrayen and finished ashore before fitting.

The twentieth century

The area most affected by modern health and safety restrictions was below decks, for it was necessary to fit an engine room with two caterpillar engines, two generators, electric lighting, sewage system, galley and mess area, refrigerator, freezer, washrooms and heads, and a modern navigation room. It was decided that air conditioning and heating were unnecessarily frivolous, although a number of people would regret this in the future. The collier's huge hold – once used for maximum cargo capacity – provided the solution for most modern requirments. Where Cook had storerooms for himself, his officers and the gentlemen, fish, bread and slop rooms, a quartermaster's cabin and a gunpowder magazine, together with storage for dozens of huge water tierces, hundreds of assorted barrels and casks, food and equipment for ninety-four men for a three-year voyage, the modern equipment could be fitted. To maintain the integrity of the eighteenth century hold all the new equip-ment was fitted in module form. Nothing was built into the hull and everything could be removed at any time with no damage. This modular structure also allowed for extra ventilation: an extra lining was added inside the hull to allow air to circulate through all

FIGURE 8

To a huge cheer *Endeavour* slides into the water just before high tide on 9 December 1993. Her ornate carvings were based on drawings by Sydney Parkinson, the artist who sailed with Cook.

(John Lancaster)

FIGURE 9

On the day of her launching *Endeavour* flew the ensign of the Royal Navy c1768.

(John Lancaster)

the decks, and the original elm-tree pumps, together with two chimneys on the weather deck, became efficient ventilators – no modern additions were necessary.

Some cabins had to be altered from their original purpose. The captain's larder on the afterfall was fitted with the modern navigation room, and one of the gentlemen's cabins became a modern bathroom for the captain and supernumeraries. A few cabins have engineering pipes running through and these have been covered by original fittings such as settle lockers or furniture. The position of all bulkheads, cabins, doors and windows throughout the ship are faithful to the original deck plans. The exception is an extra door cut into the midi-mate's mess bulkhead for quicker emergency exit from this low stern area. When voyaging all cabins are occupied by the crew and it was necessary to fit out the carpenter's and bosun's cabins to sleep three crew in each. However, their storerooms still fulfil their original function. Out of the thirteen original

FIGURES 10 AND 11

When in port, and now on display at the Australian Maritime Museum, Sydney, the cabins (such as these, the great cabin and the mess deck) are set up as museum exhibits depicting life on board in Cook's day.

(John Lancaster and Roger Daniels)

cabins, nine can be arranged as if Cook and his people had just walked off the ship.

Further research was carried out in the UK in order to build the 'time capsule' below decks – designs were found for bulkheads, doors, windows, glass, hinges, hooks, fixtures and fittings, paint, floorcloth, fixed bunks, swinging cots, hammocks, seachests, swinging tables, mess traps, armaments, cooperage, cooking items and all the eighteenth-century personal items – uniforms, books, linens and furniture – needed to create the museum display. Most of the textiles were hand-loomed and -sewn, and many other display items were hand-crafted.

As the ship neared completion the magnificent wooden hull had everyone eyeing each other and asking about the finish. There would have been a mutiny if it had to be painted. Thankfully, it was agreed that varnishing was the correct way to go – according to eighteenth century master Robert Molyneux who had *Endeavour*'s men regularly scraping the sides and 'paying them with varnish of pine'.[12]

The Fremantle team decided against sheathing and filling the hull below the waterline (the original had thin wood planks fitted and filled-in with large flat-headed nails) as it would be more difficult to check for damage; however, a modern white antifouling was applied in imitation of the original 'white stuff', which was a toxic mixture of lead and arsenic.

The colour scheme, both internally and externally, was chosen from extant ship models, paintings and documents of the period, and modern paints were matched to eighteenth century samples. As HM Bark *Endeavour* was the king's ship she was painted externally in the Royal Navy colours of the period: blue, yellow, red and black; internally the mess deck was painted to look like whitewash, and the cabins and officers' mess areas received an oil-based paint of a light-stone shade.

Weather deck

A number of modern navigation items had to be accommodated on the quarterdeck – the navigational instruments and engine controls are housed in two eighteenth-century

binnacles set in front of the helm. These are canvas-covered when the replica is open to the public. Compulsory modern safety additions include two large boxes at the stern for life jackets and buoyancy aids, four inflatable liferafts in the waist, and modern SAT navigation equipment painted black and hidden in the mass of rigging, where few people notice it. In the waist the heavy windlass has a hydraulic motor fitted to raise the anchor and save the modern crew from ruptures and strains; however, at the captain's discretion the crew may raise the anchor using the capstan and muscle power.

Rigging

Cook's *Endeavour* was ship-rigged and the replica follows suit. This means she has square sails on all three masts – top gallants, topsails and courses on the fore and main mast, topsail and fore and aft course (or driver) on the mizzen. The bowsprit supports a lighter jib boom and hangs spritsail and sprit topsail. Between the square sails, are fore and aft staysails. Large rectangular stunsails can also be rigged from the course and topsail yards to the channels, to take advantage of light to moderate breezes; she is, indeed, a magnificent sight when carrying her full set of twenty-eight sails.

Originally the sails were made of flax, which is heavy to work and very expensive. Thus, Duradon, a Scottish man-made material that both feels and looks like flax but is lighter and resistant to rot, was chosen. (Curiously, Duradon dirties easily, making it unpopular with modern yachtsmen but a decided favourite for an eighteenth-century replica.) Most of the sails are machine-sewn and finished by hand.

To find the length of the masts and spars, the team studied the only extant figures available – those taken at Deptford Yard represent survey length, which is not necessarily true length. It was common to measure and pay for only the good wood, while leaving out any damaged or rotten sections. Thus, the modern team worked from Steele's eighteenth century tables, where the size of the main lower mast was calculated by adding the length of the lower deck to the extreme breadth of the ship and dividing by two. From this one measurement all other lengths of masts and spars were calculated. For example, the main topmast is three-fifths of the main mast and the topgallant mast is half of the topmast.[13] Further calculations from these also provided the dimensions of the sails and the standing and running rigging.

On the original ship the small masts and yards were built from solid wood, the lower masts being from solid pieces held together by woldings (lashings). Nothing large enough was available in modern-day Australia, so lengths of Douglas fir were ordered from the USA. These arrived in the middle of a dry 30°+ Australian summer from a 5°- American winter and severe splitting occurred in most of the wood. It left just enough to build the lightest masts and spars but the remainder had to be laminated. All have proven strong and resilient, and during eleven years of sailing only the spritsail and crow jack yard have broken. Again Master Molyneux confirms the masts and spars were varnished.[14]

More than eighteen miles of four-strand left-laid hemp rope were needed to rig *Endeavour*. Hemp was not available and the only natural alternative, manila, has enormous initial stretch. Man-made fibres – polyester and polypropylene – were considered as they have the additional advantages of long life and easy maintenance.

Before making any final decision, the design team developed various mathematical models of the rig and tested all available fibres, with some frightening results: under test conditions the linear stretch of the polypropylene – when used for the long shrouds and stays supporting the masts – produced a domino effect that would have brought the lot crashing down.[15] So the team went back to the drawing board. It was finally decided to use a combination of fibres – polyester for the short, labour-intensive strops, polpropylene for the running rigging, and traditional manila for the long sections of standing rigging and the lanyards between deadeyes and hearts. But where could left-laid manila be purchased?

One of Australia's leading rope manufacturers, Kinnears, came to the rescue. They owned an operational ropewalk and agreed to restore the nineteenth-century machinery especially to make all *Endeavour*'s manila cordage. The rope was pre-stretched by attaching blocks of concrete and hanging the rope from a large construction crane – not very elegant, but it did the job.[16]

The rigging team – many of them experienced square-rig sailors – set to on the immense task of constructing the complete rig. They attached more than 700 hand-made wooden blocks and dozens of deadeyes, belaying pins, hearts and cleats. The blacksmiths wrought countless rigging items including bolts, rings, ring-bolts, plates and hooks, and the whole rig was put together, mast by mast, in a jig outside the main shipyard. When *Endeavour* was launched in December 1993, the rigging was ready and waiting to be installed.

How does she sail?

Various eighteenth-century books on seamanship and John Harland's excellent *Seamanship in the Age of Sail* (1984) clearly outline the theory of sailing square riggers. *Endeavour*'s original logs gave an insight into the amount of sail the ship had carried in various wind conditions, but interpreting 'light airs', 'fresh breezes' and 'moderate gales' as wind speeds took some very creative thinking – before 1805, when Sir Francis Beaufort introduced an empirical measurement for determining wind velocity based mainly on sea conditions, one man's gale was another man's stiff breeze. There remained just one piece of extant evidence: James Cook's report on *Endeavour*'s sailing qualities sent to the Admiralty after returning to England. This report answers a number of standard questions, and comparisons with the replica are neither easy nor always valid. However, the following has been observed.[17]

Cook held his *Endeavour* in high regard and wrote, on his return to England in 1771, 'I sayled from England as well provided For such a voyage as possible and a better ship For such a Service I never would wish for.' Whitby colliers were his chosen vessels from then on. The replica also rates highly with those who have sailed her. Captain Chris Blake,

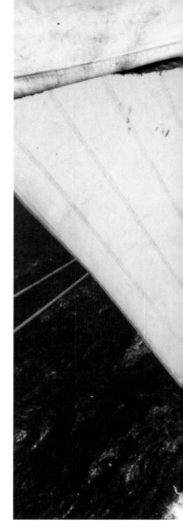

FIGURE 12
HM Bark *Endeavour* under
full sail in the Bass Strait.
(Jenny Bennett)

FIGURE 13
Furling sail on the
bowsprit.
(Richard Polden)

FIGURE 14
The rigging has some 750
blocks, handmade from
she-oak.
(John Lancaster)

Endeavour's master 1994–2005, agrees with Cook and says that in ideal conditions the ship just steers herself. During the crossing from Galapagos to Tahiti in 2005, captain-of-tops, Malcolm Evans, confirms that the ship remained on course with no assistance from the helmsperson for over three hours.

Regarding *Endeavour*'s best speed, Cook reported that 'with the wind a point or two abaft the beam she will then run 7 or 8 knots and carry a weather helm.' Bosun Anthony Longhurst states that with winds 25–30 knots aft of the replica's beam, she will run in excess of 9 knots. She can also exceed this. When caught by an offshore wind of 48 knots off the big island of Hawaii in a flat sea with too much sail up, the ship averaged 11.8 knots for one hour. Captain Blake notes, however: 'we

were caught by surprise and it seemed prudent to leave the sails where they were rather than try to bring them in.'[18] Sailing from Cape Horn towards the Falkland Islands, the replica sustained 10.24 knots over twenty-four hours, with winds averaging between 30 and 40 knots over the port quarter (often reaching more than 50 knots with gusts 65–70). It is doubtful that Cook would have risked his sails in such conditions.

The collier's tendency to carry 'a weather helm' is true also of the replica. Falconer defines griping (weather helm) as 'the inclination of a ship to run to windward of her course, particularly when she sails with the wind on her beam or quarter. This effect is partly occasioned by the shock of the waves that strike the ship perpetually on the weather

quarter, and force the stern to leeward; but chiefly by the arrangement of the sails which disposes the ship continually to edge to windward, while in this situation of sailing.'

Cook further reported that when close-hauled the ship steered well and ran about 5 knots; while in a 'topsail gale' she ran 6 knots. (Cook probably defined a 'topsail gale' as one in which the topsails did not have to be reefed. The *Endeavour* replica sails with topsails set in winds of up to 25–30 knots, so perhaps we can interpret an eighteenth century gale as such wind speeds.) In a letter to his old employer, John Walker of Whitby, Cook continue: 'in about 3 Weeks time got round Cape Horn into the South Sea without ever being once brought under our close reefed Topsails, however, we had no want of Wind.'[19]

The replica sails in winds of up to 55 knots and her 'high topsides and buoyant bow easily lift her and let the seas pass under, and it is rare for a big sea to break onto the decks'.[20]

When winds exceed 55 knots, however, *Endeavour* has to lie to – in other words she must stop sailing. The original ship did this on 7 January 1769 and Cook reported:

First part Strong gales with excessive hard Squales accompney'd with rain, at 9pm wore and brought too her head to the westward under the Main sail, and reff'd the Fore sail for the first time; the Storm continued with little intermission until toward Noon when it abated so as we could set the Topsails close reef'd.[21]

And the eighteenth-century naturalist Joseph Banks confirmed:

> The ship during this gale has shewn her excellence in laying too remarkably well, shipping scarce any water tho it blew at times vastly strong; the seamen in general say that they never knew a ship lay too so well as this does, so lively & at the same time so easy.[22]

In similar conditions on the replica, the fore-course is usually set with a first reef, some-times a second reef, which lifts the bow and counteracts the downward force generated by the fore topsail. In high winds the fore topsail is usually set in third reef, or handed com-pletely. By handing the topsails the centre of gravity is lowered making the ship more com-fortable, as Captain Blake comments: 'not quite what is usually depicted in paintings, but then you always have artistic licence to think about'. Here the replica's natural tendency to round up helps her to sit out a storm.

To change course on a square rigger it is usual to 'wear ship' or 'go about' and the replica will tack[23] through approximately 120 degrees. This is borne out by Banks:

> Wind as hard hearted as ever, we turnd all day without loosing any thing, much to the credit of our old Collier; who we never fail to praise if she turns as well as this.[24]

Thank goodness for a landlubber on the original voyage – Banks recorded many things that a sailor of the day would rarely have mentioned.

The collier's easy manoeuvrability is frequently recorded in the original journals as Cook sailed her through many difficult coastal situations, and his future voyages on Whitby colliers *Resolution*, *Adventure* and *Discovery* also bore this out – wearing, tack-ing, box hauling, sailing backwards, off lee shores, on and off anchorages were all easily done, and the replica is as manoeuvrable.

As previously discussed, without Cook's wind speeds it is difficult to make definitive comparisons; both vessels record the same average speed of 2.5 knots. The replica recorded this when under continuous sail during a six-week voyage from Cairns, Queensland, to Bali, Indonesia, filming the BBC documentary *The Ship* in 2001.

Armaments and anchors

When *Endeavour* left Deptford in 1768 she picked up her armament of ten 4-pounder guns and twelve swivel guns from Galleons Reach on her way down the Thames. She also carried six anchors. During the grounding on the Great Barrier Reef in 1770, six guns were among the stores thrown overboard to help lighten the ship, and an anchor was lost. In recent years all of these have been recovered, restored and replicated.[25]

Build *Endeavour* – why bother?

Historical replica ships are difficult and challenging to build and even more so to maintain, so why bother?

Although financially challenging to operate, *Endeavour* has proven the ideal size for voyaging as she can offer forty places to paying crew and earns additional income from port exhibitions.

The replica has added to our knowledge of eighteenth-century building and sailing tech-niques in a way that a book or static display could not, for neither needs to weather storms at sea. And it's not all about sailing – the iron firehearth was used to cook two traditional hot meals for fifty-six people each day of the BBC six-week voyage in 2001, probably the first in-situ use of an eighteenth-century ship's stove ever carried out in the last 200 years.

Endeavour has been described by the National Maritime Museum in Greenwich as the best eighteenth century replica ship built and the ANMM will make sure that *Endeavour* is kept historically accurate. With guaranteed funding from the Australian government and a commitment to keep her in survey and sailing for many years to come, the future looks promising for the replica of Captain James Cook's first ship of discovery – a great legacy to the many years of hard work and commitment by the Fremantle team, the Board of Directors, and the office and shore staff.

ANTONIA MACARTHUR

HM Bark *Endeavour* specifications

Launched:	9 December 1993
Commissioned:	16 April 1994
Dockyard:	Mews Road, Fremantle, Western Australia
Displacement:	550 tonnes
Gross tonnage:	397
Length extreme (end bowsprit to end stern)	143ft 5in (43.7m)
Length overall:	109ft 3in (33.3m)
Length waterline:	101ft 5in (30.92m)
Beam:	29'ft in (8.89m)
Depth of hold:	11ft 4in (3.45m)
Draught:	11ft 10in (3.6m)
Sails:	27; 9 square, 8 fore and aft, 10 studding sails
Height of mizzenmast:	78ft 9in (24m)
Height of mainmast:	127ft 11in (39m)
Height of foremast:	109ft 10in (33.5m)
Machinery:	Two 405hp, 6-cylinder Caterpillar diesels with 4.5:1 reduction gear boxes driving 3-bladed, 4ft diameter controllable-pitch, fully-feathering propellers. Two diesel generators, one for day running and one for overload and night operations. Fuel capacity of 24,600 litres.
Speed:	Average under sail 2.5 knots; under engine 5 knots
Sea crew – professional:	16
Voyaging crew – amateur:	36
Supernumeraries – passengers:	4

Photographs of HM Bark *Endeavour* reproduced coutesy of the Australian National Maratime Museum

NOTES
[1] William Falconer, *An Universal Dictionary of the Marine.* 1769.
[2] Alan McGowan, 'The Dutch influence on British Shipbuilding', paper from thesis by Prof Ralph Davis, *1688, The Seaborne Alliance and Diplomatic Revolution*, edited Charles Wilson and David Proctor, Greenwich, Bendwood Press, UK 1989.
[3] Ibid
[4] By the late 1740s London needed 1 million tons of coal a year for industry and homes, delivered by some 1,000 ships.
[5] Daniel Defoe, *Tour through the Eastern Counties of England 1722*. Can be downloaded free from www.gutenberg.org.
[6] Fredrik Henrik Chapman, *Architectura Navalais Mercatoria*, Stockholm 1768.
[7] NMM Greenwich Admiralty Draughts.
[8] PRO Adm106/3315 Yard Officers to Navy Board, 19 April 1768.
[9] David White, 'The Frigate Diana', *Anatomy of the Ship*, Conway Maritime Press, Annapolis 1987.
[10] Les and Rose Oxenbridge and Neville Casey camped out and cut these stumps near Herons Creek south of Port Macquarie, NSW, Nov–Dec 1991. Highway contractors Cooks Ltd helped with moving big logs. Oxenbridge/author's email Nov 2007.
[11] One trunnel was taken around the world in the US space shuttle *Endeavour* on her maiden flight in 1992. On her return to earth, shuttle commander Captain Dan Brandenstein hammered it into the replica's sternpost, thus establishing a link between past and future.
[12] PRO Adm55/39, ff.57d–62d. Master Robert Molyneux, *Endeavour* journal.
[13] David Steele, *The Elements and Practice of Rigging and Seamanship*, 1794, facsimile Sim Comfort Associates, London 1978.
[14] PRO Adm55/39, ff.57d–62d.
[15] 'The stretch characteristics of polypropylene have a domino effect as you go higher up the rig, as the shrouds for the topmasts are attached to the shrouds for the lower mast just below the top. As the lower shrouds stretch under the load from the topmast, the point of attachment effectively moves up, which then throws unbearable twist movements on the lower mast caps, which in bad weather would have failed. The same would have happened with the topmast, and consequently the topmast caps would also have failed. Basically the rig above the lower masts would have all come crashing down even though not a single rope would have failed.' John Longley, General Manager, *Endeavour* replica project.
[16] 'The stretch characteristics of manila are very different. The rope for the lower shrouds would fail at about 8 tons, but after the initial construction stretch is taken up, the stretch gets much less as the microscopic natural hooks in the fibres start catching on each other. In fact as it nears its breaking point the stretch characteristics of manila (and indeed hemp) are similar to a modern aramid fibre like Kevlar. So if you take up the construction stretch and then preload the shrouds with the deadeyes and lanyards, you end up with a very stretch resistant set of lower shrouds that provide a fixed takeoff point for the topmast shrouds, and subsequently the topgallant shrouds and the whole thing works.' John Longley.
[17] PRO Adm95/30 Cook's report 3 August 1771 to Admiralty is on a pre-printed requirement sheet with standard questions.
[18] Personal email 2007.
[19] Letter sent from his home in Mile End, London, 17 August 1771.
[20] Anthony Longhurst, one of the replica's bosuns on the first world voyage; he now works as *Endeavour* shipwright at ANMM Sydney.
[21] Cook's log 7 January 1769 p 40
[22] *The Endeavour Journal of Sir Joseph Banks*, DVD University of Sydney. p81.
[23] At this time 'tacking' meant the operation of 'going about', not the modern meaning which includes a progress. For full description see John Harland's *Seamanship in the Age of Sail*, Conway Maritime Press, 1984, p12.
[24] 11 Dec 1769 northern New Zealand p 285
[25] The guns were recovered between 1969–1972 by Defence Standards Laboratories. The anchor was recovered by David Hume, Endeavour board member 1988–2005, and is now on display in the Endeavour Wing of the Cooktown Museum, Queensland. Full details: *Cook's Cannon and Anchor: the recovery and conservations of relics from* HMB *Endeavour* by Dennis Callegari. Kangaroo Press, 1994.

13 The pride of Baltimore

The authentic wooden water cask broke its lashings, crashed across the sole and capsized a 5-gallon drum of authentic (and molten) beef tallow in its mad wake. Several sea chests went adrift and sailed about in the tallow, as did half a cord of loose firewood. The authentic, brick, wood-burning stove had been stifled, filling the hold with black smoke. Waking with a start, I jumped on the cordwood to avoid the tallow, ran up the forward ladder and puked (authentically) to leeward.

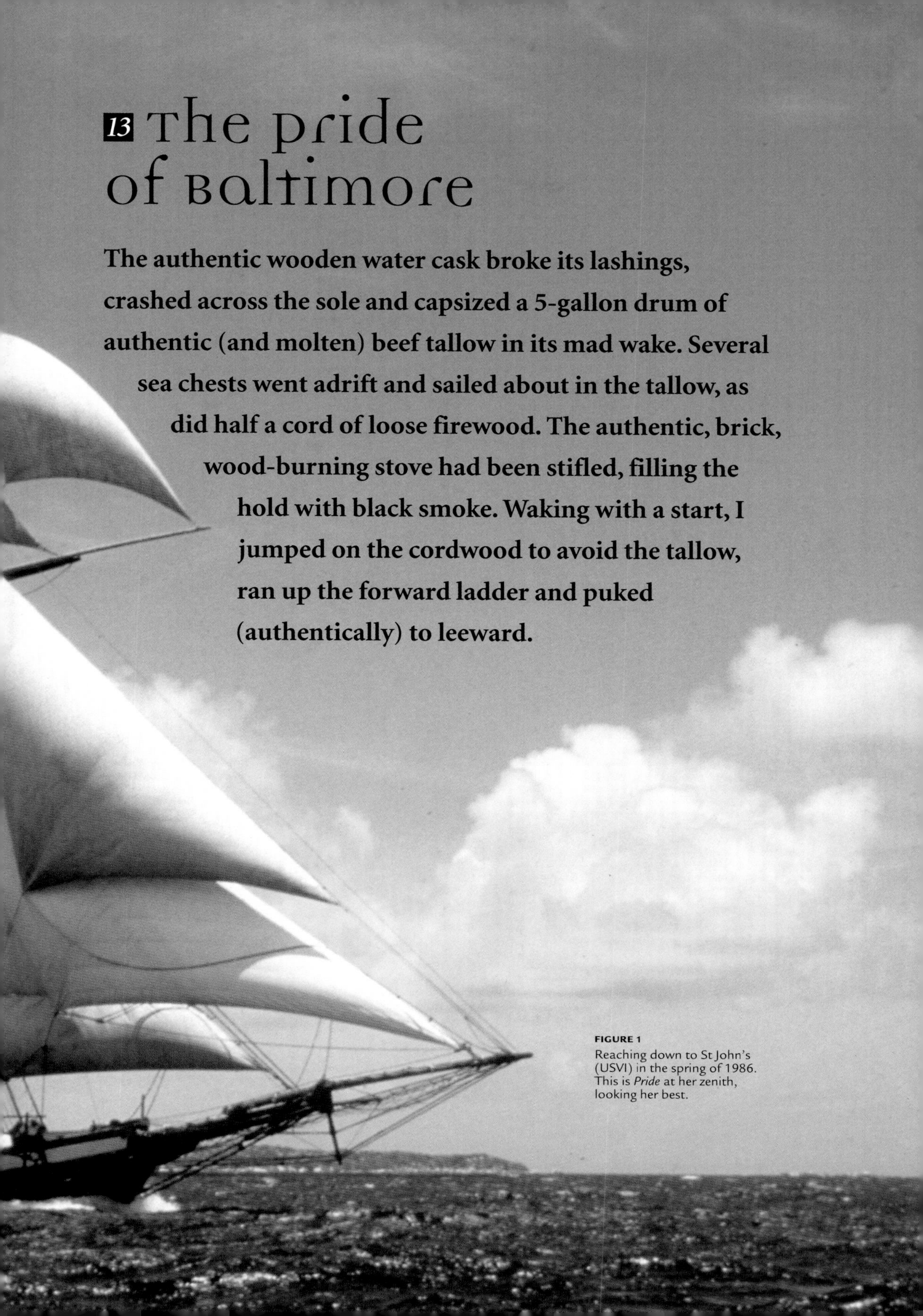

FIGURE 1
Reaching down to St John's (USVI) in the spring of 1986. This is *Pride* at her zenith, looking her best.

On deck it was little better. A northeasterly gale was smashing straight into the Gulf Stream. Under bare poles, *Pride* was running down the edge of a bleak and lumpy Atlantic with no lights, no navigation, no radio and no other vessels in sight. We were sailing a ship we'd built from wood, rope and iron with our own hands. It was authentic... *it was real.*

Pride of Baltimore was a low, black, furious little ship with too much sail on her sharply raked spars; by any measure a 'Baltimore clipper'. Unconstrained by regulation, she was the first, perhaps the only, replica of that much-eulogised type where the designer and builder attempted to make everything truly authentic. Indeed, launched in February 1977, she was the most authentic operational replica vessel ever built in the US. On 14 May 1986 she capsized, filled and sank in mid-ocean, taking four young sailors[2] to the bottom of the sea, three miles below.

Baltimore clippers
The history of the Baltimore clipper has been told.[3] It is short but rich with danger, ingenuity, bravery, trickery and crime. In eponymous Baltimore it is mythological, a purely heroic story of privateers and innovative builders.

It was during the first fifteen years of the nineteenth century that Baltimore clippers emerged as a type and flourished. They did not spring into an unsuspecting world like the first ironclad or the V2 rocket, but were equally radical and effective. Although claimed by Baltimore, the class had many antecedents in the US and abroad. They were the immediate descendants of large, fast American schooners and brigs, built in different ports by different shipbuilders and, although they became known as *Baltimore clippers*, they were built elsewhere in the fifteen American states and even abroad.

What made a Baltimore clipper? No two were alike but in common they had huge, versatile sail plans with extremely tall and raking masts and minimal standing rigging. Contemporary paintings all show flush-decked ships nearly devoid of ornamentation, with flat sheers and little freeboard. The bow and sterns were raked and the midship sections had large deadrise with slack bilges; by shape and contract, they were all 'sharp built'. But the two truly defining character-istics were that they were radically fast and weatherly.

A short history
The type was built for evasion and capture: first smuggling and blockade running, then privateering and, finally, illegal slaving. Although between 1783 and 1812 the US was mostly at peace with Europe, it was a time of upheaval and uncertainty in international trade. Britain and France were almost con-stantly at war from 1793 and strove mightily over trade and control of the West Indies. American merchants prospered and so did American shipbuilders, who profited by supplying fast ships. The development of the Baltimore clipper was not completely linear but the type did broadly evolve in response to historical circumstances.

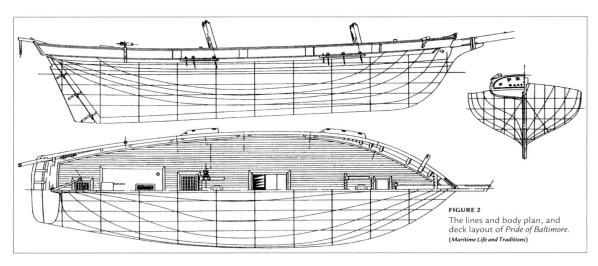

FIGURE 2
The lines and body plan, and deck layout of *Pride of Baltimore.*
(*Maritime Life and Traditions*)

During the American Revolution (War of Independence) Britain imposed a general blockade on shipping, and the large, fast schooners then built were the immediate antecedents of the Baltimore clipper. After the war, the domestic need for speedy vessels dried up as British (and French) interference in American trade decreased; however, the surplus found a ready market abroad. The Caribbean became a hotly contested sideshow to the European wars and most of the islands changed hands at least once. Several countries, but principally France and Britain, employed numerous fast vessels to defend their valuable West Indian trade, or to attack that of other countries. In the late eighteenth century the American sharp schooner was widely known and replicated in European shipyards.

The first ships that we would now recognise as Baltimore clippers were built specifically for blockade running. The year 1803 marked the beginning of the first Napoleonic War, an increased dominance of the British fleet and its total blockade of French trade. In response the French made use of the Baltimore clipper, mainly to enable continued commerce with their West Indian colonies – these were fast vessels that could still carry substantial cargo.

In 1805 Britain destroyed the combined Spanish and French fleet. The British Royal Navy was now supreme and only the swiftest of vessels could hope to slip in or out of French ports. French naval shipbuilding essentially ceased; instead, the French had built abroad a series of Baltimore clipper

armed private warships – privateers, carrying *lettres de marque*. (A 'letter of marque and reprisal' was a rule of war, an official commission authorising a privateer to cross the frontier [*marque*] and seize or destroy specified assets of the enemy nation – in this case Britain. According to international law, a privateer was only entitled to attack enemy vessels under specific conditions and, in return, the crew of such a vessel should be treated as prisoners of war. However, potential profits to owners and crew were huge and sometimes mistakes were made…. The line between privateering and piracy was fine.[4])

With no hostile foreign fleet to oppose her, Britannia ruled the waves and with that absolute command came absolute contempt for the smaller, newer, somewhat annoying seafaring countries. But, although supreme after Trafalgar, Britain's sea power was stretched to its limit blockading French ports and interdicting their trade.

In 1812 the Americans launched their puny navy against the mighty British to early, and somewhat surprising, success. Some of the American ships were sharp naval schooners, the apotheosis of the 'Baltimore clipper' type – the fast, versatile, heavily armed and heavily manned vessels, generally beamier and sharper but with less depth of hold than previous ships.

Peace came to Europe and the US with the Treaty of Ghent in 1815 – a catastrophe for Baltimore's shipyards, as contracts for sharp schooners ceased. But there is always a war somewhere and some of the best former privateers were soon sold to the Caribbean and South America where Spanish American colonies were rebelling and fast sailing ships were in great demand. Some also turned to trades where the requirement was for fast transport of perishable, high-value items: fruit from the West Indies, slaves from Africa.

In the eighteenth century most slavers had been large, relatively slow ships, which proudly carried the flag of their country. Slaving was still legal and there was no call for fast vessels that couldn't stow much human cargo. However, early in the 1800s public sentiment against slavery, and particularly slaving, was increasing, especially in Britain. Although slavery itself was not abolished until

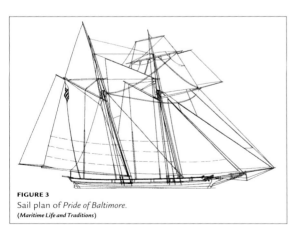

FIGURE 3
Sail plan of *Pride of Baltimore*.
(*Maritime Life and Traditions*)

later – 1833 in Britain, 1865 in the US – enslavement and slaving were banned by international treaty in 1807. The Royal Navy was fully occupied with war until 1815 but by 1816 had established a permanent anti-slaving squadron off West Africa. After that, abolitionist pressure only strengthened and by the mid-1820s the Royal Navy was strongly enforcing anti-slaving laws at sea. The result was a renewed demand for small, fast sailing ships. So began the final career for the Baltimore clippers.

Some former privateers went directly into the slave trade and the first Baltimore clippers built specifically for slaving were close models of these earlier ships. However, the hull form did evolve to greater depth of hold and tonnage: since slaving vessels principally survived by speed and evasion, they generally carried no cannon, which meant the main deck could rise to increase interior volume without adversely affecting stability.

Privateers had to be exceptional all-around

FIGURE 6
The heavy bowsprit spreaders, fondly called 'B-52's' by the crew, were added to stay the jibboom. They may have been anachronistic, but before they were installed it was impossible to carry the jibs in a wind over 15 knots.

FIGURE 7
The main is unfortunately hung up on the topping lift in this otherwise lovely photograph. The ringtail could only be set in moderate conditions. Note the hump in the sheer, evidence of the weak construction and lack of longitudinal strength.

FIGURE 4
Leaving Tortola. The leeward studdingsail is ineffective and was not normally set. The headsails were always less than optimal due to the staying and sheeting angles.

FIGURE 5
Pride of Baltimore during the first year of operation when the sails and crew shirts were still clean. The author notes that the wretched little skiff he built in five days, seen here on the main hatch, has not yet been lost overboard.

sailers both to attack and evade, near shore, in mid-ocean and in all types of weather. Slavers merely had to evade. Consequently their rigs were optimised for the limited areas in which they operated: the West Coast of Africa, the Middle Passage and the Caribbean – light air off Africa and pretty consistent leeward sailing elsewhere. Although the topsail schooner persisted, the rig of choice for the purpose-built slaver became the brig.

The Baltimore clipper did not suddenly disappear; it just changed into something else. Baltimore yards continued to build sharp schooners for many years, although the type became progressively more burdensome and less extreme. Many sharp topsail schooners and brigs were built specifically for the new West Indian fruit trade as late as the 1850s and some later vessels found their way to China to trade opium.

The vessel often identified as the last Baltimore clipper was *Ann McKim*, built in Baltimore in 1832. However, she was a relatively large ship-rigged vessel built for general cargo and probably should be remembered rather as the first of the extreme clippers. In the end the vessels now immortalised as

'Baltimore clippers' wore out, were wrecked or simply forgotten.

Sailing fast

If there was a single defining characteristic of the Baltimore clipper it was pure speed; speed downwind, speed to weather, speed in all conditions. In retrospect, there was no single technological advance that enabled the creation of the Baltimore clipper; rather it was a rational combination of existing craft and knowledge along with a single advance in technology.

Hull form

To make any vehicle go fast, the forces that propel it must be increased while the forces that impede are decreased. On sailing vessels, there is also a coupling between these two sets of forces. To go faster and more efficiently, the sailing rig and hull form must be enhanced together. It makes no physical sense to put a highly efficient rig on an inherently slow and leewardly vessel. To sail to weather, the hull has to develop lift force in the water to counter-balance the leeward sail force; generally, the more sharp or foil-shaped a hull, the more lift it can make to weather. Unfortunately, there are

few remaining plans of the Baltimore clippers
and the few records that do survive show vessels
that varied greatly in length, beam, depth and
tonnage, but they were all 'sharp built'.

Another facet in making a sailing vessel go
fast is keeping it upright under canvas sufficient
to propel it forward. In short, heeling is bad, it
increases the drag force of the sails, reduces the
available propulsive force, increases the
displacement and creates weather helm. In
purely displacement sailing vessels, stability
comes from a low centre of gravity and form
stability. The lower the centre of gravity is
relative to its buoyancy, the more stable the
vessel. With its extreme deadrise the sharp hull
of a Baltimore clipper contributes in two ways
towards its stability: ballast can be stowed lower
and the centre of buoyancy is relatively high.

Versatile rig

Pride was a topsail schooner – square topsail
and topgallant on the foremast. There were
Baltimore clipper topsail schooners, double
topsail schooners, brigs, hermaphrodite brigs,
brigantines and even sloops. However,
evidence suggests that the topsail schooner
was the most prevalent rig.

Sails were typically of tightly woven
American cotton canvas. Cotton duck was
invented in 1811 in the US and was, at first,
considered ersatz, a cheap replacement for
flax. However, it was soon found that tightly
woven canvas held its shape better and was
less porous than flax. Throughout the war of
1812 British sails were flax, but most
American heavy sails were cotton. This is
believed to be one of the main sources of the
sailing superiority of the clippers.

To sail closer to the wind, sails must be
sheeted or braced closer to the centreline.
Baltimore clippers succeeded because they
were able to hold the critical sail shape closer
to the wind and thus reduce drag. Furthermore, with their fore-and-aft rig, Baltimore
clippers were more weatherly than the ships
of the enemy. The ship-rigged British frigates
were fuller, bigger, heavier and almost entirely
square rigged: competently sailed, such a ship
could tack in about 140°; conversely, the sharp
schooner could tack through about 90°.

Thus, any time a clipper wished to escape

from a pursuing frigate, she merely had to
point higher and sail away to weather. During
the war with the British, privateers gleefully
reported luring a frigate escort to leeward and
then, when it was sufficiently removed from
the convoy, turning back to windward to
capture one of the merchantmen.

Huge crews

Part of the general success of Baltimore
clippers was the relatively numerous and
motivated crews. Though supreme at sea, the
Royal Navy in 1812 was under-manned and
stretched to its limit. Some sailors were con-
scripts and often lacked for zeal. In contrast,
the under-employed, blockaded, American
sailors were numerous and, on privateers,
always eager and greedy volunteers. The
following is part of a table from Coggeshall's
History of American Privateers showing vessels
that fitted out in Baltimore early in the war:

Name	Long guns	Short guns	Crew	Types of guns
Rossie	1	13	120	12s, 24s, 6s
Comet	2	12	120	9s, 12s
Dolphin	2	10	100	9s, 12s, 6s
Nonsuch		12	100	12s
Highflyer	1	7	100	12s, 6s
Globe	1	7	90	9s, 12s, 18s
America	2	14	115	9s, 24s, 6s

More than 100 crewmen on a flush-deck
sailing ship less than 100ft long – where did
they all sleep?

Building *Pride*

In September 1975 the City of Baltimore
issued a Request For Proposal (RFP), to build
a 'Baltimore clipper Ship'. Although the RFP[5]
specified the vessel was to be 'an authentic
example', it never seemed that the civic leaders
cared too much about the authenticity. The
city was undergoing a massive redevelopment
and the Inner Harbor was being cleaned up
and made ready for the public. Principally the
city wanted something, *anything*, floating in
the water that people would want to come
and see. It was to be an ornament; luckily,
there were two men who had a rather
different vision.

Thomas Gillmer[6] was the designer. After

retiring from teaching at the US Naval Academy, Professor Gillmer pursued his interest in the history of naval architecture and ship design. For his research on the new vessel, he went back to the source material. He used standard naval architectural methods to compare forms and rigs of those vessels for which he could find records, and derived a typical Baltimore clipper hull form and rig. The result was *not* a replica of a particular hull or rig but, rather, a new design.

Melbourne Smith was the shipbuilder, although he had had no previous experience. He was an artist and illustrator who worked principally for the Naval Institute Press in Annapolis and his bid to build the vessel was surely helped by the fact that the only image the city had of a Baltimore clipper was a painting by Melbourne himself. But both Gillmer and Smith were serious about trying to determine how these vessels were built and operated and they made substantial efforts to use authentic materials for the new vessel.

Iron

The defining engineering material of the eighteenth century was 'puddled iron' made in coal-fired furnaces. Iron and steel are not synonymous; steel is an alloy made principally of iron, and a means of industrial steel production was not invented until 1856. Thus, there was no steel structure on any historic Baltimore clipper. Steel is stronger, tougher and harder than iron but iron works well when hot and resists corrosion[7] after fabrication. Iron in shipbuilding had been completely supplanted by steel early in the twentieth century and by the 1970s had essentially disappeared.[8] However, for *Pride*, all the fittings were wrought on site[9] from historically correct iron.

Hemp and hand-laid rigging

Wire rope, which has been the standard material for ship rigging since the 1860s, was not even invented until the 1830s. Even the largest ships had natural-fibre standing rigging prior to that and hemp was the rope of choice, preferred for its long fibre length, rot resistance and low stretch. By 1976 good-quality hemp rope was history. Industrial hemp had disappeared and, short of planting

and harvesting it (illegal in the US!), processing the fibres and then creating a ropewalk, there was little possibility of creating authentic hemp standing rigging.

Without hemp the builder did his best to be authentic. Wire-rope standing rigging, though strong and available, does not look like the historic, relatively massive, rope rigging. So, instead, the designer and builder decided to substitute spun polyester (Dacron) for hemp. Naturally, they were well aware that polyester was more elastic than hemp, but had the idea that if the lower shrouds, for example, were cable laid (by hand) and then pre-tensioned and prevented from relaxing, the result would be authentic in appearance, strong and sufficiently stiff. So the standing rigging was laid up, stretched, then wormed, parcelled and served along its entire length. It had the right dimensions and feel but lacked genuine authenticity.[10] Unfortunately, it also proved to be not functional – though stronger than hemp, polyester is inherently stretchier.

Hand-made blocks

British naval blocks of the early 1800s were machine-made with great precision, generally with elm shells and lignum vitae sheaves on iron pins. However, due to trade restrictions and lack of machine manufacturing in the US, the blocks on historic Baltimore clippers were probably hand-made with wooden shells and sheaves, iron pins and mostly stropped with hemp rope; some of the more highly loaded blocks would have been stropped with iron. *Pride*'s blocks were handmade with ash shells and steel pins. The sheaves were turned from a phenolic laminate. When built, all the blocks were stropped with three-strand, spun polyester rope.

Flax sails

Three of *Pride*'s original sails were made in England from flax; they were wonderfully soft and had a lovely feel to them.

Ballast

Baltimore clippers were quite heavily ballasted, typically with a mixture of iron and stone. Being denser and immensely more valuable, the permanent iron ballast was stowed tightly in the bilges under stone. As anyone who has ever emptied the bilge of a vessel ballasted with loose cast iron knows, the material corrodes in seawater, making a huge mess. *Pride*'s iron ballast consisted of iron granules cast in polyester blocks with a resultant density only slightly greater than the granite cobbles placed on top.

Tarred seams

Deck seams on traditionally built wooden ships are still filled with 'tar'. Today this is a proprietary mix[11] or a concoction of asphalt roofing tar, pine tar and other additives; either mixture is heated and then poured into the deck seams. Two hundred years ago there was no asphalt and the 'tar' was a now unknown mixture of cooked-down pine tar and other ingredients. *Pride*'s seams were filled with unadulterated hot roofing asphalt. The hull seams were filled by saturating a brush made from a stick wrapped in hemp marline. It was a hot and ineffective process.

Beef tallow

Just as there was no asphalt roofing tar in 1800, nor was there any mineral-oil-based grease. Prior to the discovery of petroleum in the mid-century, animal fat was used for both lighting and lubrication. Beef tallow is just crudely rendered beef fat further cooked and processed to make a variety of goods: candle wax, soap, axle grease. On *Pride* the unprocessed, raw tallow was applied liberally to the bearings of the windlass, the blocks and deadeye lanyards. It rotted and it smelled.

Sailing *Pride*

It is clear that *Pride* was less of a vessel than the purpose-built letters-of-marque and privateer schooners she was supposed to replicate – in fact, less than any Baltimore clipper for which there are records. It could be that paintings, lines plans and logs of only the best exist and, to enhance the collective myth, the records of the non-performers have been lost or purged. However, by any measure *Pride* was poorly built and weakly rigged. She worked and distorted visibly under load, leaking miserably through hull and deck, even when new. Rigging parted, chainplates broke

and blocks exploded. Parts simply failed and broke off and started to do so immediately after she was built. But, most frustratingly, her performance under sail was abysmal.

Structural weakness

The modern tendency is to imagine that ships of the early nineteenth century must have been crude, poorly finished and weak because of ill-fitting joints, cheap construction and substandard fasteners – after all, they did not have electric planes, electric drills, any kind of electricity, they didn't even have steam power, so how good could the workmanship have been? The answer, we know, is very good indeed. These vessels were built by skilled professionals, who were paid well for their work. All the records agree that the Baltimore clippers were well built from the best materials. Long lengths of dense, virgin wood were used for planking and hull structures; the planking and ceiling were well fastened with trunnels, generally black locust.

Pride was clearly under-built in certain ways: she was poorly and lightly fastened and had thin, short, badly made planking that was not well caulked. Light passed through many large structural joints even when new. A builder from 1805 would have been shocked by the poor quality of construction.

Shortcomings of construction

Pride's builder had a fantastic artistic eye but had never built a ship nor organised a project of such magnitude. Early on he relied on a hard-working, Belizean boatbuilder, Simeon Young, invariably named 'Master Shipwright' in the newspapers and the project's own publicity. He was supported by two other builders from Belize, neither of whom had any boatbuilding experience. Unfortunately, the Belizeans could endure neither the rigours of the project nor life in a city. They stayed as long as they were able, but had all left by the end of 1976. They were intermittently replaced by a succession of third-world craftsmen with differing skill levels, but the real constant in the project was the team of hard-working but untutored young men who ended up actually building the vessel. To be truthful, while we were better adapted to the cold and to city life, we knew nothing about shipbuilding either. We learned by doing and, having built and sailed *Pride*, were proud of our work. It was only later, after going aboard vessels like *Gazela Primeiro*,[12] that we realised how poor our workmanship really was.

In short, there was a complete lack of shipbuilding skills, particularly hull-building skills, on the project and the result was that *Pride*'s hull, especially when new, was excep-

tionally weak. The planking was of poor quality and the fasteners of too small diameter. Joints in the deck structure would work, opening and closing visibly when under sail. Doors hung open on port tack and stuck fast on starboard. Very early in the ship's life, the deck began to separate from the beams. When the decking was later replaced it was found that those beams located aft of the bowsprit, fore and main masts had capsized on the clamp. The decking at the two masts had completely separated from the beams.

Poor sailing performance

It is the modern conceit, in any era, that anything from an earlier time must have been primitive. Hence, many of us imagine that sailing ships of the past were burdensome tubs that dragged their way ever leeward. For the most part, most 'replica' vessels today validate that belief – since they don't race equally, claw off lee shores, beat their peers to market, or sail very much at all, there simply is no evolutionary pressure to make them sail better. People are generally so pleased to be aboard a 'traditional' sailing vessel that they are uncritical when performance is not optimal. Such was the case with *Pride*: for all her failings, the crew loved her.

It is safe to say that *Pride*'s equipment was probably less efficient than on historic clippers. The cast-iron winch sat in iron

FIGURE 9
The leeward studdingsail and ringtail have been struck in a freshening breeze. This photograph was taken in the spring of 1986 just weeks before *Pride*'s fatal end.

FIGURE 8
Pride after the major structural overhaul. The vessel was much stronger after the deck was rebuilt. She remained, however, as wet as ever in a seaway.

bearings, greased with unadulterated tallow; the phenolic sheaves in handmade blocks swelled when wet so they could barely turn. Raising the main required all hands. In short, she was not easy to sail. She was a bear to steer and in any kind of a sea two hands on relieving tackles were needed just to manage the tiller. Over nine years many of these kinks were worked out, but the poor windward performance was never much improved.

The cold truth is **that** *Pride* was never weatherly. Her historic antecedents were famously good at going to weather and could probably tack in less than 90°, which any lump of a cruising yacht can do today. *Pride* never tacked in less than 120°.[13] Historical paintings of sharp topsail schooners may have been romanticised, but they must have been *based* on reality. Yet, over nine years of operation and 150,000 nautical miles, there isn't a single picture of *Pride* showing beautifully set sails. She could never effectively carry her headsails nor close-brace her yards to weather in a stiff breeze. The designer blamed the sailing flaws on poorly made sails. Although there is some truth in this, it was only a fraction of the problem. In fact, *Pride* never had a matched set of sails by a single sailmaker. Also there was a tendency to over emphasise the antiquity of the sails – the boltropes were too big, the cringles too heavy, ad so on. One of the interesting features of the rig was the use of bonnets on the foresail and staysail. (Bonnets were sail panels attached by a series of slip hitches to the foot of a sail.) On *Pride* the bonnets were invariably taken off for an ocean passage and stowed below; meanwhile the canvas foresail and staysail stretched with use – inevitably the stretched sails and unstretched bonnets never went back together easily or neatly.

However, the sails were just part of what prevented *Pride* from sailing well. Mostly the poor performance stemmed from an inability to maintain rig tension and sail trim, especially to windward.

Inadequate rig

Pride broke two jib booms and a bowsprit in her short life, because they were never adequately stayed. As previously mentioned, when first built, *Pride* was rigged with soft and stretchy polyester. However, this was soon replaced with wire-core hemp hoisting rope, and finally by steel wire rigging. In spite of these changes and the strengthening of all attachments and fittings, the whole rig continued to sag alarmingly to leeward even in a moderate wind, and the head rigging was by far the worst. The main reason for this was an incorrect rigging geometry: principally, the bowsprit and jib boom were too long. It is possible, of course, that those spars were correctly proportioned, and all that was needed was to make the rig effective were some changes in rigging geometry. However, there was great resistance to experimentation and no significant changes were ever made. (*Pride*'s rig was essentially copied onto *Pride II*, which is a much larger vessel. However, there were some changes: the bowsprit and jib boom are shorter, and some of the positions of the stays have been slightly changed. *Pride II* is very weatherly.)

Weak structure

Another factor in *Pride*'s inability to sail well came from the weak hull. Traditionally built, plank-on-frame ships are notoriously weak longitudinally and in torsion. This degrades performance in several ways: as a sailing-ship hull twists to leeward in response to either sail or wave forces, the mast and sails move outboard, which increases weather helm (and drag) and changes the angle of attack and set of the sails. Generally, a sailing vessel that flexes will perform less well than a more rigid sistership. *Pride* was famously flexible.

Hull form

Although there was no single Baltimore clipper hull form, *Pride*'s designer attempted to come up with a representational model. Two common characteristics of the historic vessels were a fine forebody, sometimes with hollow waterlines, and a wide deck carried well forward. Gillmer may have slightly overemphasised both of these. Baltimore clippers were also 'low' and *Pride* was made with less depth relative to her size than was the historic norm. The net result was that she did not respond in pitch to even relatively small waves, and exposed her bluff topside bow to the sea. Close hauled, the high leeway angle exacerbated the characteristic – instead of slicing to weather with a sharp bow, *Pride* bulldozed into it.

Propeller aperture

Putting a propeller aperture in a rudder is perhaps the best way to degrade sailing performance to weather. Water flows through the hole and creates drag out of proportion to it size. In addition, the aperture decreases the effectiveness of the rudder, which requires a higher angle of attack to hold course, making yet more drag. A small amount of weather helm is good for performance but a large amount is always detrimental; quite often *Pride* carried 15° or more of helm. In sum, the rudder was much less effective and total drag was far greater than on a similar historic vessel.

Replica ships in the western world

What makes a ship replica authentic? Surely it has to do with replicating all aspects of its progenitor, including shape, form, materials, method of construction, mechanisms, performance, and the experience of sailing it. *Pride* definitely succeeded in the last: sailing her was undoubtedly a voyage into the past.

There have been several recent European examples of zeal in adherence to correct method and materials. *Duyfken* (Chapter 8) and *Batavia* are two examples, both rigged with hemp standing rigging and setting hand-sewn flaxen sails.

Yet what made sailing the early, unrecon-structed, *Pride* so real was a general *lack,* as well as the fear. At first *Pride* definitely lacked – for strength, seaworthiness and speed, but also for navigation, communication, lights, heat, refrigeration, fresh water and often food. On watch at 3am we talked about food we had eaten, food we would eat, food we might still have, food we hoped to get. As for fear, there was plenty to be afraid of. Maybe fear is too strong a word; it was more like a constant, annoying, tiring anxiety, formed from the fears of hitting something, being hit by something else, or just plain being lost. The last has definitely changed – today it is unthinkable that even the most rigorous replica would leave port without at least GPS, and probably radar and an effective means to communicate to shore.

The problem with building an 'authentic' large replica vessel, especially in a country like the US, is that it has to make its own living. Today, freight is more economically carried by huge steel ships and smuggling is pretty much confined to speedboats – which leaves adventurers, sea cadets and passengers. Ships that carry people, regardless of how they are characterised, must conform to passenger-vessel rules, which regulate construction, structural fire protections, stability and manning. At a minimum, such vessels must meet safety requirements for flooding, stability and fire protection. A ninteenth-century replica vessel simply cannot meet these requirements and claim to be authentic – *Pride* met none of them.

Loss of *Pride of Baltimore*

When *Pride* sank, four young people who believed in her died. Nothing could be worse. There was an official USCG investigation and report, and there is no dispute about what happened: *Pride* was sailing in severe weather under shortened sail when she was knocked down by a 'microburst of wind'. She filled and sank in seconds. Any ship is vulnerable at sea, yet *Pride* went down hard and fast in bad, but not exceptional, conditions.

By the time of her sinking *Pride* was superior to her historic counterparts in some ways – principally in navigation and com-munication equipment: by 1985 she had GPS, radar, SSB, an EPIRB and weather fax. She had also been substantially rebuilt and was far stronger than she had been at the time of her launching. Yet she had inherent anachronistic deficiencies that may have contributed to the sinking; in other words, a historic counterpart might well have survived a similar situation. The ineffective rudder may have contributed to the loss. Although heavily ballasted, *Pride* probably had a lower ballast density and a lower range of positive stability than com-parable historic vessels. The freeboard was lower than comparable historic vessels. Con-sequently, she had less reserve buoyancy and righting 'energy'. Furthermore, by historic standards, she was under-manned. This can-not be underestimated as a contributor to the sinking, not only of *Pride* but also of other similar ships. Historically large, hardened, professional crews would have been able more rapidly to set or strike sail, cast off sheets, assist at the helm, and so on.

Pride II

After *Pride* sank there was a large and spontaneous public demand to build a replacement.[14] Gillmer designed it and Peter Boudreau[15] acted as Master Shipwright and Project Manager. Without explicitly acknowledging the faults of *Pride*, the new ship was designed and built to be safer and abler. Her mission was to carry passengers and to do so she had to meet federal requirements and be built under supervision of the US Coast Guard. Professor Gillmer's inclination was to make only those changes explicitly required for licensing. But Captain Boudreau, having sailed many thousands of nautical miles on *Pride*, was more inclined to make changes that he knew would improve the sailing performance. Thus, there were some deliberate anachronisms in the construction of the new ship:

- transverse watertight bulkheads for subdivision
- twin auxiliary engines
- exterior permanent lead ballast
- permanently stowed inside lead ballast
- extensive metal reinforcements, eg, bronze floor trusses
- bolted structural fastenings; lag bolt fastening of hull planking
- wire rope standing rigging
- fisherman-style main topsail
- wheel steering.

Apart from these, there were other changes, which may have distinguished *Pride II* from the historic norm:

- smaller sail area/displacement ratio
- shorter bowsprit and jib boom relative to displacement
- greater depth of hold
- all polyester sailcloth (with bonnets omitted).

Thus had most of *Pride*'s lessons been learned. *Pride II* has now been sailing for more than twenty years and is everything her namesake was not: stiff, weatherly, fast and able.

FIGURE 10
Leaving the Chesapeake Bay Bridge to leeward, *Pride II* shows herself to be much more weatherly than her predecessor.
All photographs courtesy of Pride of Baltimore, Inc.

ANDREW DAVIS

BIBLIOGRAPHY
Chapelle, H.I., *The Search for Speed Under Sail*, W.W. Norton, 1968.
———, *The Baltimore Clipper, Its Origin and Development*, Marine Research Society, 1930.
Gillmer, Thomas C., *The Pride of Baltimore*, International Marine, 1992.
Morris, E.P., *The Fore and Aft Rig in America*, Yale University Press, 1927.

1 The author helped build *Pride of Baltimore* in 1976 and 1977 and was part of her first sailing crew. He is now a naval architect and a licensed professional engineer. His firm, Tri-Coastal Mazrine, designs and builds large, wooden sailing ships.
2 Armin Elsaesser, Captain, Vince Lazzaro, Engineer; Barry Duckworth, Carpenter; Nina Schack, Seaman, 23 years old.
3 Howard I. Chapelle, *The Baltimore Clipper, Its Origin and Development*, 1930.
4 For this reason, *lettres de marque* were eradicated from international law by the Treaty of Paris in 1856. Interestingly, the US never signed.
5 Baltimore bid contract BP-18876.
6 Thomas C. Gillmer, author, historian, and former professor of naval architecture, chairman of naval engineering, and director of naval architecture and the Ship Hydrodynamic Laboratory at the US Naval Academy. Since leaving academia he has researched the history of naval architecture and ship design. Professor Gillmer has designed numerous historic sailing vessels and yachts, including *Pride of Baltimore* and *Pride II*.
7 Due to the inclusion of non-corrodible slags in the structure of the metal.
8 There has been a resurgence of manufacture of iron for craft such as

wrought-iron furniture, and for historic reproduction of armour, weaponry, etc.
9 It was not an unending litany of incompetence. Jerry Trowbridge, the blacksmith stood alone with his ability. Trained as an engineer in pre-WWII South African mines, he was a beacon of knowledge to us. He made all the ironwork, fittings and specialised fastenings for the project and was a marvel at making and repairing tools, welding bits, forging unique tools.
10 Historically, standing rigging, like the lower shrouds, would not have been served over their length.
11 eg Jeffries Marine Glue.
12 *Gazela Primeiro* was built in the shipyard of J.M. Mendes in Setubal, Portugal. Now *Gazela Philadelphia*, she is homeported at Independence Seaport, Philadelphia, PA.
13 Although *Pride* may have been able to change headings in less than 120°, she could not actually hold a course of 60° to weather, even in the best circumstances.
14 'A New *Pride* for Baltimore', Andy Davis, *WoodenBoat* 96, pp.50–57.
15 Guy Peter Boudreau was born to a seafaring family and was a professional, big-ship sailor before joining the construction team of *Pride*. He was the original mate and served as *Pride*'s captain for several years. Prior to building *Pride II*, he was Master Shipwright of *Lady Maryland*. Notable in his work has been the reconstruction of the 1853 Sloop of War *Constellation*, the largest wooden ship rebuild in 100 years. Today Boudreau is the Chief Designer and Vice President of Tri-Coastal Marine, Inc. Several of his recent replica vessel designs, *Amistad*, *Virginia*, *Spirit of South Carolina*, are operating successfully in the US.

Index

EDITOR

Jenny Bennett is an experienced sailing journalist specialising in the traditional boat world and has worked for *WoodenBoat* in the US and for *Classic Boat* in the UK. She teaches Elements of Seamanship at Wooden Boat School, Brooklin, Maine, each year, and recently wrote the well-received *Sailing Rigs: An Illustrated History*.

CONTRIBUTORS

Burkhard Bange is a freelance journalist. After serving in the Federal German Navy he retained his links to the sea by documenting the building of the caravel *Lisa von Lübeck* in a book and crewing aboard the Hanseatic ship in his spare time.

Douglas Brooks is a boatbuilder, writer and researcher specialising in the construction of traditional wooden boats for museums and private clients. He has been researching traditional Japanese boatbuilding since 1990 and was apprenticed with four boatbuilders in Japan, most recently as part of a one-year research grant funded by the Freeman Foundation.

Nick Burningham is a nautical archaeologist who has specialised in the ethno-archaeology of Asian watercraft. He has designed and supervised the construction of replica sailing vessels including the *Duyfken* replica, *Hati Marege*, a replica Macassan perahu, and a ninth-century dhow currently (2009) under construction in the Sultanate of Oman.

Andrew Davis is a naval architect and engineer who has worked as a shipwright on large wooden sailing vessels including *Pride of Baltimore*, *John F. Leavitt*, and *Spirit of Massachusetts*. His now designs and builds traditional ships, among which have recently been *Amistad*, *Spirit of South Carolina*, *Godspeed*, *Discovery*, and *Virginia*.

Wolf-Dieter Hoheisel graduated as a naval architect in 1965 and from 1970 until his retirement in 1999 was on the staff of the German Maritime Museum, becoming its Technical Director in 1971. He was President of the International Association of Transport Museums from 1986 to 1992.

Rikke Johansen, a graduate in prehistoric archaeology, is currently employed at the Viking Ship Museum in Roskilde. She has specialised in the experimental aspects of maritime technology and has been sailing Viking ship replicas throughout Scandinavia for the past fifteen years.

Antonia Macarthur is a maritime historian specialising in historic ships. She worked for the HM Bark Endeavour Foundation as historian and curator from 1991 to 2005, and sailed in *Endeavour* extensively. She has since worked with the Australian National Maritime Museum in Sydney after the transfer of the ship to the Australian Government in 2005.

Seán McGrail was Chief Archaeologist at the National Maritime Museum, Greenwich, where, amongst other tasks, he built and tested a copy of a Viking boat. From 1986 to 1993 he was Professor of Maritime Archaeology in the University of Oxford and was involved with the building and sea trials of the reconstruction of a fifth-century BC trireme. He has published extensively on experimental boat archaeology.

Drew McMullen is President of Sultana Projects and helped oversee the construction of the schooner *Sultana*. A graduate of St Paul's School and Amherst College, McMullen is a licensed United States Coast Guard captain who has directed and consulted on a variety of historic vessel restorations and replicas.

Colin Palmer began his career with the Wolfson Unit at Southampton University, providing consultancy to the small craft industry and he subsequently worked on wave energy and sail-assisted propulsion. He has established two wind energy companies but now devotes much of his time to traditional boat design.

Boris Rankov is Professor of Ancient History at Royal Holloway, University of London. He led Oxford to six victories in the Oxford-Cambridge Boat Race and was the rowing master for the Trireme Trust's trireme *Olympias*. He is currently directing a project on the ship sheds of the ancient Mediterranean.

Richard Woodman spent more than thirty years with Trinity House maintaining lighthouses, lightvessels and other seamarks around the British coast. He has written widely on the sea, both as a novelist and historian, and in 2005 was awarded the Anderson Medal by the Society of Nautical Research.

Pete Wrike is a historian and former history professor who began his career at the Smithsonian Institution under Howard I Chapelle. He was the research historian for the Jamestown-Yorktown Foundation's replica vessels *Godspeed* and *Discovery*, and is currently in Colonial Williamsburg's Division of Research and Historical Interpretation.